CUTTING-EDGE ISSUES IN BUSINESS ETHICS

Issues in Business Ethics

VOLUME 24

For other titles published in this series, go to
www.springer.com/series/6077

Cutting-edge issues in Business Ethics

Continental Challenges to Tradition and Practice

by

MOLLIE PAINTER-MORLAND

Institute for Business and Professional Ethics
DePaul University, Chicago, IL, USA

and

PATRICIA WERHANE

Institute for Business and Professional Ethics
DePaul University, Chicago, IL, USA

Springer

Mollie Painter-Morland
Institute for Business
and Professional Ethics
DePaul University
2352 North Clifton Avenue
Chicago, IL 60614-3208
USA
mpainter@depaul.edu

Patricia Werhane
Institute for Business
and Professional Ethics
DePaul University
2352 North Clifton Avenue
Chicago, IL 60614-3208
USA
pwerhane@depaul.edu

ISBN: 978-90-481-7868-1 e-ISBN: 978-1-4020-8401-0

Softcover reprint of the hardcover 1st edition 2008

Printed on acid-free paper

9 8 7 6 5 4 3 2 1

springer.com

In memory of Robert C. Solomon

Foreword

Business ethics originated in the United States as an offshoot of theoretical ethics and as part of a movement in applied ethics that was initiated with medical ethics. Although a few small religious-based colleges and universities offered courses in business ethics just after the Second World War, business ethics as an academic field developed most seriously in many universities in the early 1970s. The field of medical ethics was well-developed by then, and it was a natural step to think about ethical issues in business as well. There was also a public reaction to a number of corporate scandals (e.g., price fixing, the Lockheed Japanese bribery allegations, the Goodyear airbrake scandal, etc. that encouraged universities to begin teaching the subject).

Business ethics as an academic field was originally developed by philosophers, most of whom had come out of the analytic or Anglo-American philosophical traditions and who had been trained in classical ethics, on Aristotle, Kant, Mill, Bentham and perhaps Dewey. The resulting field then, has been dominated by this thinking. Although to date there are over 50 textbooks in business ethics, most textbooks in business ethics do not take into account contemporary continental philosophy. Although Marxism is sometimes taught in these courses, other more contemporary continental thinkers who could contribute substantially to the field have been ignored. This phenomenon is iterated in the professional journals and in theoretical books on the topic.

This collection is one of the first attempts to remedy that 30 year old tradition. The authors of the papers in this collection are scholars in continental philosophy and have taught business ethics from a continental perspective despite the paucity of texts and literature in the field. They are anxious, as are the editors, to develop this branch of business ethics. There is a vast literature in continental philosophy, particularly contemporary continental philosophy, that has much to say not only about politics and public life, but also about ethics and its applications, including commerce. While some of these writers are staunch critics of capitalism, as least as it is widely practiced currently, their works are important so that often-ignored thorny issues can be analyzed from different perspectives.

We were delighted to see that a whole issue of *Business Ethics: A European Review* (June 2007) was devoted to the philosophy of Emmanuel Levinas and business ethics, and Mollie Painter-Morland's new book, "*Business Ethics as Practice:*

Ethics as the Everyday Business of Business", will also contribute substantially to this continental perspective. We encourage scholars and teachers to engage in this new thinking and to challenge approaches that seem deadlocked in Anglo-American ways of approaching issues in commerce.

Virginia, VA Patricia Werhane

Professor of Patricia Werhane is the Ruffin Professor of Business Ethics at the Darden School, University of Virginia and she holds the Wicklander Chair in Business Ethics at DePaul University in Chicago.

Acknowledgements

We would like to thank the Institute for Business and Professional Ethics (IBPE) and the Department of Philosophy at De Paul University for their support in producing this text. A special word of thanks goes to Justin Sheehan, who was largely responsible for proofreading and editing the manuscript. We are also indebted to the graduate students at both De Paul University and Darden Business School at the University of Virginia for stimulating discussions on the relationship between Continental thought and Business Ethics, and for exploring with us the challenges in teaching Business Ethics from this perspective.

Contents

Introduction 1
Mollie Painter-Morland

Are We Victims of Circumstances? Hegel and Jean-Paul Sartre on Corporate Responsibility and Bad Faith 9
Robert C. Solomon

"It's Business; We're Soldiers": ***The Sopranos*****, Liberal Business Ethics, and this American Thing of Ours** 21
H. Peter Steeves

Redefining Accountability as Relational Responsiveness 33
Mollie Painter-Morland

Hegel on the Place of Corporations Within Ethical Life 47
Nathan Ross

Abjection, Ambiguity, and Female Sweatshop Workers: Is Alienated Labor ***Really*** **an Ethical Problem?** 59
Robin James

The Grameen Bank and Capitalist Challenges 75
Sokthan Yeng

Building an Ethics of Visual Representation: Contesting Epistemic Closure in Marketing Communication 87
Janet L. Borgerson and Jonathan E. Schroeder

Of Dice and Men 109
Russell Ford

Business, Ethics and the Hope of Society in Hannah Arendt: The Notion of Responsible Business Entrepreneurship 121
Angelo Carlo S. Carrascoso

Continental Philosophy: A Grounded Theory Approach and the Emergence of Convenient and Inconvenient Ethics 131
David Bevan

Contribution Towards a Phenomenological Approach to Business Ethics . 153
Stephen Meinster

Mental Models, Moral Imagination and System Thinking in the Age of Globalization: A Post-Colonial Proposal 169
Patricia H. Werhane

Business Ethics Beyond the Moral Imagination: A Response to Richard Rorty 187
Paul T. Harper

An Arendtian Approach to Business Ethics 207
Peter Gratton

A Marxist in the Business Ethics Classroom 215
Bill Martin

Index 225

Contributors

David Bevan
Management Department of the Royal Holloway, University of London,
e-mail: david.bevan@rhul.ac.uk

Janet L. Borgerson
Department of Management, University of Exeter, England,
e-mail: J.L.Borgenson@exeter.ac.uk

Angelo Carlo S. Carrascoso
Darden Business School, University of Virginia,
e-mail: carrascosoAos@darden.virginia.edu

Russell Ford
Assistant Professor in the Department of Philosophy, Elmhurst College,
e-mail: fordr@elmhurst.edu

Peter Gratton
Assistant Professor of Philosophy, at the University of San Diego,
e-mail: pgratton@sandiego.edu

Paul T. Harper
Doctoral candidate at the University of Virginia, e-mail: harperpos@gmail.com

Robin James
Department of Philosophy, University of North Carolina, Charlotte, North Carolina,
e-mail: rjames7@uncc.edu

Bill Martin
Professor of Philosophy, DePaul University, Chicago, IL, USA,
e-mail: woodbug1@aol.com

Stephen Meinster
Doctoral candidate and Assistant Professor of Philosophy, DePaul University,
Chicago, IL, USA, e-mail: smeinster@depaul.edu

Mollie Painter-Morland
Department of Philosophy, DePaul University, Chicago, IL, USA; University of Pretoria, Pretoria, South Africa, e-mail: mpainter@depaul.edu

Nathan Ross
Assistant Professor of Philsophy, DePaul University, Chicago, IL, USA, e-mail: nross77@yahoo.com

Jonathan E. Schroeder
Department of Philosophy and Management, University of Exeter, England, e-mail: J.E.Schroeder@exeter.ac.uk

Robert C. Solomon
Quincy Lee Centennial Professor of Business and Philosophy University of Texas at Austin, Austin, TX, USA

H. Peter Steeves
Professor of Philosophy, DePaul University, Chicago, IL, USA, e-mail: psteeves@depaul.edu

Sokthan Yeng
Assistant Professor in Philosophy at DePaul University, Chicago, IL, USA, e-mail: syeng@depaul.edu

Patricia Werhane
DePaul University, Chicago, IL, USA, e-mail: pwerhane@depaul.edu

Introduction

Mollie Painter-Morland

Business Ethics, like any discipline, reflects the alliance of its central figures to specific schools of thought, as well as the impact of a particular set of contextual circumstances. Over time, certain figures, texts and themes migrate to the center of our attention in theory and practice, and others are relegated to the margins, or ignored altogether.[1] The danger is that if these contingent preferences are allowed to sediment, particular epistemological and ontological frameworks gain such saliency that a radical interrogation of their basic presuppositions becomes unlikely. In a very real sense, such sedimentation forecloses the possibility that questions that were relegated to the margins of theory and practice receive the attention they deserve. This anthology wants to draw attention to what at this juncture has been relegated to the fringes, and grapple with the marginal. It wants to cut through the comfort-zones within which most business ethicists have come to operate, and draw attention to the limitations that the tradition as it has developed up till now, present to theory and practice.

Some of the central complaints of critics of the discipline of Business Ethics, such as Jones, Parker and ten Bos (2005), relate to the fact that it pays little attention to the insights of certain important figures within Continental thought, particularly the contributions of 19th and 20th century Continental philosophers. As such, it has been alleged that business ethicists fail to draw on the full wealth that the history of Western thought has to offer in deliberating ethical issues in business and society. It will be impossible to fully interrogate the validity of these charges in this introduction. However, it seems pertinent to indicate how this anthology hopes to respond to the absence of certain central Continental figures within the ambit of Business Ethics scholarship. In order to do so, it would have to be established what exactly makes "Continental" philosophy so different from the approach taken in most Business Ethics texts. We do not want to suggest that those working in Business Ethics come at this topic from an Anglo-American or Analytic philosophy perspective in the technical use of those terms. Seldom does one find discussions

M. Painter-Morland
Department of Philosophy, DePaul University, Chicago, IL, USA; University of Pretoria, Pretoria, South Africa
e-mail: mpainter@depaul.edu

M. Painter-Morland, P. Werhane (eds.), *Cutting-edge issues in Business Ethics*,

of Russell, Wittgenstein, Austin or Flew in business ethics. Rather, the common approach is to focus on a select group of central figures in Western philosophy, for example, Aristotle, Locke, Smith, Kant, Bentham, and/or Mill, sometimes Rawls or Nozick, as the foundational texts out of which practical ethical thinking in commerce is developed and critiqued. Sometimes, too, references are made to Marx or Engels as the classical challengers to free enterprise. What is missing, however, is often a solid critique of business practices from a Continental perspective.

The paucity of Continental perspectives in Business Ethics has been recently ameliorated by a special issue of *Business Ethics: A European Review* devoted exclusively to the philosophy of Emmanuel Levinas and Business Ethics. A future issue on Derrida, Business, Ethics is forthcoming. This anthology continues in this direction. However in pursuing an anthology that purports to have a focus on the contribution that "Continental philosophy" could make to Business Ethics, a few caveats are in order. "Continental thought" is a broad term, within which many different schools of thought coexist and many disparate points of view are defended. It would be a mistake to portray "Continental thought" as a homogeneous whole, or to assume that everyone would agree on which authors or themes constitute this somewhat amorphous "category" within philosophy. In fact, the term "Continental philosophy" is often employed as a means of self-description amongst philosophers operating in the US or the UK, who want to distinguish their way of approaching philosophy from the more common "Analytic" approach that characterizes most of Anglo-American thought.[2] As such, it is not something that many of the continental figures who are read within Continental philosophy departments, would have necessarily subscribed to or identified with. Heidegger, Derrida, Foucault etc. would hardly have felt the need to signal to others that they pursue "Continental philosophy".[3]

Why then, would it be important for scholars operating in the US, UK, or other parts of the world that are not part of "the Continent", to signal their alliance with and interest in "Continental thought"? Presumably, the need to do so arises from a distinctly different set of agendas, particular preoccupations and certain stylistic preferences. It functions as a kind of "Buyer-beware" label that signal to readers, editors and reviewers that what they are about to encounter may not fit comfortably with what is evident in most of the Business Ethics journals and textbooks. For the purposes of this introduction, we shall focus on the substantive and stylistic concerns of Continental thought. Simon Critchley (2001) argues that the Continental tradition has a unique preoccupation with bridging the gap between knowledge and wisdom that has plagued much of the history of Western thought. For instance, Continental thought remains committed to exploring the polysemic, ambiguous and opaque in ways that are often seen as elusive within economic thought. Another important characteristic of Continental thought is its interest in reading the history of Western thought from the critical vantage points of the present and the future. Continental thought is committed to portraying a specific point of view as contingent upon historical, political, and socio-economic particularities. It reflects a belief that all meaning is constructed by individuals who participate in particular social dynamics, and as such, can be reconstructed. Continental scholars are therefore preoccupied with grappling with tradition in a critical, self-reflexive manner. They seek to analyze their engagements with tradition carefully to explore the possibility of it being read differently, or to find the openings for a radical reconfiguration of their current epistemological presuppositions. Often, this entails portraying the salient tradition(s) as having led us astray, creating a crisis that threatens our agency, or foreclosing certain possibilities of being human. The relationship between Continental thought and criticism cannot be overestimated. It is their self-reflexive, self-critical, sometimes even self-deprecating style that sets many Continental scholars apart from their analytic counterparts.

According to Simon Critchley, one of the main concerns regarding Continental thought is that it seems preoccupied with "proper names" instead of with "problems". The fact that Continental thought pays careful attention to the central texts of certain important Continental figures, has led to the accusation that it loses sight of problems that cut across the work of its central figures. The Continental tradition's preoccupation with hermeneutics and the historical particularity of figures and texts, practiced through the rigorous pursuit of close-reading, has made its contributions seem inaccessible, and less relevant to practice, than the contributions of analytic thought. It is Continental thought's fascination with the ambiguity of thought and experience that has led to its being accused of obscurantism. This is a common charge leveled against certain specific branches of Continental thought, such as 20th century Phenomenology and certain strands of Poststructuralism. It has to be acknowledged that Continental scholars tend to employ a very distinct style, and display a preference for the inclusion of narrative, poetry, and other artistic genres in their writing. In a very real sense, it signals their acknowledgement of the intricate relationship between form and content. Continental scholars' commitment to the acknowledgement of ambiguity is reflected in the poetic quality of many Continental texts, which allows them to suggest, hint at, or ponder, rather than to depict, define and prescribe. It is not at all the case that Continental thought is not preoccupied with problems. In fact, it wants to address real problems by exploring areas where criticism has been foreclosed.

This anthology brings together papers that utilize the insights of Continental philosophers whose work remains largely untapped in Business Ethics literature. By drawing on the work of these Continental thinkers, business ethicists could increase the variety of their conceptual tools and sharpen the critical skills of their discipline. An analysis of the thought of certain Continental thinkers allows us to reconsider the way in which the discipline poses its questions, approaches pedagogy and pursues its corporate engagements. There are very few scholars who pursue this kind of research, and as such, finding business ethicists and Continental scholars to facilitate this unique "opening" within the discipline of Business Ethics was no easy task. It entailed challenging graduate students and faculty to relate their research in Continental thought to issues in Business Ethics. In some cases, we challenged graduate students in Management programs to reflect on what reading texts by Continental figures contributed to their understanding of ethical issues in business. As part of this selection process, the editors requested that Business Ethics professors in Continental philosophy departments reflect on their pedagogy. We also had to challenge ourselves and other business ethicists to critically reflect on our own tradition.

We were intent on creating the opportunity for conversation between business ethicists and Continental scholars. Readers of this anthology will notice that in an attempt to further this conversation, we have included a wide variety of papers. Some papers clearly display the Continental preference for focusing of specific figures and texts. Others address problems within business ethics in a way that is informed by Continental perspectives, though they do not necessarily offer close readings of Continental texts. We have also chosen to include the work of business ethicists who may not pursue their writing exclusively from a "Continental" perspective and who would not necessarily describe themselves as "Continental scholars". However, their work occasions the opportunity for conversation with Continental figures and texts. We are, for instance, greatly honored that Robert Solomon wrote a piece for this anthology. Solomon is a philosopher who, over the course of his career in an impressive breadth of writings, employed both Continental philosophical thinking as well as appealing to many classical traditions in ethical theory, in particular, Aristotle. The piece that Solomon contributed to this anthology also happens to be one of the very last pieces he wrote before his untimely death in December 2006. We are greatly honored by this piece, and saddened by the fact that he is no longer with us to further this conversation.

Solomon's essay is an excellent illustration of just how difficult it is to make statements about "The Continental Tradition". He quite rightly points out that "Continental thought", read through Sartre, could lead us in a very different direction than the "Husserl-Heidegger-Poststructuralism" trajectory, which many Continentalists follow. In this way, Robert Solomon carries out what many Continental scholars would consider an essential philosophical labor, i.e. carefully scrutinizing one's own tradition, and others' depiction of it, for clues on how to read it differently. He is also quick to point out the dangers that particular readings pose to moral agency, and to offer alternative readings. Peter Steeves' piece provides an interesting critical counterpoint to Solomon's position on moral agency. Again, Steeves helps us to cast a critical eye at who we have become from within our own tradition(s). In this piece, he confronts us with the implications of an uncritical acceptance of the tradition of "Liberalism" and a neglect of more "Communitarian" perspectives. Steeves' lucid employment of the popular television show, "The Sopranos", and his candid reflection on his own personal narrative, is illustrative of the way in which Continental scholars "argue" without drawing syllogistic relationships between distinct propositions. This author is brilliant in drawing readers into his and their own particular narratives in a way that poses an extremely convincing perspective on who they are as moral agents.

The question of moral agency has always been central concern within the Business Ethics field, but a careful consideration of the presuppositions that underpin many of these discussions is long overdue. Many decision-making models that are currently used within the field of Business Ethics are designed exclusively with an individual moral agent in mind. As such, this approach discounts the effects systemic influences within organizational contexts. It often ignores tacit cultural and societal assumptions, and underestimates the effect of power dynamics outside of the individual's control. A growing body of philosophical, psychological and sociological literature insists on the imbrication of individuals in the groups and contexts within which they function. These insights precipitate a reconsideration of certain central elements of the notion of moral agency. How do broader cultural and societal narratives impact moral agency? How do the various dynamics of organizational systems contribute to the intricacies of the moral dilemmas that individuals face? What are the philosophical presuppositions, handed down to us by the tradition, that make it difficult to interrogate our own sense of agency?

The paper by Painter-Morland furthers the critical interrogation of the presuppositions that underpin agency concepts within Business Ethics. She focuses on the notion of "accountability" to expose the flawed assumptions that are operative in the employment of this term. In pointing out the relational character of both individual and corporate moral agency, she proposes that "accountability" be redefined as a form of responsiveness to the various stakeholders (Others) that sustain both individual and corporate lives.

The paper by Ross examines the nature of Hegel's claim that "corporations" have a vital role to play in the manner in which individuals find ethical meaning and a political voice within their economic activities. The paper begins by explaining Hegel's theory of the corporation and comparing his theory to certain recent business developments. Ross points out that institutional environments have a crucial role to play in the development of responsible moral agents, and as such, the ways in which corporation could be controlled, both from within and without, deserve to undergo critical scrutiny.

The contributions by James and Yen help us to critically interrogate some of the central assumptions around subject-object distinctions that is operative in much of Western thought and that greatly impact our ability to understand ourselves as subjects and as such, as moral agents. From the perspectives of feminist and poststructuralist philosophy, it becomes clear that a critical consideration the conventional conception of moral agency may in fact yield other fruitful perspectives.

The paper by James draws on feminist thought to argue that the essentialism and binary oppositions inherent in our understanding of human subjectivity affect our understanding of ethical problems. As a result, our strategies for dealing with these problems may be misdirected. She focuses her attention on how well intentioned Marxist critiques of the "alienation" that sweatshop-workers experience may in fact misrepresent their problems and aggravate their disempowerment. Through her employment of Julia Kristeva's analysis of the abject and Simon de Beauvoir's "*Ethics of Ambiguity*", she problematizes the strict subject-object distinctions that underpin our thinking about agency, and criticizes our limited understanding of the ethical issues at stake in business. James' piece cuts through the generally accepted positions around alienation and offers a more radical interrogation of the wide array of ethical issues facing women in the capitalist labor force.

Soktan Yeng combines Foucaultian insights with the social and political thought of bell hooks in order to rethink both the repressive and the productive employment of capital. Yeng argues that hooks' theory about the strong influence of capitalism in undermining the black community, could be enhanced by considering how the force of capitalism transforms the body. Yeng further explores how Foucault's theory of power as a productive force may be used to explain the success of micro-lending projects like that of Grameen Bank. She also interrogates the social, economic and political implications, and potential costs, of such transformations.

This anthology hopes to illustrate that is often the way in which business ethicists' frame their questions that may foreclose important ethical labors from being effected. For instance, its preoccupation with distinguishing "truth" from "lie" may undermine its ability to interrogate the ethical failures inherent in the act of representation itself. While business ethicists would be quick to chastise corporations for engaging in deceptive marketing techniques or barring consumers' access to crucial information, there is very little awareness of the implications that all representations have on the establishment of identity and agency. It may be that many ethical infractions lie precisely in this area. Borgenson and Schroeder explore the cultural, aesthetic, and ethical implications of the act of representation itself to highlight the ways in which representation changes our world and our view of ourselves. As such, it impacts the very heart of moral agency that influences all other ethical deliberations.

Ford's contribution presents a challenge to way in which the analogy between business and poker sustains certain false premises about the nature of business life. He argues that in portraying business and poker as games, a more important characteristic, namely that of "play," is under-emphasized. In viewing business life as play, much more productive avenues are opened for understanding the normative boundaries that are operative in business life. Carrascoso's piece lends further support to viewing business activity as more than just the instrumental pursuit of profit. It draws on Hannah Arendt's discussion of labor, work and activity in *The Human Condition* to argue for the importance of creative activity within entrepreneurial pursuits. He also stresses the importance of an ongoing ethical interrogation of the potential negative effects of new business ventures.

Continental thought has much more to offer in terms of casting a critical eye at the broader ontological and epistemological presuppositions that inform the way in which ethical problems are framed and addressed within business ethics. In fact, the interrogation it precipitates may at times be uncomfortable, or in the words of our next author "inconvenient", but it offers us the opportunity to reconsider some themes that have been excluded from much of Business Ethics scholarship. David Bevan offers an analysis of the way in which business ethicists work within a paradigm that co-opt them into practices of which the ethical legitimacy may and should be radically questioned. By accepting the terms dictated to them, business ethicists risk becoming convenient partners in attempts to provide some inkling of moral legitimacy to an otherwise amoral capitalist system. Bevan portrays Continental thought as the bearer of a distinctly inconvenient ontology that in many ways makes an uncritical incorporation or even cooperation within the ambit of "business-as-usual" impossible. This piece is a good example of how Continental thought provides a critical perspective on how a discipline that continues without any critical self-reflection and a radical interrogation of its basic presuppositions can become incorporated into an ultimately dehumanizing project.

Stephen Meinster furthers the problematization of the way in which Business Ethics identifies its basic themes and pursues its ethical labors. Meinster argues that instead of questioning the basic assumptions made by economic theory business ethicists attempt to address its effects. As such, it could merely provide "band-aids" for the more serious wound that lies at the heart of capitalist economic theory. He argues that Continental scholars provide us with the point of departure for a more radical critique of the empiricism, naturalism and psychologism inherent in much of economic theory. With the help of Edmund Husserl's phenomenological critique of modern science, Meinster indicated how Joseph Schumpeter's empiricist model of science causes him to confuse his theoretical constructions for real economic progress. This analysis allows Meinster to unmask the morally problematic effects of the employment of Schumpeter's ideas by the likes of Alan Greenspan to motivate his arguments against increasing the minimum wage in America. This essay exposes the dangers of an uncritical acceptance of economic theory. It unmasks the harm occurring in the lives of real individuals who are on the receiving end of sophisticated economic theories that purport to possess "objective" validity.

Continental scholars are often accused of being so preoccupied with formulating critical counter-positions that they undermine current theoretical paradigms without proposing any alternative. This anthology wants to hint in the direction of potential avenues that may be considered in developing alternatives to current theory and practice. This anthology does not purport to counter this objection with a set of systematic "Continental proposals", but seeks to explore areas where continental thought may assist in providing concepts, skills and perspectives that can have an important impact on business ethics practice.

Moral imagination has become a prominent area of research within Business Ethics literature. Continental thought might have much to offer in scholars who want to explore the various iterations of moral imagination in a corporate environment. Werhane's essay offers a perspective that enables us to think about moral imagination from an organizational and systems perspective, thus challenging a preoccupation with a focus on the individual manager-decision-maker.

Paul Harper argues that the notion of the moral imagination, in the way that influential thinkers like Werhane and Rorty discuss it is not robust enough to procure moral progress. He seeks to explicate the intellectual paradigm that both explains and produces the desired innovations in our moral understanding, namely critique. Through a consideration of Michel Foucault's contributions, Harper demonstrates why critique allows for a broader and clearer pedagogical platform for moral development and leadership. Harper also outlines the shape of the pedagogy that would not only serve to reinvigorate Business Ethics, but would make ethical discourse more of a reflection of our contemporary concerns.

The last essays in the anthology focuses on interventions that are aimed at influencing individuals and groups through Business Ethics education. All pedagogical strategies rely on particular anthropological assumptions. As conventional conceptions of moral agency are being challenged, the need for a fundamental reconsideration of Business Ethics pedagogy asserts itself with even greater urgency. A more complex understanding of human subjectivity and moral agency precipitates a creative reconsideration of Business Ethics pedagogy. Within the Business Ethics classroom, it is important to bring students to a critical analysis of their own interactions with corporations, whether it is as consumers, employees, investors, or as members of the community. However, any such analysis is always already inscribed within the structure of theoretical concepts, societal practices and economic realities, which may foreclose the ability to criticize. It seems that alternative approaches to teaching business ethics should urgently be explored. For instance, the rich potential of narrative for Business Ethics pedagogy is made apparent by Peter Gratton's discussion of the use of Hannah Arendt's discussion of Eichmann in Jerusalem in Business Ethics teaching. Bill Martin's paper provide us with a clear exposé of the multiple challenges that we face in drawing on various philosophical resources in the Business Ethics classroom. It is perhaps fitting that Martin should have the final word in this anthology. His criticism of much of what is done in Business Ethics teaching brings us right back to the drawing board, and challenges us to rethink both our research agendas and pedagogical practices.

This collection of papers has been prepared in anticipation of a more meaningful conversation between business ethicists and Continental scholars. At the very least, it will hopefully provide scholars and practitioners with some new perspectives by drawing on the insights of philosophers that are often overlooked in the Business Ethics field. Much remains to be done, but all conversations have to start with establishing at least some insight into the interlocuters' points of view. This collection is a step in that direction.

Notes

1. For a variety of reasons, much of the business ethics literature in the US has come to draw predominantly on a limited selection of the rich heritage of Western thought. Some, have argued that business ethics as a discipline focuses only on three streams of ethical thinking, i.e. one that originates from the Ancient Greeks (virtue-ethics), one from 18th century Germany (deontology) and another from two eighteenth and nineteenth century Englishmen (utilitarianism). See: Jones, Parker and ten Bos. 2005. *For Business Ethics*. London: Routledge.
2. For concise exposé of the differences between Continental and Analytic thought, see: Critchley, S. 2001. *Continental Philosophy: A very short introduction*. Oxford: Oxford University Press.
3. As Simon Critchley points out, is also important to note that "Continental Philosophy", as a distinct area of study, only arose as a description of certain Philosophy courses in the1970's (US) and 1980's (UK).

Are We Victims of Circumstances? Hegel and Jean-Paul Sartre on Corporate Responsibility and Bad Faith

Robert C. Solomon

> *The share in the total work of Spirit that falls to the individual can only be very small. Because of this, the individual must all the more forget himself.... Of course, he must make of himself and achieve what he can, but less should demanded of him, just as he in turn can expect less of himself, and may demand less for himself.*
>
> –*G.W.F. Hegel in the Preface of the* Phenomenolgie des Geistes
>
> *Shall we not say that such a person is in bad faith?*
>
> –*Jean-Paul Sartre,* L'etre et le Neant

Business ethics, for the most part, has been blessedly innocent of philosophical methodology. Happily, the question "what is philosophy" has not played much of a role in business ethics (whereas it has been known to destroy whole philosophy departments). It has been noted, however, (by the editors of this volume) that business ethics has nevertheless betrayed a certain bias toward the Anglo-American analytic philosophical tradition and has more or less excluded (or in any case not shown substantial interest in) the philosophical traditions of Europe. As they say,

> ...much of the current literature has not dealt or dealt adequately with the rich array of contemporary writings in continental philosophy. The fact that the business ethics field sometimes ignores this group of thinkers means that certain types of questioning are not brought in to the discussion in its analyses, a discussion that might precipitate a more critical analysis of its assumptions

I think that this is true and significant, and in itself worth the effort of producing this volume. But "continental philosophy" is by no means all of a piece. Among the many splits in emphases and methodology are those between those philosophies that loosely fall under the rubric of existentialism and phenomenology, "postmodernism," and the much more political and sociological philosophies defined by the Frankfurt School, those that follow the "Structuralist" line and those that insist on a "Post-Structuralist" positions, and those that follow a more or less psychoanalytic approach and those that do not. Historically, there are substantial differences

---

R.C. Solomon
Quincy Lee Centennial Professor of Business and Philosophy University of Texas at Austin, Austin, TX, USA

M. Painter-Morland, P. Werhane (eds.), *Cutting-edge issues in Business Ethics,* between what I call "classical" (or "Pre-Postmodern") Continental Philosophy and that odd collection of Postmodern positions that are now already part of philosophical history themselves. A Continental approach to business ethics, accordingly, must inevitably choose where to situate itself in a complex demography of personalities, approaches, and positions.

Along with these other splits in European philosophical approaches, there is one that I find particularly challenging that cuts through these various approaches and positions. I would locate it in a classic dispute in the history of Continental Philosophy, that between the German Idealist G.W.F. Hegel and the Danish "Existentialist" Søren Kierkegaard, but it certainly applies as well to the tensions that separate Jean-Paul Sartre from his Post-Structuralist successors (however much it can be argued that they nevertheless owe substantial debts to him). The dispute has to do with the basic philosophical question about the source and nature of agency and responsibility. Hegel, defending the idea of an all-embracing Spirit (*Geist*) that includes us all, concludes that :"the individual must all the more forget himself... that [his] individual responsibility does not amount to much" (even though Hegel adds, "Of course, he must make of himself and achieve what he can"). Kierkegaard, in a witty response, suggests that if someone took Hegel seriously in this, "he would not even be in a position to have a letter addressed to him." In this reply, Kierkegaard captures the essential insight of existentialism, that one's personal identity, indeed his or her very *existence*, depends on our individuality, and that in turns depends on our taking responsibility for what we do and, most importantly, who we are.

Jean-Paul Sartre famously continues this emphasis on individual responsibility, and looking back form our present position, we can also see some affinity between Hegel (as Kierkegaard read him) and the postmodernists, however vigorously they may have protested against Hegel's "totalization" and his systematic "meta-narratives." The affinity in question has to do with diminishing individual responsibility. The postmodernists, of course, do not appeal as Hegel does to a larger all-embracing Spirit or system. Instead, they appeal to the Nietzschean discovery of a fragmented self, which compromises the traditional notion of agency and undermines the idea of individual identity on which the existentialists Kierkegaard and Sartre place so much emphasis. Thus the editors of this volume write,

> Some decision-making models that are currently used within the field of Business Ethics are designed with an individual moral agent in mind. Some of these further assume that this individual will be engaging in deliberate rational decision-making processes. As such, one has to be careful not to discount the effects that systemic influences within organizational contexts, taking into account tacit cultural and societal assumptions, and measuring the effects of power dynamics outside of the individual's control. The growing body of philosophical, psychological and sociological literature insists on the analysis of individuals in the groups and contexts within which they function. These insights may even precipitate a reconsideration of certain central elements of the notion of moral agency. What is the influence of organizational culture and climate on individual moral decision-making? How do the various dynamics of organizational systems contribute to the intricacies of the moral dilemmas that individuals face? Who are the role models that individuals tacitly refer to in their moral judgments? How do broader cultural and societal narratives impact moral agency?

I have already pointed out why I think this describes only some trends in Continental Philosophy and not others, but it does describe one particular feature of postmodern philosophy rather well. The notion of moral agency, which forms the centerpiece of Kierkegaard's and Sartre's philosophy, is under attack. Moral agency is not just a feature of contemporary Anglo-American philosophy but an essential element in Continental existentialism as well. From a Sartrian viewpoint, the Hegelian-Postmodern position illustrates an exemplary case of what he calls "bad faith," a refusal to take full responsibility for who one is and what one does. It is, in short, the making of *excuses*. Applying all of this to the problematic of business ethics, we might say that any effort to deny one's own responsibilities by appealing to larger forces, most notoriously "market forces," is a case of bad faith. From the existentialist point of view, a person in business makes choices, takes responsibility for them, and takes the consequences. Market forces may be in the background, they may even serve as the opposition against which stakeholder-friendly business decisions and choices *not* to maximize profits get made. (A good contemporary example is Whole Foods in Austin Texas.) But also, business life is filled with efforts to deflect personal responsibility by reference to more particular forces outside of oneself, for example, by employing the common excuse "everyone's doing it" or by appealing to the more localized excuses of pressure from one's boss ("just doing what I was told") or peer pressure ("I couldn't have shown my face around the office if I hadn't"). In this essay, I would like to explore Sartre's notion of bad faith with particular reference to corporate and personal responsibility.

Sartre's Bad Faith

Jean-Paul Sartre's philosophy is best known for its harsh, uncompromising insistence that we are free and responsible for virtually everything we do, for what we are, and for the way our world is. His concept of "bad faith" (*mauvaise foi*) has much to do with freedom and responsibility as the *denial* of one's freedom and thus his or her responsibility. In the business world, we find a fertile field for examining both the freedom and responsibility thesis and bad faith. The first is an essential ingredient in the very idea of executive agency (or if this is redundant, just "agency"). No matter what the organizational structure, decisions get made, and someone makes them. The questions of freedom and responsibility follow. But, of course, the corporation can even be defined as the evasion of accountability. The great E.F. Schumacher insisted that the free market is "the institutionalization of irresponsibility," and one of the main selling points of incorporation is the avoidance of liability. This is reflected and given philosophical credentials by the literature of post-structuralism, which insists that the fragmentation and diffusion of decision-making undermines agency and responsibility. Thus corporate life consists for the most part of finger pointing and the energetic dodging of responsibility, with the ultimate bad faith gesture of blaming "market forces" or one's organization for choices for which one ought to take full responsibility. It is no surprise, therefore, that Sartre would have a good deal to say about this – however much he may have despised bourgeois capitalism not to mention how horrified he would have been at the very thought of corporate life.

Sartre tellingly insists, "bad faith is *faith*," despite the fact that he is a notorious atheist who grants no role whatever for religion (although he plays with it in several of his novels and plays as well as, famously, in his philosophy. "(Man wants to be God.") Bad faith typically involves *belief* (as opposed to knowledge), but more importantly (and with Kierkegaard in mind), Sartre insists that it involves an act, a commitment, a practical project, and not merely belief. Thus, according to many people (Kierkegaard among them), we can have no knowledge of God, but *belief* in God requires faith. Bad faith is faith insofar as it requires a belief that cannot be proven and a way of behaving that denies our own free will at the same time that we are clearly exercising it. It is acting *as if* we are not responsible. But also, Kierkegaard insists that faith in God requires a motivated ("passionate") commitment, a "*leap* of faith." It is a practical and very personal phenomenon, not a theoretical curiosity. Sartre's notion of faith is not intended to be at all religious, of course, but I think that there is a plausible suggestion that bad faith is Sartre's secular and "ontological" version of Christian "original sin," that is, an intrinsic flaw in the human character, something that no matter how one acts or what one does cannot be transcended or resolved. Like human sin, it is both blameworthy and unavoidable. But in corporate life, it is just accepted as a matter of course. Everyone is a mere victim of circumstances, forgetting about the fact that the very basis of the free market (and employment therein) is voluntary association and freedom of choice.

At the end of his discussion of bad faith in *Being and Nothingness*, Sartre insists that there is "no way out," that we are stuck in bad faith by our very natures. (This despite the fact that Sartre insists, at least in his popular writings, that human beings have no "natures.") I find his insistence on the inevitability of bad faith more unconvincing than disturbing, but I think that what Sartre has in fact achieved is to point out the considerable difficulty one faces in acknowledging one's own responsibilities in the face of powerful pressures in the world.

Sartre's official theory, the one that is most easily promulgated with the aid of two of his more famous pieces of jargon, is this: we (as consciousness or "Being-for-Itself") are essentially, phenomenologically/ontologically, free. That is to say, we have *transcendence*, the ability to intend and reach *beyond* any factual situation in which we find ourselves. We have desires. We hope. We fear. We have ambitions. We make plans and resolutions. The factual situation Sartre calls our *facticity* (a term borrowed directly from Heidegger). Thus we find ourselves "abandoned" or "thrown" into a world not of our choosing – born into a violent century, an unjust society, a troubled family, a religious tradition, stuck with a sickly body, a homely face, a troubled personality, a bad job with a horrible boss, a falling stock market, a tightening of credit. We have facticity, the facts that are true of us, and we have transcendence, so we can always imagine "possibilities," alternative ways that the world and we might be and devices by which we might try to bring these about. Thus human reality has two very different aspects, the facts that are true of us, the "given," if you like, and our ability to choose, to aspire, to "transcend" ourselves.

The facticity and transcendence formula provides a nice simple model, and it is the one Sartre uses (for the most part) throughout the chapter on "Bad Faith." His famous waiter in the café, for instance, is described as in bad faith because he imagines that he *is* just a waiter, that is, he is thoroughly defined by the fact of his job and its duties. (That heavily ontological "*is*" is characteristic of Sartre's discussion.) One can imagine similar but more serious cases in which Nazi soldiers or Vichy policemen conceive of themselves as thoroughly defined by their jobs and their duties and thereby refusing to disobey or even to scrutinize orders no matter how immoral, cruel, or criminal. So, too, in the corporate world. An executive who has to decide to "downsize" a company and lay off thousands of workers could just appeal to "market forces" and convince himself that he had no choice. But the authentic decision is one that is made *in the face of* market forces but not determined by market forces. Robert Allen, when he was CEO of AT&T, had to downsize the company, he made it well-known that he personally regretted his having to do so and if he was sincere (I have good reason to think so, but one never knows) he accepted the responsibility for his action. By contrast, Al "Chainsaw" Dunlap similarly downsized Sunbeam and was perfectly happy to insist that he had no choice, "the company was dead when I got there," and everyone got the impression that he was delighted to go along with necessity. (The employees all cheered when he was felled by the same market forces.)

It is easy to understand both why Sartre thinks that bad faith is so central to his overall defense of freedom and why he tends to be so moralistic about it. (I take his insistence that he is not doing ethics but rather only ontology, which I read as parroting Heidegger, to be both absurd and self-undermining.) But the facticity and transcendence formula, as neat as it is, fails to capture the complexity of the phenomenon that Sartre seeks to understand. For one thing, Sartre makes it very clear throughout *Being and Nothingness* that facticity and transcendence are not so easily distinguished, and that confusing them is not simply a matter of bad faith but of the human predicament as such. Here is both the wisdom and the pathos of that well-known Reinhold Niebuhr (1892–1971) "Serenity Prayer," "*God grant me the serenity to accept the things I cannot change; the courage to change the things I can; and the wisdom to know the difference*." Unfortunately, there is no decision procedure to discern the difference. Who is in a position to definitely say what is possible and what is not? People who try to do the impossible sometimes do, and so do companies. Indeed, the story of entrepreneurship in the world is filled with people who defied the wisdom of the market and succeeded, sometimes extravagantly.

But if facticity and transcendence cannot be readily distinguished, then we can see how Sartre might have concluded that we cannot escape from bad faith. If bad faith is the confusion of facticity and transcendence, the denial of one or the other, and if facticity and transcendence cannot be adequately distinguished, then we might well find ourselves doomed to bad faith. If in defying the wisdom of the market one is simply going along with one's personal rebelliousness and perhaps a different kind of peer pressure (one's fellow entrepreneurial students, for example), one might claim that one is simply being determined by one source of facticity rather than another. So where do freedom and choice get in here? Couple this with Sartre's rather infuriating but typical philosophical bad habit of thinking in stark "either/or" dichotomies, and it becomes clear why he seems so hesitant to evaluate bad faith in terms of degrees of blameworthiness. In the classic formulation of Parmenides, either this *is* or *is not.* There is no room for "sort of," "more or less," "in a way," or "in a sense." But we are not talking ontology here but ethics, and we are talking about a very common but problematic range of human experiences in which we are not straight with ourselves about who we are and what we can and should do. Though the huge range and the multitude of experiences that fall under the rubric of "bad faith" cannot be captured by so crude a set of dimensions as "the facts that are true of us" and "our possibilities." At the same time, however, this dichotomy allows us to understand and appreciate some of Sartre's most provocative and broadly philosophical declarations about human nature and, for us, an important tool for criticizing corporate irresponsibility.

Bad Faith and Being-for-Others

There are at least two different and quite opposed conceptions of self-consciousness that are evident in Sartre's discussions. The first is a matter of more or less "immediate" reflection (that is, consciousness of myself which I achieve just by being aware of myself). This is not just the awareness of awareness that Sartre insists is essential to all consciousness but also that reflection which brings the self as an "I" into the picture. (Sartre's examples: "I am counting cards," "I am running for the streetcar.") But second is that sense of self that Sartre inherits from Hegel, of reflection *mediated* by the awareness or the possible awareness of others. One might argue that neither sort of reflection is strictly immediate in that all reflection involves the mediation of the "me," but in the first third of *Being and Nothingness*, which includes the "Bad Faith" chapter, it is the first conception of self-consciousness that gets most of the attention, in the guise of the "For-Itself." Beginning with Part III, in which "Being-for-Others" is formally introduced, it is the Hegelian conception that is most in play (though we might point out that in Sartre's discussion of "The Reef of Solipsism," Hegel is shown to be "*aufheben*'d" [overcome and improved upon] by Husserl, Heidegger, and, finally, Sartre.)

Sartre's discussion of "Concrete Relations with Others" is notoriously dependent on Hegel, and on his "Master Slave" parable in the *Phenomenology* in particular. In that parable, selfhood emerges only out of a life and death conflict as each tries to gain the "recognition" of the other. The outcome of the battle is mutual personal identity, one becomes the "master" or "Lord" the other the "slave" or servant, *Knecht.*) It does not involve much of a stretch of imagination to interpret corporate hierarchies in much the same way, as one's very existence in the company depends wholly on one's recognition by one's superiors, that is, the recognition (real or merely illusory) that one is contributing to the prosperity of the firm. (One might occasionally recognize one's self as a self independently of his or her life on the job, but this would be quite rare. It would typically occur in those moments just before one decides to quit.)

This suggests a distinction also suggested by Hegel in his parable, between self-consciousness *as such*, the self-consciousness of the self as agent, "the self in itself," what Kant called "the Will," and having a *particular* self-consciousness, that is, self-consciousness of oneself *as* such-and-such, as the bearer of certain feature, of being a skillful negotiator, of being out of place in a meeting of employees, of being the best salesman in the department. Such features are clearly constitutive of the "me." There is some question whether the first and more general sense is presupposed by the latter more or less particularized senses or is rather derived from them. This is the source of Hegel's slave's bad faith, shifting his claim from the supposed involuntariness of the self as loser to the alleged helplessness of the self as such, and this, too, is the typical ploy of the hapless employee or manager who shifts attention from the particular fact that one has made a disastrous decision to one's overall characteristic weakness of will or "market forces." It is also the *modus operandi* of corporations who "externalize" their responsibilities, whether to consumers, the taxpayers, or the community.

The origins of self-consciousness by way of mediation by other people suggests a problem with the facticity and transcendence formula of bad faith. Sartre's discussion of bad faith sometimes makes it look as if bad faith might be just a matter of one's opinion of oneself qualified, in some troublesome way, by the facts about oneself. Other people enter in only as persons from whom one wants something, people to be coped with, sexual partners, or the source of problems. But if self-consciousness is itself the product of one's relations with other people, as in Hegel's parable, it is easy to see how other people might not be at all tangential or incidental to bad faith and to one's opinion of oneself. In fact, even the chapter on "Bad Faith" is shot through with considerations of bad faith via the looks and opinions of others, including virtually all of Sartre's examples. So bad faith turns out not to be a two-way tension but a three way tension between one's facticity, one's transcendence, and what Sartre calls "Being-for-Others." But as we saw with facticity and transcendence, the distinction between these supposed dimensions of human reality is none too clear. So what the facts are and what people widely believe (for example, one's skill as a manager) is often problematic, and what one thinks of oneself and what one "internalizes" as other people's opinions of oneself (as in the "hero" CEO) turns out to be an enormous issue and a complicated source of tension.

In most of the chapter on "Bad Faith," Sartre maintains the misleadingly simple and therefore seductive thesis that bad faith is a denial or a confusion of two very different and opposed aspects of ourselves, facticity, the facts that are true one oneself, and transcendence, that which goes beyond the facts. To be sure, there are examples of self-deception that are a lot like this, and Sartre plays with them, notably, with the waiter in the café who pretends *to be* a waiter, in his novel, *Age of Reason*, where his character Mathieu insists (a la Sartre) that he is not what he obviously is, and in the play *No Exit*, where the male protagonist wrestles with the question whether he is (or was) nothing but the sum of his actions (and of *which* actions?). But most of Sartre's examples of this supposed phenomenon are demonstrably something quite different, in which it is the view of *other people* that creates the problem of bad faith and not just the self-reflection of the subject. In other, bad faith is not only the product of facticity and transcendence ("being-in-itself" and "being-for-itself") but of what Sartre calls "Being-for-Others" as well. We shall see that this complicates matters enormously.

There are times, as in some of Sartre's literary examples, when bad faith may devour the whole of one's life. But even so, it is not as if one just *is* in bad faith. Again, people might say this ("Well, I guess I'm just in bad faith.") but this, quite palpably, is just another case of bad faith, another way of refusing to face up to one's responsibilities, and a way of trying to justify one's bad behavior to other people and change their expectations. No one, however, is "just in bad faith." Some people are more conflicted, less consistent and less coherent in their values and their ideals, and more willfully distracted. But many are not. It is the nature of consciousness that, short of extreme trauma or psychopathology, few of us are all that conflicted, inconsistent, or incoherent. Our lives (more or less) "hang together," and the right hand usually has a good idea what the left hand is doing. We may all occasionally fool ourselves about what we are doing with our lives and conceptualize ourselves in self-serving (or in some cases self-denigrating) terms, but there are almost always limits to how extensively we can do so. And Sartre has pointedly insisted on the most important of these limits, the fact of our freedom, and with it the idea that we are always choosing what to do and are responsible for those choices.

Are We Victims of Circumstances? The Notion of *Character*

Sartre's conception of bad faith and Hegel's conception of the mediated self have both been bolstered and exemplified not only by postmodern philosophy but also by current empirical psychology. Both bad faith and the mediated self can be found in business ethics, for example, in the now perennial arguments whether corporations can be or cannot be held responsible.[1] One familiar line of argument holds that only individuals, not corporations, can be held responsible for their actions. But then corporate executives excuse their actions by reference to "market forces" which render them helpless, mere victims of economic circumstances, and everyone who works in the corporation similarly excuses their bad behavior by reference to those who set their agenda and policies. They are mere "victims of circumstances." They thus betray their utter lack of leadership. Moreover, it doesn't take a whole lot of research to show that people in corporations tend to behave in conformity with the people and expectations that surround them, even when what they are told to do violates their "personal morality." But what might count as "character" outside of the corporation tends to be more of an obstacle than a boon to corporate success, for what seems to count as "character" in the corporation is a disposition to please others, obey superiors, follow others, and avoid personal responsibility.

This notion of character can cut different ways in any discussion of responsibility. On the one hand, the celebration of character may emphasize will power, independence, autonomy, and taking responsibility for one's choices. On the other hand, the concept of character can be used to mitigate responsibility and accept what philosophers refer to as "determinism" which in turn is commonly thought to undermine agency and responsibility. Thus David Hume and John Stuart Mill, the two most illustrious empiricist promoters of this strategy, suggested that an act is free (and an agent responsible) if it flows from the person's character[2] where character stood for a reasonably stable set of established character traits that were both morally significant and served as the antecedent causal conditions demanded by determinism. Adam Smith, Hume's best friend and the father of not only modern economics but of business ethics too, agreed with this thesis. It was a reasonable solution that saves the notions of agency and responsibility and is in line with our ordinary intuitions about people's behavior. (Also, it did not try to challenge the scientific establishment, the main promoter of determinism.) Sartre, notoriously, does not believe in character, I think mainly for this reason. If character is considered to be the determinant of actions (as opposed to the result of many particular actions and decisions) one can readily fob off responsibility onto one's character, blaming one's character for one's poor decisions and one's disastrous choices instead of taking responsibility for them. I think that this is short-sighted on Sartre's part, however, since character can take on a meaning that he would very much approve of, namely, character as will power, autonomy, and taking responsibility.

Accordingly, I consider myself a "virtue ethicist." I take the concept of character (and with it the related notions of virtue and integrity) to be central to the idea of being a good and responsible person in business. But I take it to be so only in the strong (Sartrian) sense, not in the bad faith prone deterministic sense. I would add here that virtue ethics, despite its heavy play in Anglo-American ethics in recent years, precedes this by many years, going back to Aristotle and, on the Continent, to Brentano and Scheler. Such an ethics is particularly appropriate for business ethics because the concept of character fills the void between institutional behaviorism ("organizational behavior") and an overblown emphasis on free will and personal autonomy that remains oblivious to context, the reality of office work, and the force of peer and corporate pressures. It provides a locus for responsibility without sacrificing the findings of "management science." Nevertheless, I have mixed feelings about the empiricist solution, in particular thus determinist-friendly Hume and Mill account. It does not account (or try to account) for actions "out of character," heroic or saintly or vicious and shockingly greedy behavior which could not have been predicted of (or even by) the subject. And it does not (as Aristotle does) rigorously hold a person responsible for the formation of his or her character. Aristotle makes it quite clear that a wicked person is responsible for his or her character not because he or she could *now* alter it but because he or she could have and should have acted differently early on and established very different habits and states of character. The corporate bully, the greedy entrepreneur, and the office snitch all would seem to be responsible for not only what they do but who they are, according to Aristotle's tough criterion.

On the other hand, however, the empiricist solution overstates the case for character. (This is what some psychologists, and Gilbert Harman, refer to as the "attribution error.") The empiricists make it sound as if character is something both settled and "robust" (the target of much of the recent psychological literature). Character consists of such traits as honesty and trustworthiness that are more or less resistant to social or interpersonal pressures. But character is never fully formed and settled. It is always vulnerable to circumstances and trauma, and it is formed, as Sartre rightly points out, through the accumulation of actions and decisions. People change, and they are malleable. They respond in interesting and sometimes immediate ways to their environment, their peers and pressures from above. Put into an unusual, pressured, or troubled environment, many people will act "out of character," sometimes in heroic but more often in disappointing and sometimes shocking ways. In the corporate setting, in particular, people joke about "leaving their integrity at the office door" and act with sometimes shocking obedience to orders and policies that they personally find unethical and even downright revolting. But they are clearly in bad faith in their willingly subjecting themselves to forces that are meant to undermine their autonomy. The corporation one joins, the jobs one accepts, the ambitions one takes on, the small bits of behavior that define the average working day, all of these contribute to the making of the character that one is. Character is never merely "given" in advance of all our behavior.

These worries can be taken care of with a Sartrian retooling of the notion of character and its place in ethics. But my worry is that in the effort to correct the excesses of the empiricist emphasis on character, the baby is being thrown out with the bath toys. In recent work by Gilbert Harman and John Doris, for example, the very notion of character is thrown into question and with it, the concept of responsibility as autonomy.[3] Indeed, Harman suggests that "there may be no such thing as character," and Doris entitles his book, tellingly, "Lack of Character." (Although Doris tries nobly, I should add, to show how responsibility can survive the absence of character). But Harman and Doris, both analytic philosophers deeply engaged with empirical psychology, provide an impressive defense of the Hegelian-postmodern thesis that we are deluding ourselves to think that we as agents are responsible for our own actions. While the ontology might be very different (Hegelian all-embracing "Spirit" versus postmodernist ill-defined "forces" versus the "subjects" in social psychology experiments), they all tend to deny and undermine responsibility by denying the idea of a responsible, more or less autonomous agent. (Doris's conclusion is candidly postmodern, and he entitles it "The Fragmentation of Character" and he explicitly defends the idea that there is no "core of character" that explains our social behavior.)

Harman and Doris argue at considerable length that a great deal of what we take as "character" is in fact (and demonstrably) due to specific social settings that reinforce virtuous conduct. To mention two often-used examples, clergy act like clergy not because of character but because they surround themselves with other clergy who expect them to act like clergy. So, too, criminals act like criminals not because of character but because they hang out with other criminals who expect them to act like criminals. Sartre would half agree, but then he would charge that this is giving way entirely to the notion of Being-for-Others, as if there is *nothing but* Being-for-Others, and this, too, is a clear example of bad faith. Harman argues vehemently against what he calls the illusion of "a robust sense of character." Doris argues at book length a very detailed and remarkably nuanced account of virtue and responsibility without character. The conclusion of both authors is that character in the sense that Sartre would endorse it, as more or less autonomous decision-making, is at best a mistake, and at worst a vicious political maneuver.

It is worth saying a word about this "vicious political maneuver" that is the political target of Harman's and Doris's arguments. I share in their concern, and I, too, would want to argue against those who, on the basis of an absurd notion of character, expect people to "pick themselves up by their own bootstraps," blaming the poor, for instance, for their own impoverishment and thus ignoring social and political (not to mention medical and racial) disadvantages that are certainly not their fault. I, too, reject such a notion of character, but I am not willing to dispense with the very notions of character and the virtues in order to do this. Nor, of course, is Sartre, who might gladly give up the deterministic notion of self but would never forget that free agents are always in a *situation* (their facticity), including other people, and of course it is against this background that any and all decision-making takes place. And some situations are debilitating. (Sartre came to appreciate this, after defending "absolute freedom" in his early work, prompted by his friend and colleague Maurice Merleau-Ponty.)

So, too, in business ethics, there is a good reason to be suspicious of any notion of character that is supposed to stand up to overwhelming pressures without peer or institutional support. I would take Harman's and Doris's arguments as well as the insights of Hegel and the Postmodernists as good reason to insist on sound ethical policies and rigorous ethical enforcement in corporations and in the business community more generally, thus maximizing the likelihood that people will conform to the right kinds of corporate expectations. Nevertheless, something extremely important gets lost in the face of that otherwise quite reasonable and desirable demand. It is the idea that a person can and should resist those pressures, even at considerable cost to oneself, depending on the severity of the situation and circumstances. That is the reason that existentialism ought to be appealing to people in business. It is the hope that they can and sometimes will resist or even rise up against pressures and policies that they find to be unethical.

Notes

1. E.g. Kenneth Goodpaster and John B. Matthews, Jr., "Can a Corporation have a Conscience?" *Harvard Business Review*, Jan.-Feb. 1982; John Ladd, "Morality and the Ideal of Rationality in Formal Organizations" *The Monist*, Oct. 1970; Peter A. French, *Collective and Corporate Responsibility* (New York: Columbia University Press, 1984); Peter A., French, "Responsibility and the Moral Role of Corporate Entities," in R. Edward Freeman, ed., *Business as a Humanity* (*Ruffin Lectures II*) (New York: Oxford University Press, 1994); Peter A. French, "The Corporation as a Moral Person," *American Philosophical Quarterly* 1979 (16:3); Manuel G Velasquez, *Business Ethics* (Engelwood Cliffs, NJ: Prentice-Hall, 1982 and further editions).
2. David Hume, *An Enquiry Concerning Human Understanding*, 2nd ed. L.A. Sleby-Biggee, Ed., (Clarendon: Oxford University Press, 1902; John Stuart Mill, *A System of Logic* (8th ed.) New York: Harper & Row, 1874; Adam Smith, *Theory of the Moral Sentiments* (London: George Bell, 1880).

3. Gilbert Harman, "Moral philosophy meets social psychology: Virtue ethics and the fundamental attribution error." *Proceedings of the Aristotelian Society* 1998–1999, 99, pp. 315–331; Revised version in Harman, G., *Explaining Value and Other Essays in Moral Philosophy* (Oxford: Clarendon Press, 2000), pp. 165–178; See also, "The nonexistence of character traits," *Proceedings of the Aristotelian Society* 1999–2000, 100, pp. 223–226; John Doris, *Lack of Character: Personality and Moral Behavior* (New York: Cambridge University Press, 2002).

References

Doris, John. 2002. *Lack of Character: Personality and Moral Behavior*. New York: Cambridge University Press.

French, Peter A. 1979. "The Corporation as a Moral Person," *American Philosophical Quarterly* (16:3).

French, Peter A. 1994. "Responsibility and the Moral Role of Corporate Entities," in R. Edward Freeman, ed., *Business as a Humanity* (*Ruffin Lectures II*). New York: Oxford University Press.

Goodpaster Kenneth and John B. Matthews, Jr. 1982. "Can a Corporation have a Conscience?" *Harvard Business Review*, Jan.-Feb. 1982

Harman, Gilbert. 1999. "Moral philosophy meets social psychology: Virtue ethics and the fundamental attribution error." *Proceedings of the Aristotelian Society* 1998–99, 99, pp. 315–331.

Harman, Gilbert. 2000. "The nonexistence of character traits," *Proceedings of the Aristotelian Society* 1999–2000, Vol. 100, pp. 223–226.

Harman, Gilbert. 2000. *Explaining Value and Other Essays in Moral Philosophy*. Oxford: Clarendon Press. pp. 165–178.

Hegel, G.W.F. 1977. *The Phenomenology of Spirit* trans. A.V. Miller. New York: Oxford University Press.

Hume, David 1902. *An Enquiry Concerning Human Understanding*, 2nd ed. L.A. Selby-Bigge, Ed., Clarendon: Oxford University Press.

Ladd, John 1970. "Morality and the Ideal of Rationality in Formal Organizations" *The Monist*, vol. 54, no. 1, October 1970, pp. 488–516.

Merleau-Ponty, Maurice 1962. *The Phenomenology of Perception*, Evanston: Northwestern University Press.

Mill, John Stuart 1874. *A System of Logic* (8th ed.) New York: Harper & Row.

Sartre, Jean-Paul 1956. *Being and Nothingness* Trans. H. Barnes, New York: Philosophical Library.

Smith, Adam 1880. *Theory of the Moral Sentiments*. London: George Bell.

Solomon, Robert C. 2006. *Dark Feeling, Grim Thoughts: Experience and Reflection in Camus and Sartre* Oxford University Press.

"It's Business; We're Soldiers": *The Sopranos*, Liberal Business Ethics, and this American Thing of Ours

H. Peter Steeves

Envelopes of Cash

I'm not sure how many connected men I've met in my life. At least three. Likely more. The number seems high to me as I've lived most of my life in the quiet American Midwest – not a hot-bed of *Cosa Nostra* activity by most regards. And yet, I have . . . stories.

When I was just out of my first year of college I was in search of a summer job and thus came to tutor the only son of a rich Italian businessman in a town in Illinois. The boy was attending summer High School and it was my job to see he passed every class, especially the math and science courses, his greatest challenges. We worked for hours each day (it was a struggle; he bore more than a passing resemblance to A. J. Soprano in body as well as mind); and I would reward myself most nights by accepting the hospitality of the family, especially happy to take home a Tupperware container of the mother's manicotti or the grandmother's freshly made and frozen *cassatta siciliana* – exotic foods to my Ohio-born, Hamburger Helper-acquainted, Velveeta-accustomed palate.

In my memories, twisted and interpreted as memories necessarily are, the grandmother was a lovely stereotype. Not a scheming Livia Soprano, but a Hollywood creation nonetheless: the happy Italian *nonna* committed to her family, talking about "the Old Country" with a tear in her eye, offering food as the solution to all of life's problems. She had been born in Italy and moved to the U.S. as a young girl; and after more than seventy years in this county she still seemed "Italian" to me in a way that was somehow deeper than her son.

Is thinking in such a stereotype itself somehow immoral? Was I wrong to think this way? Am I wrong to remember this way? Was I wrong to care so much for this woman and her family, knowing – no, not quite *knowing* – but "knowing" how it was that the bills were paid? Where is the beginning and the end of my own complicity?

Have another plate of *mani-got* for now, my "adopted" grandmother would say. Don't worry. You'll figure it all out tomorrow.

H.P. Steeves
Professor of Philosophy, DePaul University, Chicago, IL, USA
e-mail: psteeves@depaul.edu

M. Painter-Morland, P. Werhane (eds.), *Cutting-edge issues in Business Ethics*,

The father's business had something to do with construction, though it was impossible for me to imagine him ever having a speck of dirt on his clothes. The materials from which his suits were made seemed flowing and smooth, like running wine. No jogging suits and see-through socks in his closets. He seemed to me such a good and kind man as well. He clearly loved his family. He slapped me on the back each day with a smile, thanked me for doing a commendable job with his son, treated me with respect and good humor, and paid me every Friday. In the middle of trying to get out of a geometry lesson one particularly sunny morning, his son once spoke of the family's boat out on the lake, eventually making a passing reference to his father's work and letting the word "construction" hang in the air with an ironic tone. But it's not as if I accidentally came across $50,000 in Krugerrands and a .45 automatic while hunting for a pencil sharpener in the house. And yet....

At the end of the summer, "A.J." passed all of his classes to the delight and surprise of his parents (and his tutor), and everyone insisted that I come to the house one last time that final Labor Day weekend as part of the family, part of the party, part of the collective celebration of the ending season and the accomplishments of the previous months.

It was an unseasonably cool September. We ate sausage cooked outside with peppers and onions grown in the family garden. We played horseshoes and bocci in the finely kept lawn beside the tennis court which I had never seen being used, and came back to sit close to the grill in the early evening, the imported handmade tiles beneath us cool and red, shadows of their surface imperfections appearing and disappearing in the blue flame light. I was in a different world, a world I was soon leaving, and I took time to take it all in as such. At the end of the day the father called me into the house, into the kitchen, and thanked me for the miracle I had worked with his son. I assured him that the boy had truly worked hard, but he wouldn't hear it. He said that he wanted to give me a bonus for having done such a fine job. I refused, sincerely needing the money but just as sincerely not wanting to take anything away from his son's accomplishment or to take a greater payment than that on which we had agreed. I had my honor as well. He definitely wouldn't hear it. With a warm smile that should have – but somehow did not – clash with his serious eyes and the determined force with which he took my hand and made the decision for me, he placed an envelope of cash against my open palm then pushed my hand up to my body toward my heart before letting go and walking away. I didn't look in the envelope but folded it and stuffed it into my pocket, playing my part. I would not see him again.

Later that evening the grandmother kissed me on the cheek and wrapped up three sausages in aluminum foil for me. The cream floodlights that shone up the sides of the house were turned on, the lightning bugs scattered out of the garden, and I left for home.

Tony and the B of A

Tony Soprano feels disappointed that he came in at the end of *this thing of ours*. "The best," he says with great remorse and in the grips of depression, "is over" ["The Sopranos" (Pilot)]. Yet regardless of the fact that the Mafia seems to have lost the code of honor that once – at least so goes the collective myth – held it together, Tony's identity, his sense of self, his set of values, are direct creations of the community in which he finds himself today. Against the tide of modern life with its constant undertow of Liberal metaphysics and relativistic ethics, Tony treads purely communitarian waters: he *is* his roles and relationships – father, husband, lover, Don, friend, and executioner; the point of overlap of the many narrative threads that converge in modern Jersey to constitute this man. And yet he is in a state of crisis. It is a crisis that can, in part, be traced to the tension between Liberalism and communitarianism in the Western world. Liberalism, finding its roots in the seventeenth century thought of Descartes and Hobbes, maintains the radical isolation of the individual: we are each radically distinct monads, separate, equal, and armed with rights to keep each other at bay. Versions of this sort of thinking essentially found our society: capitalism, contemporary democracy, the U.S. Bill of Rights, our justice system, our educational institutions, our cultural myths all take this individualism – this view of what it is to be a self – as fundamental. To Liberal eyes, even, the Mob boss comes close to a Hobbesian Sovereign, with the *Omertá* oath which one swears upon entering the Mob akin to signing a social contract. The Mafia requires a Sovereign, not a community, in charge, goes the thinking – or as Sylvio Dante remarks: "We need a supreme commander at the top, not the fucking Dave Clark Five" ["Meadowlands"].

And yet, the Mafia is all about community, being-together, defining one's self in terms of one's relationship to the group. It is, at its very core, more communitarian than Liberal. Communitarianism rejects the assumption that all we can know, count on, or take to be fundamental in our politics, metaphysics, and ethics is the isolated individual. Instead, to be is to be a member of a group. We are born into – and throughout our life find ourselves caught up in – roles and relationships that, at a fundamental level, define who we are. The self is thus defined in terms of its relation to Others. First and foremost, one is someone's son or daughter, brother or sister, a member of this culture or that. We might then make decisions to go one direction or another, but it is always from a starting point over which we have no choice and by means of which we found our core identity. And even after we leave this initial position, we continue to be communally defined. The rejection of Liberalism is not the rejection of free will, but it is the acknowledgment that one's will is always tied to others' and thus is not radically individual. When his psychiatrist, Dr. Melfi, for instance, ushers in a discussion of free will with Tony, he rejects any radically individual formulation of it as a cause for his "chosen" line of work. "How come I'm not making pots in Peru?" he responds. "You're born to this shit" ["Down Neck"].

Saying one is born to a line of work and a way of life seems to be a way of sidestepping ethics – not just business ethics, but ethics in general. It seems to be saying that one has no choice. But *choice* is a Liberal value – the ultimate individual noninterference right for the ultimate radically self-creating individual. Choice is thus at the forefront of Liberal business ethics: did you choose the correct thing in releasing that product, blowing that whistle, hiring that person, cooking those books? Business ethics in America faces crises, though, under this Liberal model. Are corporations, for instance, individuals? Can they choose?

Can they be held accountable? As a culture, we have yet to come to terms with such questions, extending first amendment rights but not fifth amendment rights to corporations.

It is easy to offer a Liberal critique of the Mob's way of doing business: individual rights of noninterference are being violated; universal human rights (based on a belief in a universal human nature) are being rejected; Tony and his crew don't play by the appropriate Liberal rules. But if we accept a communitarian metaphysic of the self and thus an ethic as well, mustn't we admit that this is the life those in this community know, this is the set of traditions they hold in esteem? If one's identity is constructed within the Mafia business community, what right does a non-made man have to come in and say it is a bad identity, a pathological community, an immoral moral code?

In "From Where to Eternity," Tony gives a defense similar to this when Dr. Melfi asks a rare judgmental leading question about whether Tony thinks his violent ways will send him to hell. Tony is clear: hell is not for him; hell is reserved

> for the twisted and demented psychos who kill people for pleasure. The cannibals, the degenerate bastards that molest and torture little kids. They kill babies. The Hitlers, the Pol Pots. Those are the evil fucks that deserve to die . . . . We're soldiers. Soldiers don't go to hell. It's war. Soldiers, they kill other soldiers. We're in a situation where everybody involved knows the stakes. And if you're gonna accept those stakes . . . . You gotta do certain things. It's business; we're soldiers. We follow codes . . . . [L]et me tell you something. When America opened the floodgates and let all us Italians in, what do you think they were doing it for? Because they were trying to save us from poverty? No, they did it because they needed us. They needed us to build their cities and dig their subways and to make them richer. The Carnegies and the Rockefellers, they needed worker bees and there we were. But some of us didn't want to swarm around their hive and lose who we were. We wanted to stay Italian and preserve the things that meant something to us: honor and family and loyalty. And some of us wanted a piece of the action. We weren't educated like the Americans, but we had the balls to take what we wanted. Those other fucks, those other . . . . The J. P. Morgans? They were crooks and killers too, but that was a business, right? The American way.

Let's first admit that this "apology" makes some sense – as hard as that is to face. Tony is actually making a nuanced, thoughtful, philosophic response to Dr. Melfi's simple black-and-white take on the Mafia. The argument is that only those who enjoy violence (as an end in itself?) are evil, and that in a community where everyone knows the standards and codes, acts of violence are not necessarily immoral – the implication being that Tony does not take pleasure in violence but merely accepts it as part of his communal code, knowing he must dish it out and may someday have to take it. Furthermore, if outsiders critique the Mob's code, they should first look to their own history and their own traditions – the implication being even clearer that the American Mafia was a response to the subjugation of Italian immigrants, and that the "American Way" has its own violence hidden just beneath the surface. Indeed, in some ways one could extend Tony's line of thinking and suggest that there is something inherently morally superior to the Mafia as opposed to the standard "American Way" of business in that Mafia violence is not hidden, its codes are out in the open to all who are involved, there is no attempt to "pretty it up."

Let us be clear. Tony lends money to people. If they don't pay, he hurts them. He beats them, runs them over with a car, takes over their business and runs it into the ground, sends Furio to shoot them in the leg, etc. How is this unlike the Bank of America?[1] The B of A loans money to people. If they don't pay, the bank hurts them. In the meantime, Bank of America uses that money to invest in all sorts of nastiness that causes bodily harm to real people (e.g., Vietnam received that much more napalming thanks to the Bank of America). If someone doesn't repay the B of A after a couple of "friendly" warnings, the bank might take over that person's business, or take the person to court and force him into bankruptcy. When the bank comes to foreclose on the house, we do not call this violence. It is part of the system, a faceless corporation merely doing what it is legally entitled to do to someone who has not paid on his or her loan as promised. That this person might be put out on the street, that his or her family might then be hungry and homeless or even dying, none of this matters or counts as violence. In America, if your business fails or your pony doesn't place or whatever your story for running out of money to make good on your debts happens to be, that's simply an instance of The Invisible Hand: you can't compete, you lose. Yet surely as much as the hand is invisible, it is bloody as well – and all the perfumes in Arabia, all the scrubbing with Lava and Clorox over a bathtub, will not render it clean.

The Liberal sees the body as the vessel for the individual and thus associates bodily violence with the most threatening type of violence. Thinking that the self is solitary and unitary, the skin barrier fools the Liberal into thinking that the body is sacred, the boundary of the individual, that which marks the difference between me and you. To do bodily violence, then, is to threaten the sanctity of the individual. One can scream at a protester all one wants (that's a right to free speech), but don't lay a hand on him. The communitarian realizes that there is nothing special about personal body violence. There are other forms of violence as well: to communities, to families, to a way of life. The communitarian realizes that there is nothing "real" about the skin barrier. Flesh is communal, bodies are socially constructed, we are all in this together. To call beating a man for not repaying a loan a form of violence, but to refuse to call foreclosing on a man for not repaying a loan the same is merely a Liberal prejudice. Both are violations, painful disruptions, castigations by those with power for failure to make good on a promise. How can we condemn one and celebrate the other? Furthermore, Tony may have whacked Matt Bevilaqua for having tried to kill Christopher, but if the State had caught up to Matt first, they would have done the same – only after a supposedly straightforward and fair trial, in a nice clean sterile environment, with public approved gas or electricity or chemical injections, all so that the death could be orderly and peaceful and just and acceptable and nice. Who's scamming who?

The Mafia code suggests there be no "collateral damage," that only those within the community who know the stakes can be harmed. The violence is thus supposedly, though not always, *controlled* – not all violence is accepted – and this seems to be based on a social construction of different categories of players: some within the business and others outside. Even within the ranks, everyone knows you cannot lay a hand on a made man without permission from the top Boss – a rule Tony forgets when he roughs up Ralphie after Tracee is murdered and later kills Ralphie after Pie-O-My is murdered. Still, such moments aside, there is indeed allowable, sanctioned violence within the Mob community, violence as a legitimate way to operate a business. Must we be silent when we are asked if whacking a guy is *generally* wrong as a community business tradition?

It's not that each community has standards and that there is no way to critique one in favor of another. It's not that communitarianism must be a form of relativism. Hopefully this much is clear. There are universal truths according to the communitarian – universal truths about how identity is constructed, how we are always intertwined with Others and our Goods are intertwined as well, how we should not treat Others as if they were something they are not, etc. None of this is relative. But the problem with thinking that life is sacred and murder is wrong or – following Levinas – the face universally commands us not to kill, is that "life" and "murder" and even "the face" can be understood and constituted quite differently in different communities. Some constructions can be critiqued if they go phenomenologically wrong, but as general place-holders for the ultimate moral commands, they don't do much work. Something more fundamental must be decided, something that tells us how these terms came to be used the way they are being used and if those uses are *right.* In our own society – the "American Way" – we use set definitions that could have been otherwise.

To put the problem another way, perhaps we could argue that the immorality of Ralphie killing Tracee (the stripper carrying his baby) centered on phenomenologically taking her to be less than a real person, less than an Other in the community. But when Tony is faced with killing Febby Petrulio, the government witness rat he encounters while visiting colleges with Meadow, would he not be taking Petrulio as somehow less than a real person, less than a true Other in the community, if he decided that Petrulio should *not* be killed? The guy took an oath. He confirmed his membership in a community in which he agreed to be killed should he ever betray his friends and business partners. If Tony did not follow through, would he not then be constituting Petrulio as less-than-an-Other, as less than a thoughtful and willing person? Petrulio must die – given the moral code to which he agreed long ago. And Tony must play his role – in order to keep up his end of the code as well. It is a strange problem for Mafia-business-ethics: at first glance it might seem a sort of anti-whistleblowing; but this would be applying Liberal categories to an illiberal tradition. The categories are all different here, the rules never the same.

But let's put aside for the moment the larger question of generally critiquing Mafia business and instead admit that many of the apparently terrible things Tony does in the course of running his business are things in which we, as an audience, take pleasure. This is not only an aesthetics question, then, but a moral one. Is it merely that we wish we could run our business this way, living above the law and only by our own codes as Tony does? I don't think so. Al Swearenger, from HBO's "Deadwood," (2004–2006) is an interesting character who runs his Old West town making the rules as he goes; but he is much harder to identify with, much less sympathetic, than Tony Soprano. Rather, we revel in Tony's violence, I think, because it is so often a symbolic attack on the institutions of Liberalism – institutions we know, we feel, are killing us and are inherently violent to our true selves. Allow me, in conclusion, to try to make this claim clear.

To Kill a Rat

Karl Marx realized that one of the main problems inherent to Liberal capitalism is the way in which the anonymous marketplace and the exchange of money as the foundation of business lead to alienation. The *use-value* of an object (that is, the actual social value the thing has as something to be used to make life better) is completely divorced from the *exchange-value* of the object (in late-capitalism, the *exchange-value* of something is whatever money one can get for it in the marketplace). This level of abstraction, where money stands in for and replaces everything, is culturally damaging. Social relationships that should exist between producers and consumers are replaced by economic relationships and, to a certain extent, get confused with the commodity itself. Commodity fetishism begins to take shape, and we instill a sort of mystical power in the commodity. When we go to the store, we interact with products not people. We pursue individual self-interest and not our communal interest. And we assume that the marketplace will take care of everything for us. When the commodity is further fetishized, as Jean Baudrillard argues, it begins to play a role in the formation of personal identity. Certain products define who we are, and money itself acts as the great common denominator, allowing abstract measurement and comparison of things that could not be compared or measured outside of the system. Given that we no longer have real personal relationships, our merit is measured by how well we do in business, how much money we make, what sort of car we drive, and the general expense of the things with which we surround ourselves. The proletariat, the working-class stiff, suffers the most. But the situation is, in reality, damaging for all classes.

The fourth season episode "Everybody Hurts" is basically a meditation on this topic, a rumination on the nature of money and the way in which we are alienated by our pursuit of it and our self-definition by it. Artie loans money to a Frenchman, Jean-Philippe, as a sort of "foreign investment," but Artie is not a good businessman. Jean-Phillipe steals the money and beats Artie up when Artie tries to act tough and get it back. What is at stake here is not just the money, but Artie's manhood, his virility, the image he has within his family and his community. Without something more than just his restaurant, he will never be "legitimate" and thus "the next Bobbie Flay." In the same episode, Tony gives money to the suicide hotline after he learns that Gloria, his ex-lover, killed herself. The exchange of money as a replacement for inter-personal communication and relationships is the main focus here. Janice asks for a drink at the end of dinner with Tony, but makes sure to point out that it is expensive; Carmela cares very much about her $3000 statue; Tony cares about his 1.5 points (only $1500 interest on the $50,000 he loaned Artie to give to Jean-Philippe); and A.J. learns – and is disappointed by the fact – that his girlfriend, Devon, has a lot more money than he has. Devon's house actually looks like the Corleone's *Godfather* mansion with gates, guards, etc. (thus suggesting once again that there is no difference between so-called legitimate business and the Mob). All of the ways in which people should be relating one-on-one and personally, they instead employ money. Tony is generous and wants to be liked, so he sets up Carmela's cousin with a new suit from Patsie and finally decides to sign the living-trust papers that Carmela always wanted him to sign (which is a bad monetary thing for him to do for himself if there is ever a divorce). In the next episode, Tony apologizes to Melfi for knocking her Kleenex box off her table by sending her an expensive arrangement of flowers, and can only show remorse through money. What had, in part, infuriated Tony was both the fact that Melfi did not act as a friend and tell him about Gloria's suicide (instead, she acted as a psychiatrist, with a commitment to confidentiality), and that she had also pointed out in a somewhat condemning way that most of Tony's money comes through usury. Which brings us full circle as we must ask two fundamental questions. Isn't this the same way a bank makes money? And isn't it essentially the lack of real friendship that Tony is bemoaning? Melfi didn't tell Tony about Gloria's death as a friend truly would; Artie didn't treat Tony as a friend but merely as someone to fear or someone from whom to get money.

Friendship is most likely the glue that keeps all communities functioning. This is a truth that goes all the way back to Aristotle, a man who knew that one can only have a limited number of friends and that a community has an upper size limit beyond which it will not function justly (for lack of real face-to-face relations and thus true community). Friendship appears in many different forms and has multiple cultural incarnations, but one way or another, without this close bonding, face-to-face connection, and the true sharing of a life in common, we could not be human. Liberalism, however, inevitably destroys friendship as a means for social organization and thus for doing business. Personal relationships are not supposed to make a difference in Liberal interactions: judges and jury members must leave a case if they know the litigants; bank loans are decided by mathematical formulae rather than acquaintance or trust; doctors see multiple strangers as patients each day; friends and strangers all pay the same price for bread at ones bakery; and Franco-American (come on, the *French*-Americans producing your macaroni?!) makes sure their SpaghettiOs are not poisonous only because the huge corporation is afraid of lawsuits, not because it cares one bit about you and me having a healthy dinner, feeling well, living or dying in horrible gastric pain. How can the corporation care: it has no feelings. And worse yet, the people that run it do not know you and me, they have no stake in how we feel as real people, only as potential customers, because we do not share a common life, we have no face-to-face interaction, we meet only as strangers on a huge playing field designed to make living morally all but impossible.

When Tony resorts to violence it is typically of a personal kind. He does not run shareholders and stakeholders into bankruptcy from high above, as the leaders of Enron did. He does not allow others to take his fall while still making money and supporting widespread violence as Dick Cheney did with his Haliburton cohorts. No. Tony shows up at your house if you do him wrong. At times he sends his most trusted friends to take care of business: Furio beats the Frenchman who swindled Artie in his bad business move; Sylvio takes Adriana for her last ride upstate. But typically, at the crisis moments, Tony himself takes care of business. He waits at the country home with a shotgun to blow away his cousin without a word; he cuts off Ralphie's head and puts it in a bowling bag; he smothers Christopher before he calls for an ambulance; he garrotes the rat and puts Pussy to bed with the fishes.

Part of the reason we take a certain pleasure in some of Tony's violence, then, is that we see him using it out of frustration in a Liberal world where friendship, acquaintance, and close personal relationships are being ignored. When Uncle Junior's doctor starts ignoring him and his worries about his cancer, for instance, we all know the feeling. Uncle Junior does not want to put faith in a system, in an HMO, in the medical *business*, or in a scientific treatment plan. He wants to put faith in another person. But Dr. Kennedy is part of the Liberal world. He doesn't care about Junior. And how could he? He doesn't really know him at all. The doctor is trained to do a job like any other, and he does his best because he does not want to be sued and have his malpractice insurance go up, not because he takes Junior's Good – a Good that is necessarily unknown to him – as such as his own. What Junior wants, what we all want, is for someone to be working to cure our illnesses because he or she cares, because he or she takes our best interest to heart and truly sees how our Goods are intertwined. When Dr. Kennedy continues to snub Junior, then, Tony and Furio pay him a visit on the golf course and convince him at least to play the part of a caring physician so that Uncle Junior does not give up hope in curing his cancer. As Tony threatens Dr. Kennedy in a "friendly" yet deadly serious way, he slowly backs him into a water-trap on the golf course. Furio "playfully" smacks the doctor's hat off because it had a fictional bee on it, and they let the man know "[t]here are worse things that can happen to people than cancer" ["Second Opinion"]. Tony knows that he needn't harm this man, that the threat will work just fine, and we are happy with this as well.[2] We are happy to see someone chip away at Liberalism.

Something similar is working in the case of Dr. Melfi's rapist ["Employee of the Month"]. When the attacker goes free on a technicality, we are outraged; but having such a rule is important in a faceless, bureaucratic, Liberal justice system. Without guaranteeing the accused his or her rights, there can be no justice on a large scale. Without guaranteeing a secure chain of custody in handling evidence, how can we go about prosecuting the millions of people we end up prosecuting each year? No matter that it is personally clear to all involved that this particular man is guilty of this particular rape. The procedure outweighs personal experience in importance in the Liberal system. And so, the attacker walks away a free man. We would understand if Dr. Melfi acted on her impulse to mention what has happened to Tony. Tony – the protective bulldog – would surely set wheels in motion that would punish this man and "squash him like a bug." And yet Dr. Melfi chooses to remain silent.

Her silence is not for fear of having Tony do something unjust. Tony's is a less Liberal, and surely more outwardly violent, system of justice, but he does not dispense punishment thoughtlessly. He will, that is, do everything he can to find out if the fellow he saw in Maine (in the first season episode "College") really was Febby Petrulio, the rat who sold out his friends. When Tony threatens a doctor, he does so in the name of what could have been, what should be, of someone truly caring for another. Is it ironic that Tony's threat of violence is actually an echo of a call for trust, caring, and friendship? When Tony murders Petrulio, he does so in the name of trust, loyalty, and honor. Petrulio, too, has rejected friendship. Is it ironic that Tony then murders in the name of friendship? Is it absurd to say that the only way left to be a true friend to Petrulio is to murder him?

We are big-pussy-footing around a dangerous point: to take this person as a true Other, one must respect him enough to kill him? There are Kantian echoes here, I know. Kant (in)famously outlawed all murder – for any reason (even self-defense) – but was in favor of capital punishment, arguing that to *not* kill the killer is to treat him with less respect and dignity than he deserves, to treat him as if he did not possess a free will, as if he were not capable of realizing that murder is a false maxim (one that cannot be universalized without logical contradiction). In order to treat the murderer as an end in and of himself, then, Kant would whack him.

A critique of this bad Kantian reasoning would take us too far off course now, but it is important to note the general sense in which Kant goes wrong. His equation of logic and ethics, his Liberal view of the individual in general, and his suspect reasoning that an executioner is not a murderer himself all deserve attention; but more to the point, we should look at the sense in which Kant would argue that the murderer freely willed to commit his crime. Free choice, as we have seen, is the ultimate value for a Liberal. Since the Liberal individual is metaphysically disconnected from all Others and from the world, the Liberal definition of freedom is having the individual will disconnected as well. This value of choice, then, becomes a foundation for Liberalism in all of its guises. We think someone is free if he or she can vote for either a Republican or a Democrat (choice!), if there are fifty different types of breakfast cereals on the shelf (choice!!), if a man is homeless and sick and destitute yet no one is physically keeping him from getting a job and becoming the next Bill Gates (choice!!!). For a communitarian, choice is a value, but it is one among many – and it is never taken to be radically free. As a communitarian I realize that other wills intersect with my own, and the narratives in which I find myself will always be setting boundaries to my choice. None of us – not Michael Corleone, not Tony Soprano, not John-Paul Sartre, not you, and not I – are doomed to radical freedom.

Still, though, it is unclear if violence is ever truly to be condoned, whether freely chosen or not. Should killing a business associate ever be anything but immoral? Could Tony – however illogically, however impossibly, however absurd it sounds – have let his best friend and greatest betrayer, Big Pussy, live and still have been Pussy's true friend? Could he have found a way to save him *and* remain true to him? Can our violently shattered postmodern identity *not* be a hallmark of our way of interacting as well? Could Tony have chosen something other than what he apparently must have done? Could Pussy have lived and the world stayed in one piece? Could Pussy have lived!?

Have another plate of *mani-got* for now. Don't worry. You'll figure it all out tomorrow.

In the end, perhaps the *agita* of identity is a sign, the trace of violence inherent in all becoming and all being. Perhaps it is an indication that we are never fully realized, never truly made, never free from the responsibility of choosing right over wrong even when the choice is less than free, less than really ours. This, then, is what it means to be in the business of a wise guy: to know just how little we know as we simultaneously refuse to accept our short cut. It is to know that even envelopes of cash stuffed into youthful pockets on quiet Midwestern nights make us who we are, and we will echo these moments the rest of our lives in a world that was never fully innocent.

Notes

1. Bank of America assets in 1998 were $618 billion; in 2004 they are $930 billion.
2. A nearly identical thing is happening when Carmela takes the pineapple ricotta pie to Jeannie Cusamano's sister and asks for a letter of recommendation to Georgetown for Meadow ["Full Leather Jacket"]. (Note that Tony also starts with a gift—a new golf club—for the doctor.) Georgetown will have tens of thousands of applications, with no way to tell who are the best students apart from mathematical, statistical analysis of GPA's and SAT's, etc. A supporting letter from someone that an admissions officer might know can make all the difference. Carmela calls on a friend's family for the favor, but the sister refuses even to look at Meadow's dossier, arguing that she only writes one letter a year and already wrote that letter (for a disadvantaged youth she obviously does not even personally know). Carmela's threat does the job and makes the Liberal process a bit more personal, even if that personalism is, in the end, a facade.

Redefining Accountability as Relational Responsiveness

Mollie Painter-Morland

Introduction

Accountability is a concept that remains central to our understanding of justice, honesty and responsibility within the contemporary business world. It is therefore not surprising that the spate of big corporate scandals that occurred over the last decade brought the importance of accountability into sharp relief. When things go wrong in the business world, society wants justice. Stakeholders, who suffer the consequences of business misconduct, demand the truth about exactly what happened, how it happened, and why it happened. They want those involved to take responsibility for their actions. Principles such as justice, honesty and responsibility require that individuals and corporations "give an account" of their decisions and actions. The implications seem simple and self-evident: If the actions and decisions of an individual or corporation bring about positive consequences, he/she/it can justly be rewarded. On the other hand, if such actions or decisions have harmful consequences, blame or punishment can rightly be appropriated to the guilty parties.

This understanding of accountability assumes a direct causal relationship between particular positive or negative business events and the actions and decisions of specific individuals or organizations. As such, this understanding of accountability lies at the heart of most efforts to ensure ethical business conduct. The legal frameworks that are usually created to curb corporate misconduct and the internal compliance processes that are implemented in many organizations are specifically designed to identify and punish those individuals and organizations that are implicated in business misconduct. These measures attempt to dissuade corporate agents from engaging in business misconduct by threatening to hold them to account for their actions and decisions.

This view of accountability relies on a number of crucial assumptions. The first of these has to do with the way in which individual and corporate moral agency is understood. Secondly, it is implicitly assumed that a direct cause and effect

M. Painter-Morland
Associate Professor of Philosophy, DePaul University, Chicago, IL, USA; Part-time Associate Professor at the University of Pretoria, South Africa
e-mail: mpainter@depaul.edu

M. Painter-Morland, P. Werhane (eds.), *Cutting-edge issues in Business Ethics*,

relationship exists between agents and the consequences of their actions. Furthermore, it is assumed that holding agents accountable for the outcomes of those business events in which they participate, or simply threatening to do so, encourages individuals and organizations commit themselves to ethical business conduct. What I will argue in this paper is that there are good philosophical reasons to question every one of these assumptions. These objections seem to call for a reconsideration of the way in which accountability is conventionally understood. I will therefore propose an alternative understanding of accountability, which is grounded in contemporary philosophical thought and the real life dynamics of contemporary business life. This alternative understanding of accountability is of a thoroughly relational nature and emphasizes moral responsiveness and innovative moral problem solving.

Moral Agency Redefined

The question as to whether business organizations can be treated as moral agents have been the topic of many papers and debates in the business ethics arena. At the heart of this controversy is the fact that individuals and organizations share many of the characteristics that apparently allow one to hold an agent morally accountable. A business organization can, for instance, make decisions just like an individual moral agent. Just like an individual, it can cause harm or be beneficent. It can also make conscious efforts to determine the likely outcomes of its actions or decisions[1]. Because of this, many business ethicists argue that business organizations should be held accountable in the same way as individuals. What this line of argumentation fails to consider however, is whether the way in which individual agency is being described, is in fact accurate. In business ethics literature, moral agents are typically described as rational agents, who make decisions on the basis of reasonable principles or calculations. This is evident from the fact that most authors utilize some form of deontological, utilitarian or rights-discourse when they describe the way in which agents make moral decisions (Jones, Parker, ten Bos 2005). Those who subscribe to this view of moral agency assume that corporate agents have a clear understanding of societal principles or values and the behavioral parameters that they suggest.

In this view of moral decision-making there is a tendency to unproblematically assume that good decisions will have positive consequences and that bad decisions will have undesirable implications. It relies heavily on the belief that decision-makers are capable of developing a clear, "objective" view of what is "right" and "wrong" in any given situation. Decisions and acts are seen as deliberate, intentional responses, over which individuals have complete control. It is based on a belief that there is a direct cause and effect relationship between the willing and acting agent and the consequences of his or her decisions and behavior. What is assumed then is that an agent, or a group of agents can be isolated and identified as *the* single cause of an event. It does not allow for the influence of organizational culture, or other factors in the workplace environment such as peer pressure, performance management and rewards to be brought into the equation. In this view, the rational moral agent is someone who is unencumbered in his/her moral determinations by personal biases and social pressures. An individual's capacity for moral behavior is determined by his/her ability to "apply" rules and principles to particular moral dilemmas.

Some contemporary moral theorists[2] propose a radical departure from the notion of an isolated, rational moral agent who makes his/her moral decisions and acts on the basis of *a priori* universal imperatives. These proposals problematize the idea that an agent can be held individually accountable for his/her "rational", "deliberate" decisions and actions. The increasingly interrelated virtualized world of contemporary business also challenges the way in which moral agency has conventionally been understood. Instead of being calculating, isolated decision-makers, business practitioners are compelled to act in relation to, and in interaction with one another. Moral agency does not reside in an isolated individual agent. Instead, it is a thoroughly relational affair. A number of 20th century philosophers have drawn attention to the way in which historical contexts (Foucault 1994), social practices (Bourdieu 1990), metaphoric language (Lakoff and Johnson 1999), as well as his/her embodiment (Merleau-Ponty 1987), shape the moral agent's judgments. In their view, moral judgments reflect tacit knowledge and social grammars that the moral agent is seldom conscious of. Judgments that are made on this basis, it is argued, are not necessarily purposeful or willful. In fact, moral knowledge is acquired through an ongoing process of trial and error (Petersen 2002). The specific actions or decisions of individuals and organizations represent a whole constellation of unarticulated beliefs and intuitive perceptions. Together, these beliefs and perceptions constitute the corporate culture of a particular organization, which informs the moral sensibilities of individual employees.

Misconceptions about the nature of individual moral agency are often reflected in the way that corporate agency is described. Business organizations are regularly portrayed as closed systems that occupy the central, pivotal position on stakeholder maps. From this perspective, it is assumed that a business organization operates as a self-contained entity that freely interacts with stakeholders on its own terms. Those who attempt to curb corporate misconduct through legislation and regulation tend to assume that responsible business behavior is a matter of staying within legal boundaries, following rules and institutionalizing systems and procedures. These legalistic parameters are supposed to provide business practitioners with "objective" behavioral guidelines. Meanwhile, corporate success is measured in terms of the bloodless protocols of the double entry accounting system while business practitioners are primarily held to account for the state of their organizations' financial bottom-lines. Even the move towards so-called "triple bottom-line" reporting has not succeeded in fundamentally altering the calculative reasoning that informs conventional views of accountability. In the minds of many business practitioners, triple bottom line reporting has simply expanded the list of items on their organization's balance sheet. This approach to corporate accountability often leads to a check-the-box mentality. In the process, the existence of compliance measures and reporting practices are mistaken for ethical responsibility.

The apparent inability of such strategies to curb corporate misconduct is indicative of the questionable assumptions on which they are based. The influence of certain modern management traditions may be partially responsible for the questionable way in which many business ethicists and practitioners continue to think about corporate agency. When Frederick Taylor started to apply precise data-gathering techniques to corporations, management theorists began to think of their discipline more in terms of a science, than an art (Kikoski and Kikoski 2004, p.24). In the process, they sought to formulate rules that could predict how a corporation would operate under certain conditions, much in the same way natural scientists try to identify natural laws and make predictions on the basis of them. In the early 20th century, modern scientific method conceived both natural and human systems as orderly, rule-driven mechanisms. From this mechanistic perspective, it was possible, and indeed necessary, to distinguish between objective fact and biased opinion, between public commitments and private allegiances and between "right" and "wrong" when various possible courses of action were weighed up against one another. It is therefore quite understandable that these expectations became such an integral part of many peoples' understanding of accountability. However, for a few decades now, this mechanistic worldview is no longer considered the best model for understanding either natural or social systems and as such, our understanding of accountability may be in serious need of revision.

Over the course of the 20th century, many leading scientists have abandoned this mechanistic view of nature (Taylor 2001). Instead, it has been proposed that the dynamics of natural forces and organisms, as well as the organization of individual and collective human life, can be described more meaningfully in terms of the dynamics of so-called "complex adaptive systems". Complex adaptive systems are open, dynamic and continually adapt to new developments. Other sciences, like management theory, are once again following suit. Kikoski and Kikoski (2004, p.28) argue that the early 20th century's manager's "book of standardized practices" is inadequate in the disruptive, nonlinear information era. Since it cannot deal with fast-paced change and is unable to foster innovation, it actually becomes more of a liability than an asset. This has led to the emergence of the so-called "postmodern" management paradigm. In this paradigm, the focus is on "learning organizations" that function as open systems and maintain a delicate equilibrium close to the edge of chaos.

From the perspective of this more complex explanatory model, the conventions and expectations that organize and guide business behavior come into being and develop on a contingent basis as colleagues, clients and competitors interact with one another and do business. In a sense, the ethos of business life is something that continually develops among people, as they do business, in order to continue to do business. The 'orderliness' of business life is a reflection of the fluid internal logic of business as a system of dynamic functional relationships. One of the advantages of this more 'organic' understanding of business is that it looks for signs of functional organization within the dynamics of business activity itself, instead of trying to force it to conform to some preconceived operational model.

It also offers an intriguing model for describing the relationship between the tacit understanding among colleagues in an organization and the unconscious dynamics that are part of an individual's own sense of self. From the perspective of complex adaptive explanatory models, there is a non-linear relationship between individual employees' own unique sense of moral propriety and the tacit expectations that exist between him/her and his/her colleagues at work. This means that both affect, and are affected by the other. The same is true of the moral sensibilities of individual employees. Colleagues may reciprocally influence one another's moral sensibilities in unexpected ways. The perceived expectations of one colleague might, for instance, combine with the observed inclinations of another to produce an unconscious disposition in a third, which no one could have foreseen. As such, the relationships of influence in a contemporary business organization defy the deterministic logic of mechanistic modern management models. These models are only meaningful and helpful as long as the relationships between agents in an organization conform to a linear, cause-and-effect chain of causality. From the perspective of complex adaptive explanatory models however, relationships of influence within the organizational system are complex, unpredictable and reciprocal. In this respect they correspond with the ideas of theorists such as Bourdieu, Butler and Merleau-Ponty, who all described the relationship of influence between an individual and his/her social milieu as something, that is reciprocal, uneven and dynamic.

Because of the complexity and singularity of the relationships and dynamics that are involved, it is simply not always possible to articulate, in a conventional manner, the tacit understanding that a business organization's employees and agents have of the way in which things work, and are supposed to work. The nature of this kind of tacit organizational knowledge makes it impossible to codify or quantify like other, more 'explicit' forms of knowledge. Tacit knowledge differs from explicit knowledge both in terms of its source and content. Explicit knowledge allows agents to point to something concrete and demonstrable and assert that they know "*that*". Such knowledge can be articulated, motivated, contested and debated. Tacit knowledge, on the other hand, is not something that an agent can put his/her finger on. The possession of tacit knowledge allows an agent only the more modest claim that they know "*how*". It is an embodied form of knowing, an understanding that is only revealed when it is used to make a decision or perform a task. Authors in the field of knowledge management recognize that agents are often not aware of much of the tacit knowledge that they rely on to make moral judgments. Tacit knowledge is the kind of intuitive grasp of something that is hard to verbalize. It is intuitive and experiential because it often involves deep-seated mental impressions of emotional and physical experiences. Because of its intuitive and experiential nature, tacit knowledge is very difficult to analyze and even more difficult to "manage".

Tacit knowledge refers to the "unwritten rules" that everyone in an organization knows about, yet no one ever openly discusses. It is what people are referring to when they vaguely talk about "the way we do things around here". Philippe Baumard (2004, p.12) ascribes the development of tacit knowledge to the irrational, ceremonial and maneuvering nature of organizational life. Employees and agents gain their understanding of the dynamics of the organization in an informal and non-systematic way. He describes organizations as fast, fragmented and multidimensional operational fields with their own ceremonial conformity. Individual agents "know" what is appropriate because of the complex interaction of a company's history, its past successes and failures, its archives, its internal mail, its customs and its rumors. It is this tacit understanding that is of crucial importance in understanding how an organizational culture or ethos can influence individual ethical decision-making.

As we have seen, the lines of influence between an organization's culture and its employees' moral sensibilities are not one-directional. It involves a multi-directional flow of verbal, visceral and mental signals about what is valued and expected by the organization's employees and agents. Employees on all levels contribute to the tacit understanding that emerges among them. Because this understanding emerges in the course of multiple interactions between employees, under various different sorts of circumstances, no one individual can control it. To be sure, certain individuals, like senior executives and charismatic leaders, may play a more prominent role than others. However, it is extremely difficult for a single individual to 'step out' of the web of unarticulated expectations, obligations and pressures that make an organizational culture what it is, in order to change or challenge it. Even if it were possible for an individual to do so, through some reflexive act of critical self-awareness, his/her agitations would simply be taken up in the multidirectional flow of tacit interpersonal signals within the organization, where it would combine with other, unarticulated expectations to produce any number of unforeseeable effects on the behavior of employees.

If the locus of moral agency lies in the reciprocal circuits of influence between individual employees' personal moral sensibilities and the complex network of relations within an organizational environment, the assumption that individuals act in a deliberate, rational and willful way becomes untenable. Complex adaptive explanatory models also question the viability of constructing direct cause and effect relationship between particular decisions and consequences. Within a complex adaptive system, seemingly insignificant events can have major effects. Furthermore, because moral agency is not exercised deliberately, it seems unlikely that the threat of being held accountable would deter individuals or organizations from wrongdoing. Individuals may never stop to deliberately ponder the potential punitive consequences of their business practices and calculate the risks. Clearly, considerations such as these seriously undermine the questionable view of accountability that many people still subscribe to. However, accountability is not an obsolete concept in contemporary business life. The notion of accountability will remain meaningful and significant in business ethics discourses, but only if it is fundamentally reconsidered and reconceived.

Redefining Accountability

If the notion of accountability in contemporary business life is not well served by the assumption that individuals or corporations act in a rational, deliberate, and willful way, what does it mean to be accountable? In a recent work, Judith Butler (2005) considers Nietzsche's claim that accountability typically only follows upon an allegation or accusation made by someone who can deal out punishment and only if causality can be established. According to Nietzsche, we start to give an account only because someone asks us to, and because that someone has power delegated from an established system of justice (Butler 2005, p.11). If Nietzsche is right about this, reflexivity within a subject only becomes possible as a consequence of fear and terror. However, Butler is convinced that there are other ways of being addressed by another, which carries another kind of weight and can motivate one to give an account for other reasons. Butler suggests that being in a relationship with another and feeling the need to maintain the relationship through narration is central to the whole process of giving an account of oneself. People tell one another stories about how particular states of affairs came about. Even where direct causality seems absent, they tell stories about how things are related and how they hang together. Giving an account through processes of narration need have no relation to the appropriation of blame. The purpose of such stories can be to persuade, build trust, or nurture relationships. Butler's (2005) understanding of accountability is thoroughly rooted in the context of relational life. In a very real sense, it is only within the context of particular relationships, that any kind of account becomes meaningful and significant. It is this emphasis on the relational nature of accounting that makes Butler's work so useful in the consideration of morality in contemporary business life.

A new understanding of accountability requires an awareness of the relational context within which responsibilities and duties develop. It demands an acknowledgement of the dynamic network of interactive relationships within which individuals and organizations are embedded in the business environment, as well as a willingness to seriously consider the very consequential role and effect of expectations and perceptions within such a context. What is required is a broadening of our understanding of accountability. We usually think of moral agents as being accountable *for* something. However, considering the interactive way in which moral knowledge comes about and moral decisions are made, we may need to re-envisage a moral agent as someone who is accountable *towards others* or *in terms of* some shared sense of normative propriety. The notion of being accountable "for" something is usually associated in the business environment with responsibility for a set of defined, concrete assets. There is naturally merit in this, but it is hardly sufficient within the context of an open network of interactive relationships where perceptions and other intangible dynamics play such a crucial role. Individual business practitioners and organizations also need to consider *"towards"* whom they have responsibilities in the determination of their moral duties. To do so would be to acknowledge that much of the value of an organization is generated in and through cooperative business relationships and that the quality of these relationships may represent an organization's most valuable assets. The emphasis in such an approach is on the way in which a business organization and its employees engage with and respond to its stakeholders within an extended network of reciprocal business relationships. In addition, the nature and limits of an individual or organization's moral responsibility towards those with whom they interact could be clarified if it was understood *"in terms of"* a particular relational form of moral orientation. This is an approach that remains cognizant of the fact that an individual's professional inclinations and an organization's moral priorities develop relationally in the course of the interpersonal interaction between agents within a system of relations as well as under the influence of contact with alternative perspectives that may enter the system from without. The tacit sense of reciprocal responsibility, loyalty and common cause that develops among colleagues and collaborators in this way may resist formal articulation in the form of rules and procedures, but they nevertheless form the normative backdrop against which the actions and decisions of individuals and organizations become intelligible. As such, it is also an understanding of the nature of accountability that acknowledges the need for discretion and discernment. The actions and responses of individuals and organizations cannot adequately be appreciated or evaluated without considering the specific business episode and context within which it is situated and of which it is a part.

Accountability, from this perspective, is all about being responsive towards ever-changing stakeholder interests. It entails responding to these interests in terms of an evolving sense of moral appropriateness that has to be nurtured within everyday business practice. Values, from this perspective, are seen as a result of the relational dynamics within an open, complex adaptive system. The values that become manifest in the behavior of individuals within a particular organization represent what may be thought of as an "emergent order" within a system of functional relationships. This "order" is unique in that it is not formulated in reference to some abstract and supposedly independent point of moral orientation, nor does any one agent or body within or outside of the organizational system unilaterally impose it. Instead it spontaneously emerges over time in and through the interaction of individuals who participate in the system. Frederick (1995) has defined values as "enduring beliefs about preferable states of existence". They express and articulate those things we care about and that we think create a better world. A more relational understanding of the responsibilities of the organization therefore requires that those who contribute to, and participate in it continually consider what they care about, and that they make these priorities integral to their organization's goals. In other words, the organization needs to align its strategic goals and organizational values. In addition, care needs to be taken to ensure that some form of congruence exist between the moral priorities of the organization as a whole and the values of its individual employees. For this kind of alignment to come into being, some self-reflection will be necessary on both an individual and corporate level.

On an individual level, the individual will have to have some grasp of where he/she comes from, in what direction he/she would like to be heading and what is important to him/her as part of the journey. Foucault (1994) describes this process of reflection as a "genealogical unpacking" of the dynamics of power and knowledge that informs the self. The individual is not an isolated, independent rational agent, and therefore the social dynamics of power and knowledge creation plays into how an individual understands him/herself as well as the nature of his/her relationships and responsibilities to others. Judith Butler (2005) draws on these Foucaultian ideas to explain why the sense of normativity, which emerges as part of the self's processes of narration, is not completely solipsistic or relativistic. Naturally there is a need for some sort of normative boundaries if the notion of accountability is to have any meaning at all in business ethics practice.

Addressing the Objections

There are indications that some business ethicists are ready to begin looking at business ethics from a more relational perspective. Ed Freeman's (2001) shift of emphasis from stockholder to stakeholder interest, for instance, suggests a growing awareness of the fact that business success can no longer be assessed solely in terms of the financial benefit that is accrued by business owners. There seems to be an implicit recognition in all of this that business success is at least as much about sustaining mutually beneficial relationships with stakeholders, as it is about profit. Recent stakeholder literature also suggests that business ethicists are beginning to appreciate the way in which power dynamics and the complex interactions between organizations and stakeholder groups dynamize stakeholder relationships in the contemporary business environment (Phillips, Freeman & Wicks 2003, p.493). Because of this, the "balancing" of stakeholder interests is not always strictly effected in conformity to simple principles of equality, but often depends on the specific purpose of a particular stakeholder interaction. Obligations exist between discrete entities, rather than as abstract, general imperatives. There is a growing realization then that the notion of "stakes", and "relationships" require constant sensitivity and a readiness to respond appropriately to the singular contingencies of every new situation. There can, in other words, be no hard and fast rules to define the parameters of a business organization or practitioner's moral responsibilities to stakeholders.

These contemporary developments in stakeholder theory are certainly encouraging, but there seems to be something that makes many business ethicists resist a more relational understanding of moral values and obligations. In my opinion, it is the fear of relativism that is preventing these insights from fundamentally changing business ethics practice. To acknowledge that the normative content of moral duties is shaped by the tacit expectations, pressures and assumptions that are circulated in the complex web of relationships in which business practitioners participate, seems to suggest that rules can be made up as one goes along. What the skeptics of a more relational approach seem to fear, is that this will amount to a form of radical subjectivism on an individual level, or a kind of "When in Rome do as the Romans do" relativism on an organizational level. While these fears are understandable, it has to be remembered that the normative content of moral responsibilities are not only shaped, but also limited by what is necessary to sustain relationships of trust with various stakeholders. What is considered appropriate can never be completely relative to the person or the problem, nor can it simply be dealt with in reference to a self-imposed and self-serving organizational environment. What is required instead, is a delicate balance between individual discretion and organizational influence. In a very real sense, what we are dealing with here is the practical implications of the free will-determinism debate.

A more relational understanding of the duties and responsibilities of business practitioners precludes the formulation of abstract general guidelines, but this does not mean that a business practitioner or organization can act in the absence of any moral expectations. Business practitioners and organizations are obliged to build and sustain relationships of trust, confidence, and respect with stakeholders and this imposes important limitations on what they can justifiably do. As a sense of moral propriety emerges in the course of specific sets of interactions, it creates strong normative expectations that guide and inform individual behavior. The kinds of moral constraints that emerge in the context of specific business relationships are often of a more demanding nature that more conventional legalistic ones. They require careful consideration and discretion in each situation. If individual employees are to build and sustain crucial relationships of trust with their organization's stakeholders, they need to participate fully in the multidirectional relational circuits within the organizational system. It is in and through these channels of reciprocal influence that the normative sensibilities of those who participate in the organizational system are continually shaped. An individual employee's participation in an organization's internal network of relations therefore helps to ensure that his/her moral sensibilities remain congruent with that of the organization system as a whole.

Even though an individual employee's sense of normative propriety develops in interaction with his/her colleagues and associates at work, it is important that an organization's ethos do not begin to function as a deterministic straightjacket. Since normative expectations emerge within the context of a particular "internal" system of organizational relationships, there is always the risk that employees will become insulated against those interests that do not fall within the ambit of their own immediate concerns. In the process, organizations run the risk of becoming inured against discourses that utilize a logic contrary to their own. What safeguards the organizational system against the potentially harmful effects of such insularity, is the fact that complex adaptive systems are organized as open networks of relations. As such they cannot function in isolation from one another. They are therefore unlikely to devolve into deterministic environments that undermine the possibility of dissent and criticism.

To both maintain a meaningful sense of moral orientation and avoid self-interested insularity, it is important for organizations to actively seek and nurture relationships. American pragmatism' relational view of moral development is very helpful in this regard. Richard Rorty is one of the more prominent contemporary proponents of pragmatist thought. He describes moral development as a matter of "re-making human selves to enlarge the variety of relationships which constitute those selves". Rorty associates morality with an agent's sensitivity and responsiveness to the needs of an ever-larger variety of people. Instead of constructing a foundation for moral truth on the basis of some arbitrary set of metaphysical first principles, pragmatists direct their efforts at the extension of existing networks of relationships. For Rorty (1999, p.87) the pragmatist emphasis, in considering moral issues, is on breadth, rather than depth. He compares this accommodating process of critical inclusion to the sewing together of a very large, elaborate, polychrome quilt. Moral obligations and duties are continually defined and redefined as a moral agents respond to the dynamics and contingencies of the relationships to which they commit and in which they participate. The relational nature of this pragmatist approach compels agents to recognize, respect and accommodate the differences between various individuals and organizations. Building relationships requires a certain amount of accommodation and inclusion. Because of this, the normative orientations of organizations remain open to challenge, reform and development. However, the tacit sense of moral propriety that informs the behavior of an organization's individual employees does not develop overnight. It develops gradually over time and it is never entirely reified. As such it is always susceptible and subject to the shaping influence of those who participate in the organizational system. An organization's agents and employees always have an opportunity to contribute to its internal process of value formation. While it may not be possible to deliberately impose a set of pre-formulated values on employees, the everyday decisions and actions of individuals, as well as the way in which an organization is structured can over time have a decisive influence on what is valued in and by the organizational system.

The way in which basic organizational functions like strategic planning, human resource management, supply chain management and reporting practices are treated can have a significant impact on the ability and willingness of individuals to remain morally responsive to the contingencies and dynamics of particular relationships and situations. Within each of these organizational functions, individual corporate agents, and the corporation as a whole, signal their values to others with whom they are in a relationship. The need to maintain trust, respect and goodwill, as well as dedication to the purpose of a particular business association, all influence how an organization or its agents interpret their duties and responsibilities in specific business episodes. The way in which an organization reports its practices is an indication of how it sees its duties and responsibilities. For instance, if an organization feels compelled to remain responsive to a variety of stakeholder constituencies, it is unlikely to limit the account that it gives of its activities to the accumulation of physical assets and financial gains. Corporate responsiveness requires that an organization explain how it perceives its relationships towards its stakeholders and how it intends to build and sustain these relationships. Suppliers, employees, customers, and the communities within which the corporation operate all have different informational needs when it comes to corporate reporting. The Global Reporting Initiative's guidelines[3] provide an example of the various types of information that an organization may include as it gives an account of its activities.

If moral responsibility depends on the ability and willingness of an individual to remain responsive to the contingencies and dynamics of ever developing relationships, then it is crucial that individual's retain a sense of critical self awareness. When individual employees are rendered subject to the expectations and pressures of an organizational system to such an extent that they lose their capacity for critical self reflection, their ability to remain morally responsive in an authentic way is also impaired. If employees are not allowed to participate in the process of defining an organization's priorities on both a strategic and operational level, they are also unlikely to buy into the organizational system's tacit operational ethos. Participative decision-making, teamwork, and cross-cultural learning are crucial elements in the facilitation of relational responsiveness. In order to nurture relational responsiveness, multiple discursive spaces must be created that challenge participants to explore new ways of narrating the corporate identity. It literally challenges agents to tell the story about who and what the corporation is and what it stands for in different ways. Openness towards difference is very important, as it facilitates the dissemination of new ideas, and can open the possibility of new relationships with important, yet previously unknown stakeholder-constituencies. It is this process that fosters innovation, growth and creative problem solving. All of these elements are crucial for survival in an intensely dynamic contemporary business environment. It enables an organization to "give an account of itself" in new ways and to continually reinvent itself in and through its relational responsiveness.

Conclusion

If we are to redefine accountability in the contemporary business environment we need to recognize ourselves as relational beings. It is also important to understand that a business organization is an entity that exists in and through its ever-evolving stakeholder relationships. Contrary to the compliance-driven approach that is favored by many business ethicists, individual or corporate moral agents can never be adequately motivated to meet their moral duties and obligations through the threat of punishment. A moral agent's sense of duty should not be imposed from without. It should be something that emerges from within the organization because it understands that what it is and what it can do is intimately bound up with the relationships in which it participates. A more relational understanding of the notion of accountability proceeds from the assumption that the most meaningful normative duties and responsibilities resist legalistic formulation and codification. This does not mean that it allows for an "anything-goes" subjectivism or relativism. The dynamic normative expectations that define an agents moral duties and obligations within a relational context provide tacit, yet meaningful guidance. While the emergence of such expectations among its employees is not something that an organization can control, everyone who participates in the organizational system have the opportunity to contribute to it. From a relational perspective, accountability is something that requires ongoing attention to "the way we do things around here". Ultimately, it is only through their everyday business interaction with others that an organization and its agents discover the true nature and extent of their moral obligations.

Notes

1. The assumption upon which this argument relies is that the corporation can be viewed as a moral agent in much the same way that an individual can. It draws, in this regard, on the work being done in agency theory by authors such as Peter French. The article by Goodpaster and Matthews (1983[2001]) "Can corporations have a conscience?" provides a rationale for extending moral agency to corporations.
2. I have outlined the philosophical critique of the rational moral agent in more detail elsewhere. See: Painter-Morland, Mollie 2007. "Redefining Accountability in a Network Society". *Business Ethics Quarterly,* 17(3): 515–533. This critique includes MacIntyre's critique of the "ghostly self" in After Virtue, Foucault's insights into the interaction between power, knowledge and self, as well as the work of Mark Johnson and Verner Petersen on moral agency.
3. See the Global Reporting Initiative's Guidelines on www.globalreporting.org.

References

Baumard, P. 2004. *Tacit Knowledge in Organizations*. SAGE, London.

Butler, J. 2005. *Giving an Account of Oneself*. Fordham University Press, NY.

Bourdieu, P. 1990. *The Logic of Practice*. Harvard University Press, Cambridge.

Foucault, M. 1972. *The Archeology of Knowledge*. Pantheon Books, NY.

Foucault, M. 1994. *Foucault: Ethics, The Essential Works I*. The Penguin Press, London.

Freeman, E.R. 2001. Stakeholder Theory of the Modern Corporation. In: Hoffman, W.M, Frederick, R.E. and Schwartz, M.S. *Business Ethics: Readings and Cases in Corporate Morality*. McGrawHill, Boston.

Jones, C., Parker, M. & Ten Bos, R. 2005. *For Business Ethics*. London: Routledge.

Kikoski, C.K. and Kikoski, J.F. 2004, *The Inquiring Organization. Tacit Knowledge, Conversation, and Knowledge Creation: Skills for 21st-Century Organizations*. Praeger, London.

Lakoff, G. and Johnson, M. 1999, *Philosophy in the Flesh. The Embodied Mind and its Challenge to Western Thought*. Basic Books, NY.

MacIntyre, A. 1988. *After Virtue*. Duckworth, London.

Merleau-Ponty, M. "Carnality" in Taylor, M.: 1987. *Alterity*. University of Chicago Press, Chicago.

Nagel, T. 1987. *What Does it All Mean? A Very Short Introduction to Philosophy*. Oxford University Press, NY.

Petersen, V.C. 1999b. *Thinking with Our Hands – The Importance of Tacit, Non-algorithmic Knowledge*. Working paper 99–10. (The Aarhus School of Business, Aarhus, Denmark).

Petersen, V.C. 2002. *Beyond Rules in Business and Society*. Edward Elgar, Northampton. p. 309–357.

Phillips, R., Freeman, R.E., Wicks, A.C. 2003. "What Stakeholder Theory is Not". *Business Ethics Quarterly*, 13(4): 479–502.

Rorty, R. 1999. *Philosophy and Social Hope*. Penguin Books, London.

Taylor, Mark C. 2001. *The Moment of Complexity. Emerging Network Culture*. University of Chicago Press, Chicago.

Hegel on the Place of Corporations Within Ethical Life

Nathan Ross

This chapter examines the relevance of the philosophy of G.W.F. Hegel (1772–1831) to the contemporary practice of business ethics. Although Hegel's philosophy is rarely discussed in this context, there are compelling reasons why it should be. As an ethical philosopher, Hegel has his own distinctive normative theory that separates it from Kant, virtue ethics and Utilitarianism. His theory of ethical life provides a prescriptive model for how social and political institutions should be configured so as to make possible the ethical agency of those who take part in them. Thus his theory removes the emphasis on individualistic, subject-oriented decision making that we find in many other ethical theories, and instead places the emphasis on the relation of individual actions to their social and institutional context. This makes Hegel's theory particularly well suited to business ethics, where the agent is always confronted with economic, social and legal parameters in attempting to make an ethical decision. Further, of the major ethical philosophers from the history of philosophy, Hegel is one of the few to devote extensive attention to economic processes and to grant a special place in his ethical theory to the kinds of ethical issues that emerge in a growing, industrial economy. Finally, his theory of ethical life involves a particular prescriptive model for the role of the corporation in the economy. Though his conception of the corporation clearly bears a resemblance to the 19th century model of the corporation, I will argue that much of his ethical argumentation is still relevant today, in the age of corporate scandals and increasing political regulation of the economy.

Hegel's 'Ethical Life' as a Normative Model

Before describing the specific meaning that Hegel attributes to corporations, I will begin by clarifying the more fundamental normative foundation that Hegel provides in his ethical philosophy. Hegel has his own distinctive way of attributing normative value to actions, which is quite different from more well known ethical models such

N. Ross
Assistant Professor of Philosophy, Oklahoma City University, Oklahoma City, OK, USA
e-mail: nross77@yahoo.com

M. Painter-Morland, P. Werhane (eds.), *Cutting-edge issues in Business Ethics*,

as virtue ethics, Kantian universalism and utilitarianism. Indeed, Hegel was quite aware of these ethical models in his own writings and he provides substantial reflections on how his own perspective is different. The key to understanding Hegel's ethical theory, and how it is different from these others, will consist in explaining the meaning that he gives to the term 'ethical life', and how he contrasts this term to what he calls 'morality'. In general, I will argue that Hegel's theory of ethical life can be understood as a method that replaces the normative analysis of individual intentions, actions and consequences of action with a normative analysis of social institutions. An action is ethically good insofar as it (1) takes place within or (2) helps to bring about a rational institutional structure. A rational institutional structure, according to Hegel, is one that promotes freedom by providing us with a clear sense of how our rights and duties relate to those of others who are affected by our actions. Any analysis of actions that attempts to judge their moral worth without taking into account this institutional context is, according to Hegel, overly abstract and incapable of providing ethical actors with grounds that will motivate them consistently to pursue the good. In this section, I will work to clarify the theoretical basis of Hegel's ethical philosophy and to counter a common objection to this theory, namely that it is merely descriptive of social practices and has no normative or critical capacity. Countering this objection will allow us to see Hegel's theory of the corporation as a prescriptive ethical model for business practices that is still applicable today.

The term 'ethical life' is the accepted English translation of Hegel's German term '*Sittlichkeit*'. The term '*Sitte*' means 'custom' in German, and *Sittlichkeit* could best be translated as: an ethics that is rooted in customs. In contrast to this notion of ethical life, Hegel uses the term 'morality' to describe a normative perspective that considers the moral worth of an action in terms of subject-oriented standards: the goodness of a person's intentions, the consistency with which one can will a course of action, the results of an action for one's own well being or that of others.[1] 'Ethical life' on the other hand implies a normative perspective that takes into account the social context of an action: how does the action represent a response to social norms and institutional structures? How does the action work to change a defective social practice, or how does it conform to a good social practice?[2]

Hegel does not completely deny the validity of the perspective that he calls morality. As agents who have a limited knowledge of the world and how our actions fit into it, we are forced to turn inwards and focus on our actions form this moral perspective. What is more, the development of a moral perspective on the world shows the autonomy that people gain in certain societies to abstract themselves from the social norms around them and take up a critical stance. Hegel considers such autonomy to be one of the most valuable aspects of modern, Western cultures. But he argues that if philosophy is to give a fully consistent account of the way in which people manage to actualize their moral goals, it must take into account the actual political and social structure of the world, how it motivates them to act, how their actions relate to it, and how the meaning that they give to their actions is shaped through institutions and practices. This argument by Hegel could be compared to the moment in Plato's *Republic* where Socrates claims that if we want to know what justice is, we might do better to turn away from the question of what makes an individual just or unjust, and ask instead what social and political structure makes a society just or unjust.[3] Plato's point is not that individual justice is not important, but that we can more concretely understand the nature of what it means for a person to be just if we consider the social world that such justice would belong to or at least strive to create.

Hegel's theory of ethical life describes three central institutions of modern life: the family, civil society (meaning the realm of economic interaction) and the state. He describes versions of each of these institutions that bear a distinct resemblance to the modern, Western, protestant context in which Hegel lived. The family he describes is a nuclear family in which children are taken care of up to maturity and then expected to leave and start their own families. The economy is an industrial economy driven by private enterprise and regulated by state intervention so as to prevent extreme poverty and unemployment. The state that he describes is a constitutional monarchy, with a bicameral legislative body. The question presents itself to most readers of Hegel: is his theory of ethical life simply a description of the dominant institutions of his time? If so, then isn't Hegel a moral relativist, who believes that a social practice is ethical simply because it is embraced by a given culture? Such charges seem to be strengthened by some of Hegel's own words in the preface to the *Philosophy of Right*, where he writes his famous dictum that "the real is the rational" and he argues that "philosophers are children of their time" (Ibid., 24–26) and hence unable to present an ethical vision that radically transcends the social reality around them. Is it the case that Hegel believes that a social practice is rational simply because it is widely practiced and instituted as binding? If this charge were true, then it would be particularly damning for Hegel's theory of the corporation, which he treats at the end of his section on civil society. His description of the corporation is obviously quite different from the corporation of today, since he views the corporation as a legal entity that requires a state charter, that has sole control over a certain sphere of production and that involves democratic participation from all of its workers. If Hegel's method were merely descriptive in nature, then this theory of the corporation could simply be dismissed by arguing that this model is no longer applicable to current business practices and hence has no theoretical value.

It can, however, be demonstrated that Hegel's method of argumentation in the ethical life section of his *Philosophy of Right* is not merely descriptive, but has a normative and critical component. This point has been demonstrated quite well by a number of Hegel scholars in recent years.[4] Hegel's method in 'ethical life' does not consist simply in sanctioning existing social practices as rational. Rather, he argues that a social practice can only be fully acceptable to humans to the degree that it allows them to actualize their most fundamental human capacity, namely their ability to will rationally. At the root of Hegel's practical philosophy is an agreement with Kant about the source of all ethical value: an action is good insofar as it follows from the freedom of a rational being, and we embody such freedom only when our actions have a sufficiently universal quality. Hegel simply disagrees with the way in which Kant seeks to describe the realization of this conception of freedom. Hegel believes that freedom or autonomy is manifest not primarily in individual actions undertaken on valid maxims, but that autonomy is only fully realized when we are 'with ourselves' (Ibid., p. 74) in the world in which we are acting. He demands not just that we apply a test to the maxim behind our actions to see if we could will these actions consistently, but that we ask whether the world that we live in (and which is a result of our actions as well) is a world that promotes the rational agency of the individual. This critique of Kant's categorical imperative is based on two dualisms that Hegel sees in Kant's ethical philosophy: (1) the categorical imperative involves a split between the maxim (or intention) of the action and its actual effects. But Hegel argues that we are not truly autonomous unless we are able to see our rational plan actually realized in the world. As rational beings, we are confronted not only with maxims, but with the drive to structure the world according to our goals. Rationality is inherently teleological. (2) Hegel also rejects the Kantian dualism between inclination and duty. Kant believes that an action that reason prescribes is good independently of any (sensual) gratification that we might get out of performing the action. Hegel argues that this leaves us with a conception of the good that cannot motivate us to act upon it. The importance of such institutions as the family, the economy and the state consists in the fact that they provide us not just with duties that make our behavior socially acceptable, but they shape our desires in such a way that we are motivated to act upon our duties. In loving my parents, in pursuing work or creating employment, or in participating in the political structure of a well realized state, I am not merely doing my duty, but I am also doing what I want. Thus Hegel's theory of ethical life is an attempt to preserve the basic Kantian value of autonomy, while overcoming these two dualisms in Kant's theory by working it out in terms of institutional prescriptions.

A closer reading of Hegel's description of ethical life reveals that he is not simply endorsing the existing Western society of his time, but making prescriptive demands on the basis of a normative model. Nowhere is this more evident than in Hegel's treatment of the corporation at the end of civil society. Hegel realizes that professional organizations of the kind that he calls corporations have been dissolved in the most advanced industrial economies of his time. He also argues that the corporation, as he is describing it, is not the same as the guilds that existed at one time in Europe and still had some hold in Germany at Hegel's time. This suggests that we read the section on the corporation not merely as Hegel's defense of a dying social institution at his time, but rather as his attempt to provide a solution to what he saw to be the ethically disastrous consequences of the modern, industrial economy. Thus the context is prepared for interpreting Hegel's theory of the corporation: it is an attempt to provide an institutional analysis, rather than a moral prescription, of how we can be ethical within an industrial economy; and the standard that Hegel uses in determining that this conception of the corporation is an ethical one in that it allows us to recognize our own rational will within our activities.

Hegel's Theory of the Corporation

Within the *Philosophy of Right*, Hegel's treatment of the corporation comes at the end of his section on civil society, right before his treatment of the state. Civil society describes for Hegel the entire sphere of market-driven, economic activities, and it plays a crucial role as a middle-term between the family and the state in his theory of ethical life. Both the family and the state describe forms of conscious, ethical community: the family describes what Hegel calls an immediate, natural form of social co-existence, because its members are tied together through the bonds of blood. The state describes the most artificial, most universalistic aspect of ethical life, since it is the creation of a long historical process and involves unification through the legislative activity of the state. Civil society, by contrast, represents a moment of difference within ethical life, a sphere in which we pursue our self-interests and only relate to the interests of others insofar as they relate to our own. And yet Hegel includes this kind of activity within his overall theory of ethical life because he argues it can, if pursued in the right way, represent a crucial, positive phase in the ethical development of individuals. Hegel is influenced by Adam Smith and David Hume in believing that economic development and the cultivation of luxury have a kind of civilizing influence on the moral life of a society. In the economy we must work for others in order to meet our own needs, and this gives us an immediate motivation to socialize our behavior, conform to universal standards and be attentive to the demands of others. Further, the development of the economy instills many new desires for luxury in the subject and Hegel believes that this development of artificial needs means that in relating to our self-interest we are not relating merely to our natural impulses, but to society. He argues that we cannot be free in answering to natural impulses, since we are relating to something merely given to us, but in acting to pursue socially instilled desires, we are relating to psychological factors that are the result of human activity. Hence Hegel argues, contra Rousseau, that the pursuit of luxury is actually a precondition for the attainment of human freedom (PR 350).

For Hegel, the development of civil-society to the level of industrial production and free exchange is one of the very preconditions of modern political life. In his early writings, Hegel glorifies the Greek *polis* and sees it as the ultimate political ideal, because it relegated the sphere of production and exchange to the un-free class of servants and merchants and thus allowed for a political class that was unencumbered by the bourgeois element of self-interest. But by the time that he wrote his *Philosophy of Right*, Hegel reversed his position and came to see the freedom of labor in modern society as the real advantage of the modern state. Because of the freedom of labor and the open pursuit of economic activities, Hegel argues, no class or no necessary aspect of human existence need be excluded from the sphere of rational autonomy in the state. Greek freedom was built around the exclusion of the experience of necessity from the political realm, while the modern state makes possible a kind of freedom in which we are 'with ourselves' as rational beings even in the pursuit of our needs.[5]

Despite the fact that Hegel recognizes such a positive ethical role in economic activities, he is also deeply critical of the most advanced industrial economies of his time. In the first part of his treatment of civil society, 'the System of Needs', Hegel describes both the positive ethical education that comes from the social development of economic activities as well as the ethical problems that he sees arising from these activities. He traces a variety of ethical problems inherent to civil society: the development of systematic economic inequality, extreme poverty and unemployment, and eventually the cultivation of a social class that feels completely deprived of the benefits of the society around it and thus incapable of participating in a common political life.[6] What is crucial in Hegel's account is that he views these consequences not merely as accidents, nor as results of an economy that does not function adequately or has not developed far enough, but as inevitable consequences of a free, industrial system of production. He argues that the very mechanisms that produce industrial efficiency in an economy also lead to over-production, unemployment and social unrest that wear at the very integrity of the political body.

The basic ethical problem that Hegel sees at the root of civil society can be summed up in one word that Hegel uses: arbitrariness. The system of production and exchange is designed to satisfy people's needs and wants. And yet if this sphere were left to its own laws, Hegel argues, the actual satisfaction of these needs would remain utterly arbitrary. Some would manage to attain to a superb level of luxury and others would be left in a state of destitution resembling a second state of nature. In a free market, individuals have no right to have their human needs satisfied, but must constantly strive to prove themselves useful to the demands of the market. Hegel contrasts this state of arbitrariness to the ethic that rules the family; as a child within a family, I have the right to an education and to have my needs satisfied. A family that does not satisfy these needs is not an ethical family. But as a "child of civil society", Hegel argues, I lose this security and am left uncertain about my basic ability to take part in civil society as a producer and consumer. As an ethical philosopher, civil society presents Hegel with an acute problem: on the one hand, he recognizes its positive ethical value in the way that it provides for the education of the subject, and yet if the satisfaction of my needs is left to chance, then I cannot be 'with myself' as a rational being in civil society. How can Hegel preserve the positive ethical aspects of the modern economy and yet resolve the ethical problems that he sees as endemic to it? The answer to the question lies in Hegel's theory of the corporation.[7]

In introducing his theory of the corporation, Hegel sees it as fulfilling an analogous ethical role to that of the family. The family provides a space in which the child can develop into an autonomous subject by securing the necessities that the child demands in order to grow up, and by giving the child an education. And yet Hegel realizes that civil society is quite different from the family. In the family, I am related to other members of the family through blood ties and through love, while in civil society, I am related to others through the way in which we satisfy each other's economic demands. And yet Hegel argues that the corporation must accomplish on the level of an industrial economy what the family accomplishes in relation to the natural act of reproduction: it stabilizes a given form of production against chance and gives the individual who takes part in it insurance against the vicissitudes of the economy. It gives the worker the right to have her needs satisfied and to have access to an education that makes her a productive member of the economy.

Hegel's theory of the corporation has several features that are clearly normative in nature. He realizes he is describing a form of business practice quite distinct from any that were present in his day. In what follows, I will elucidate the features and functions that Hegel prescribes for the corporation, and clarify how the corporation fits into his overall theory of ethical life.

Prevention of Overproduction

For Hegel the problem of arbitrariness in the modern economy consists in the fact that the law of supply and demand is not capable of ensuring the economy against over-production. Market oriented mechanisms will promote efficiency in the production process, but they will not provide any security for the worker who relies on the production process. What is needed, according to Hegel, are countervailing mechanisms that take into account the interest of the worker in having stable employment, as well as the interest of society as a whole in the efficiency of the production process. Thus he charges a centralized, public authority with controlling price levels on necessary goods and insuring workers against unemployment. Yet Hegel also has qualms about excessive state welfare and regulation of the economy, for he realizes that state regulation interferes with the aspects of the market that lead to efficiency and that welfare takes away the formation of individual workers through their own activity. (Ibid., p.390) The solution, in Hegel's view, is that there should exist a balance between centralized regulation from the state and industry-specific self-regulation. Thus he describes two interlocking institutions with the same basic interests: the public authority and the corporations. The corporation is a self-regulating industrial organization, in which the members of the industry address the ethical concerns of the workers. He charges the corporation with the specific tasks of controlling prices, production levels and the number of employees, asserting professional standards to which workers must conform, and setting the benefits and wages of the workers in the corporation at a standard commensurate with the general standard of living.

State Mandate

For Hegel the right of the corporation to control the production processes of an industry and ensure its workers against unemployment must be balanced against the broader concern that the corporation provides a useful service to society. The mere fact that a group of people relies on a certain mode of production to make their living does not in Hegel's view justify this industry having corporate privileges. It must, in Hegel's terminology, represent a form of production that is 'substantial', i.e. which makes a valuable contribution to the demands of society as a whole. Thus he distinguishes his conception of the corporation from the historical existence of guilds in pre-capitalist economies. Guilds tend towards 'ossification' in Hegel's terms, because they take it as their interest to protect a form of labor and the people who pursue it from economic change. Hence they are blind to new production methods and do not allow entrance of members based on qualification, but based on tradition. The corporation must be responsive to the demands posed by a changing economy to pursue greater proficiency, as well as keep the profession open to all those who might be qualified to take part in it. Hegel submits the corporation to these demands by arguing that it must receive its mandate from the state, from a bureaucracy that has a more universal perspective on society and that represents the interests of the whole of society. This notion of a state mandate also makes clear that in Hegel's view the corporation must be charged with a specific form of production and not deviate from this mandate. Its mission is not to serve the owners (indeed Hegel does not even think of the corporation as an entity that is owned) but to fulfill a particular task with which society has charged it.

Representation

Though the corporation must be chartered by the state, it is essentially a self-organizing aspect of an industry. In Hegel's view, membership in the corporation is open to everyone who is involved in the mandated form of production, both owners and workers. It is structured in such a way that it allows everyone involved in the industry to have a voice in the affairs of the industry. Thus Hegel's theory represents a clear objection to the contemporary notion of the corporation as ruled in the interest of maximizing the profits for the owners. Hegel's reasoning on this point is rooted in the basic normative structure of his theory of ethical life: an ethical duty is only present in Hegel's view where there is a concomitant ethical right. Where I have no voice and no rights, I also have no obligations and there is no possibility for ethical agency. Thus in Hegel's view, industrial economies can only make up a part of ethical life insofar as they involve self-organizing corporate activity that is open to all of the members of the industry.

Employment Security

Members of the corporation gain the security that their place in the economy is not simply a matter left to the uncertainties of the market, but makes up a stable aspect of their personhood. Hegel distinguishes between a day laborer and a professional: to be a day laborer means to be ready to fulfill whatever need the economy might have at a given moment, while to be a professional means to have the honor that comes from knowing that one has secured the right to perform a particular kind of work and to count on a stable subsistence from this work. Even if the professional should become unable to work through no fault of her own, the corporation will step in to cover her subsistence. Further, this support and security does not have the degrading aspect that comes from being the recipient of charity or welfare, but rather contains the dignity that follows from a right that one has earned through ones activity. The particular ethical value of the corporation consists in the fact that it provides within each sphere of production the possibility to become a professional and gain the rights that follow from this status. Hegel justifies the importance of such security with reference to the family: in the family, we gain our personhood, our ability to become rational subjects, through the obligation of the parents to provide for the child. In economic affairs, the corporation gives us a similar security, with the difference that here we also gain the honor that comes from knowing that we have earned our security through our own contribution to society.

Unity of Duty and Right

For Hegel, the corporation does not remove the basic demand of civil society that individuals fend for themselves and that they only have their needs met insofar as they serve the needs of society. He merely thinks that the corporation raises this process to a level of rationality that it would lack if industry were left merely to the market. One of the cornerstones of Hegel's analysis of ethical life is the notion that ethical institutions must unify duty and right. We are only free in our duties if through them we also gain corresponding rights, and vice versa. This unity of right and duty is quite evident in Hegel's analysis of the corporation: the member of the corporation only gains job security and the dignity of belonging to the profession by proving that she is willing to live up to the professional standards laid out by the corporation. And the corporation only has the ability to impose standards of behavior as true ethical duties if the worker has the sense that in performing these duties, she is not merely obeying the demands of a boss, but is gaining a stable identity that cannot be taken away by the whims of the economy.

Hegel's Theory of the Corporation Today

After undertaking this description of Hegel's theory of the corporation, it seems necessary to ask what his theory has to say about modern business practices. His conception of the corporation, as a state mandated charter to perform a certain business function, seems today to be rooted in the 19th century legal reality and to bear little similarity to what we today call a corporation. Since corporations today are instead privately owned business entities designed to maximize profits through flexible business functions, his conception seems hopelessly outdated. Yet the question remains: has his description of the ethical dilemma at the root of all business activity really lost its relevance in today's post-industrial economy? And has his basic prescription regarding the role of the corporation as a part of ethical life lost its value completely? In this final section I will address these questions of relevance by pointing to some ways in which Hegel's theory must be up-dated, and by applying the basic arguments behind his theory to some contemporary issues in business ethics.

Clearly, Hegel's emphasis on over-production and the ensuing cycle of poverty and unemployment seems to have lost some of its bite in the context of the modern post-industrial economy of Western nations. To be a worker today does not necessarily mean to be engaged in the production of a commodity, but more likely involves facilitating the transfer of goods and services on some level. But the core of Hegel's argument about the system of needs is that the mechanisms that produce efficiency of production and exchange in an economy do not insure of their own accord that individuals will be able to find their human needs met by the economy. Hegel is worried not just by the cycle of unemployment that follows from over-production, but more fundamentally about the issue of arbitrariness in economic development: just because a system of production is efficient does not mean that it will promote the kind of ethical agency that Hegel makes the cornerstone of his ethical theory. Even if one argues that the problem of over-production is not the fundamental challenge to the modern economy that it was in Hegel's time, the basic problem to which he is pointing manifests itself in many other ways in the modern economy. The recent string of corporate scandals in American and European firms stems from a break-down in honest and effective accounting practices. This ethical vacuum was caused by the fact that accountants and fiduciary institutions were not able to maintain a clear sense of the difference between performing their professional obligation to society and rendering a service to the firm that had hired them. This lack of professional standards is merely one example of an economic environment in which individuals were rendered unable to think about the social consequences of their action by the lack of clear regulatory mechanisms. Accountants, consultants, as well as corporate managers were unable to see themselves as anything other than servants of the short-term interests of the corporation as a profit generating entity, and did not experience themselves as having any stable, professional identity.

This view of the ethical problems behind the corporate scandals is supported by some of the discussions following the shake-up of accounting practices through the new Sarbanes-Oxley legislation. This new legislation reacted to the lack of professional standards in the accounting practice by essentially removing the self-regulatory capacities of accounting firms and organizations. Yet in the wake of this legislation, some members of the accounting industry have argued that the way for accountants to regain clear ethical standards is not to strip them of their ability to impose their own standards, but to return to the understanding of accounting as a profession, that is, as a form of work in which one does not merely serve the interests of the client, but in which one acts based on deeper professional commitments to the profession and to society. (Oliverio 2003) Accountants can only regain this status if they are given the ability to develop their own professional standards in a forum that is independent from the business pressures placed on them by their clients. This conception of self-regulation as a path towards ethical agency seems quite parallel to what Hegel has in mind with his theory of the corporation. The core of Hegel's argument regarding the role of the corporation consists in the need for some self-regulating organizations within each industry, which allow individuals to separate themselves from the pressures of the market long enough to gain a stable ethical identity and reflect on their rights and duties within the economy. Hegel does not believe that this is possible without state oversight, but he allows each profession the right to organize in this manner.

In many cases today arguments in favor of corporate self-regulation rather than state regulation are founded in the interests of business to avoid regulation altogether. Nowhere is this more evident than in the call by some politicians to let industries impose their own pollution standards. This is certainly not the kind of self-regulation that Hegel has in mind in his theory of the corporation. First of all, Hegel considers the corporation not as a single business entity, but as representing the interests of all of the members of a specific kind of industry (thus in the case of accounting, the corporation is more like the AICPA than any specific accounting firm). Secondly, Hegel does not consider the corporation as managed in the interest of maximizing the profits for the owners, but rather as representing the voices of all the members of the industry, and aiming instead to balance the need for professional stability with the needs of society for that which the industry contributes. Finally, Hegel does not see a dichotomy between state regulation of an industry and self-regulation within the corporation: where society has a pressing interest in the positive or negative effects of an industry upon the whole community (as in the case of pollution), Hegel believes that the public authority must step in to impose standards. But he holds that the imposition of ethical standards upon any business practice cannot be fully effective if those who are engaged in the practice are not also given a forum for determining the specific manner in which the ethical standards can be coordinated with the long term interests of those employed within the industry.

Hegel's conception of the corporation is the attempt to resolve a fundamental ethical conflict that he sees in modern society: he believes that economic activity in modern industrial society contributes vitally to the ethical formation of the individual. In and through participation in the market we learn that we can only meet our own desires if we work to fulfill the desires of others. But Hegel also realizes that the very mechanisms that provide this ethical formation are not capable of ensuring that individuals actually find their needs met within the economy. Thus he introduces his theory of the corporation in order to avoid the extremes of a free market economy in which individual fulfillment is left to chance, on the one hand, and a regulatory state apparatus in which individuals are not able to form their ethical identities through their own activities. He believes there must be self-regulating, political structures built into industry that provide economic activity with the sense that right and duty are intimately bound together. In today's economy, we can multiply the number of ethical problems confronted by businesses to include many that Hegel had no way of anticipating, such as environmental costs of industry, global labor distribution and lack of clear professional standards for corporate mangers and accounting firms. But the essence of Hegel's theory is fundamentally applicable to each of these issues: how can we maintain the social benefits of economic development that economists such as Smith prophesied, while also dealing with the kinds of political issues that the market is not able to solve through its own activity? In Hegel's view, the only way that we can address this question is by thinking in new ways about the role of the corporation as a legal entity and as a forum for ethical debate within economic enterprises.

Notes

1. Hegel contrasts morality and ethical life in the last two divisions of his *Philosophy of Right* (1821) as well as in the 'objective spirit' section of the *Encyclopedia* (1817). Under morality, he describes theories that sound quite similar to Kantian ethics, virtue ethics, as well as Utilitarianism. He gives specific critiques of each of these theories, but he also attempts to group them together in order to clarify how his notion of ethical life is different than all three.
2. The difference between morality and ethical life is not simply the difference between a teleological theory and a deontological theory of ethics. In his treatment of morality, Hegel considers

how a theory such as utilitarianism that focuses on the consequences of action can still be subjectivist, since it uses the inherently subjective standard of pleasure or happiness to analyze the value of actions. The key contrast between morality and ethical life rests not in the difference between intentions and consequences, but rather in the difference between an individualistic evaluation of actions and an evaluation that takes into account the relation between actions and social practices and institutions.

3. Plato, *Republic*, 357b.
4. Cf. Siep (1987), p. 157–178, Wood (1990), p. 8–17 and Thompson (2000). These authors provide extended reinterpretations of Hegel's famous dictum that the 'rational is the real', which demonstrate that by actuality Hegel does not mean the factual, historical existence of a social practice, but the sustainability of a social practice insofar as it satisfies the demands of human rationality.
5. "In this social aspect (of dependence on others for luxuries) there is a liberating side, in that the strict natural necessity of our needs is hidden and the human being comports himself to something that is his own, namely a universal opinion and a self-made necessity, rather than to an internally arbitrary factor" (*Philosophy of Right*, p. 350).
6. Hegel develops these consequences in detail in §§ 236–245 of PR. For a strong account of why, in Hegel's view, these economic failures are inherent to the system of needs, c.f. Avineri (1972), pp. 86–98.
7. There are a great many differences in the secondary literature on Hegel's social philosophy regarding how he sought to solve the problem of poverty. Marx argues that Hegel grasps the problem of poverty in an astute manner, but is unable to venture a solution and hence advances a philosophy of resignation towards social injustices. Aveneri (1972) and Peperzak (2001) essentially agree with Marx in arguing that poverty represents a fundamental impasse in Hegel's social theory, with no real solution. Houlgate (1991) argues, as I will, that the corporation represents Hegel's structural solution to the problem of overproduction and social injustice in the modern economy. I have only a slight disagreement with Houlgate's account, which will be developed in subsequent footnotes.

References

Avineri, Shlomo. 1972. *Hegel's Theory of the Modern State*. Cambridge: Cambridge University Press.

Hegel, G.W.F. 1986. *Grunlinien der Philosophie des Rechts. Suhrkamp Werke VII*. Suhrkamp: Frankfurt a.M. (Also refered to as PR: Hegel's *Philosohy of Right* C.f. *Grundlinien* below)

Houlgate, Stephen. 1991. *An Introduction to Hegel: Freedom, Truth and History*. New York: Routledge.

Marx, Karl. 1978. 'Contribution to the Crique of Hegel's *Philosophy of Right*'. In: *The Marx-Engels Reader*. Ed. By Robert C. Tucker. New York: Princeton University Press.

Oliverio, Mary Ellen. 2003. 'Sarbanes-Oxley: Is Reconsideration Warranted?' *The CPA Journal*, September: 6–8.

Peperzak, Adriaan. 2001. *Modern Freedom: Hegel's Legal, Moral and Political Philosophy*. Dordrecht: Kluver.

Siep, Ludwig. 1987. *Praktische Philosophie im Deutschen Idealismus*. Frankfurt am Main: Suhrkamp

Thompson, Kevin. 2000. 'Reason and Objective Spirit: Method and Ontology in Hegel's Philosophy of Right'. In. Spindel Conference, Vol. 39.

Wood, Allen. 1990. *Hegel's Ethical Thought*. New York; Cambridge University Press.

Abjection, Ambiguity, and Female Sweatshop Workers: Is Alienated Labor *Really* an Ethical Problem?

Robin James

> *While the determinations of class, race, and gender make possible the continuation of labor exploitation for women of color, it may also precisely constitute the ground from which the cross-generational, cross-national, cross-class, anti-racist, and feminist struggles against those dominations emerge*
> (Love 1997, p. 275).

We're all familiar with the stereotypical sweatshop worker: the Asian woman working in a free-trade zone, the Latina in the maquilladora. In the early 21st century, the face of alienated labor is that of a woman of color, particularly, the third-world woman of color. For example, in the film version of *The Corporation*, we hear about women of color who work in sweatshops making Kathy Lee Gifford apparel for Wal-Mart. Assembly-line work at its most brutal, sweatshop labor is the contemporary paradigm for labor exploitation and alienation. However, it is my contention that standard narratives of labor exploitation, particularly those which focus on alienation and the "objectification" of (third-world) women of color, are further exploitative insofar as these narratives continue to place women of color in a structurally passive position, thus reproducing the colonial and patriarchal schemes wherein non-Western people and women need to be "saved" by those in the privileged classes (like philosophers). Marxian discourses of alienation and Kantian notions of ethics assume as normative a "pure" or "natural" state of agency in terms of which "alienation" and "objectification" stand as states of corruption and disempowerment. But what if one is a third-world woman of color, who is, in many ways, always-already objectified by and misrepresented in intersecting systems of race, class, and gender privilege, for whom any iota of agency and self-determination has come in the context of this objectification and alienation? Is it really "alienation" that makes these women's jobs so pitiful, or is it something(s) else (e.g., sexism, racism)? Is "alienation" the correct term to describe this kind of labor? Is alienation itself a corrupted, undesirable state?

R. James
Assistant Professor, Department of Philosophy, University of North Carolina, Charlotte, North Carolina
e-mail: rjames7@uncc.edu

M. Painter-Morland, P. Werhane (eds.), *Cutting-edge issues in Business Ethics*,

Critiques of "immediacy" and "presence" could constitute an entire subdiscipline in continental philosophy: determinate negation, negative dialectics, deconstruction, Lacanian psychoanalysis, docile bodies, performative identity. However, it seems to be a given that "alienation" is an undesirable and unfortunate phenomenon. In this essay, I consider a somewhat bold proposition, namely, that alienated labor is neither a flaw in need of correction or a symptom of capitalism's inherent brutality, but is in fact fundamental to (Western) subjectivity and society. Using Julia Kristeva's theory of the abject, I argue that the objectification of the self and of social relations in, for example, commodities, is not a hindrance to ethical actions and a just society, but their very condition. Indeed, the experiences of oppressed groups (women, people of color) demonstrate that social marginalization and objectification, while certainly disempowering, aren't absolutely disabling; as Lisa Love suggests in the epigraph, the fact that oppressed groups have organized to effectively promote social justice proves that it is incorrect to view objectified, alienated individuals as completely lacking in agency.

None of this is meant to justify sweatshop labor, or as a Milton Friedman-esque absolution of business from social and ethical responsibility. Rather, this paper is meant to demonstrate that the problems with sweatshop labor, with commodity fetishism, and ethical problems within business generally do not result from "alienation," objectification, or, in a more general sense, violating the "means-ends" formulation of Kant's Categorical Imperative (i.e., using someone as a means and not treating him or her as an end in him or herself). Because she considers humans in terms of *both* subjectivity (ends in themselves) and objectivity (means towards an end), I turn to Simone de Beauvoir's *Ethics of Ambiguity* both to critique the Kantian and Marxist assumptions about alienation, and to assess what, if not alienation, are the ethical problems with sweatshop labor and discourses about it.

Estranged Labor and the Categorical Imperative

A brief survey of the business ethics textbooks on my shelf yields the following observations: all contain some reference – either via primary or secondary sources – to Kant's categorical imperative, and two reprint the "Estranged Labor" section of Marx's *Economic and Philosophic Manuscripts of 1844*.[1] Examining these two works together, it becomes evident that both share the belief that it is wrong to use a human being as a means to an end. Although Marx is usually offered in business ethics readers as a somewhat "radical" ethical challenge to capitalism, it is my contention that Marx's views on estranged labor offer a fairly conservative view of agency, subjectivity, and ethics.

Kant's categorical imperative is one of the most well-known and widely discussed aspects of Western ethical theory. Because a full treatment of Kant's categorical imperative and its volumes of secondary literature would be an excessively lengthy detour to my task in this paper, I will provide only a brief overview of the categorical imperative as it pertains to my discussion of Marx. Although Kant thinks we can never have knowledge of them, he believes that things-in-themselves do exist. Similarly, he posits the existence of universally valid, purely rational principles or "ends" which can, and moreover, must, be known.[2] Indeed, this is what a categorical imperative is: something which must be true, and must be done, universally in all circumstances. One formulation of such a categorical imperative is to always treat humans as subjects, and never as objects: "all rational beings," argues Kant, "stand under the law that each of them should treat himself and all others never merely as a means but always at the same time as an end in himself" (Pojman 1993, p. 173). In other words, humans have an obligation to regard themselves and others as valuable for their own sake, and thus not to act towards anyone in a way that ignores this inalienable dignity in order to receive some other sort of gain from them.

In his passage on "Estranged Labor," Marx describes the commodification of labor and argues that then-present economic conditions produce laborers as objects, not as subjects, citizens, or "ends-in-themselves," According to Marx (1978), alienation is a necessary and inevitable consequence of the commodification of labor. All labor has a use value (either its product or its process, the concrete purpose of working); commodified labor, however, is labor considered only in terms of its exchange value, i.e., its value, expressed in money, relative to other commodities. Thus, when one offers one's labor as a commodity, one does not work for the purpose of producing objects necessary to and meaningful for one's self; rather, one works for the purpose of collecting the exchange value of his or her labor. In other words, labor ceases to be an end in itself, and becomes merely a means to the resource (money) necessary to meet other needs and desires. "[A]fter all," argues Marx, "in the wage of labor, labor does not appear as an end in itself but as the servant of the wage" (Ibid., p. 79). It seems, for Marx, that because the commodity is inaugurated by the substitution of something contingent (exchange value) for something concrete (use value), the commodity is inherently and characteristically estranged and/or estranging. In other words, the commodity is not valued in and of itself (i.e., according to it's "use" or concrete character), but in terms of and as a means to something else. Labor, and as I will soon demonstrate, the laborer him/herself "is therefore not the satisfaction of a need; it is merely a *means* to satisfy needs external to it" (Ibid., p.74).

This means/ends language is quite pervasive in the "Estranged Labor" passage. Exchanged as a commodity, labor – i.e., human life activity – becomes a means for the procurement of money, and thus an end other than itself. "[L]abor, life-activity, productive life itself, appears to man merely as a *means* of satisfying a need – the need to maintain the physical existence... Life itself appears only as a means to life" (Ibid., p. 75–76). Because human life activity is not performed for its own sake, human life is not regarded as an end in itself. Consequently, insofar as labor produces not only products but also the laborer him/herself, the system of wage labor positions humans as means to other (and others') ends.[3] Claiming that "in degrading spontaneous activity, free activity, to a means, estranged labor makes man's species life a means to his physical existence" (Ibid., p. 77), Marx argues that commodified labor creates a situation in which what is most "human" about *homo sapiens* – namely, creativity, thought, and sociality – become the skills and activities the laborer exchanges for the means of his or her subsistence. Not only the individual human laborer, but humanity itself becomes a "means,"[4]

When, according to Marx, human life-activity is treated as an end in itself, the result is freedom. Unlike the bee, who "produces only under the dominion of immediate physical need" (Ibid., p. 76), human beings are able to reflect on their situation, their needs, their desires, and their capacities in order to *choose* when, how, and what to produce; humans are also capable of using this same conscious reflection in order to understand their role as producers and the role of their products in the world at large. Because we are self-conscious beings, we are capable of choice, and thus freedom: in Marx's terms, "his own life is an object for him. Only because of that is his activity free activity" (Ibid., p. 77). When labor is commodified and human life-activity treated as a means toward other(s') ends, consciousness and/of labor ceases to be a source of human freedom, and turns instead into its opposite: objectification, the treatment of humans not as subjects, but as things.[5]

It seems to be this "objectification" – namely, the "estrangement" of human beings from their normative state of freedom – that Marx finds most morally problematic about commodified labor. The very possibility of labeling certain forms of labor "estranged" assumes the existence of natural, normal, and/or "whole" forms of labor and human life-activity. Discussing the ways in which commodified labor is a force of both individual and social alienation, Marx posits the existence of such a normative "authentic" state: "the proposition that man's species nature is estranged from him means that one man is estranged from the other, as each of them is from *man's essential nature*" (Ibid., p. 77; emphasis mine). Here Marx makes the claim that "estrangement" involves the separation from some proper (original, natural, unique, appropriate) state of affairs. To be "estranged" is to be deviant, abnormal, and even perhaps perverse. In a commodity economy, "[l]abor's realization is its objectification" (Ibid., p. 72). This objectification, argues Marx, "appears as *a loss of reality* for the workers; objectification as *loss of the object* and object-bondage; appropriation as *estrangement*, as *alienation* [Entaeusserung]" (Ibid., p. 72). Marx's language here is quite revealing: alienated labor is the "loss" of some truth or "reality" which, in normal or natural circumstances, humans *ought necessarily* possess and/or be. Having lost his or her freedom, "the worker becomes a slave of his object" (Ibid., p. 73). In a quite binary fashion, objectification functions here as the lack of subjectivity, an "unnatural," morally problematic situation.

That Marx proposes communism as a remedy for this supposedly abnormal state is further evidence that he views alienation as undesirable and morally problematic. Indeed, explaining communism as "the complete *return* of man to himself as a social (i.e., human) being" (Ibid., p. 84; emphasis mine), Marx assumes a logic of lack and fulfillment, symptom and remedy. Communism "returns" what commodified labor takes from us or estranges us from . . . namely, individual and social authenticity, the "natural" relations to ourselves and to others. The antidote to alienation, "[t]his communism, as fully-developed naturalism, equals humanism, and as fully-developed humanism equals naturalism" (Ibid., p. 84). Now, Marx does admit that this "natural" humanism could be a normative state produced by social forces.[6] Whether this "nature" is given or developed over years of social custom and physiological adaptation, the fact that Marx's analysis and evaluation of "estranged" labor rests upon the assumption of a normative "natural" state remains unchanged.

But what happens to Marx's analysis if we reject his essentialist supposition of a "natural" human condition and his binary opposition between subject and object? What if there is no "reality" to be lost? What if subjectivity is predicated upon this very lack? What if agency and subjectivity require "objectification," i.e., require, to some extent, one to treat oneself and others as things, as means to ends other than themselves?

If we understand agency, freedom, and ethics in terms of the ambiguity of the abject, the picture that Kant and Marx sketch of alienated labor dissolves along with their essentialisms and commitments to binary oppositions. Turning to Julia Kristeva's theory of the abject and Simone de Beauvoir's *Ethics of Ambiguity*, I argue that alienation and objectification are necessary, if not foundational, components of Western subjectivity, and consequently, that ethical problems with estranged labor lie not in the "estranged" or "estranging" character of commodities, but elsewhere.

The Limitations of Fetishism and the Excessive Ambiguity of the Abject

Marx's own text provides evidence for viewing the process of commodification not as "alienation" or "objectification," but rather as a process of abjection. Describing the estranged laborer negatively, as "[w]hatever the product of his labor is, he is not", Marx (1978, p. 72) calls upon the idea – which I will elaborate shortly – that the abject is the "negative" of the subject, the "not-me" (unlike the object, which is the opposite of the subject). Further, in his claim that "in the very act of production he [the laborer] was estranging himself from himself" (Ibid., p. 73), Marx addresses the notion that abjection is first and foremost an abjection of self. However, where Marx believes this rendering "other" of the self to be crippling,[7] the notion of abjection establishes it as the condition of agency, choice, and freedom. This is possible because the abject recognizes the non-binary, non-exclusive – indeed, *ambiguous* – relationship between inside and outside, subject and object, activity and passivity. Kristeva's concept of the abject questions any strict opposition between activity and passivity, acknowledges the empty yet overdetermined nature of the signifier and, most importantly, allows us to examine the ways in which "estrangement" is not a reduction to, but the foundation of agency.

Kristeva: Abjection and the "Impossible Real"

I read Kristeva's *Powers of Horror* (1982) as a means to explore in more detail the reasons why abjection's emphasis on the impossibility of the real and the intersectionality of difference make it a more appropriate model for understanding inter and intrasubjective (ethical) relations in a commodity economy.

In Kristeva's work, abjection is used to mark humanity off from animality, on the one hand, and the speaking subject off from maternity/femininity on the other: something "becomes abject only if it is a border between two distinct entities or territories. A boundary between nature and culture, between the human and the non-human" (Kristeva 1982, p. 75). She examines the work of anthropologists like Claude Levi-Strauss and Mary Douglas alongside the more ontogenic writings of Freud (e.g., *Totem and Taboo*, *Moses and Monotheism*) in order to demonstrate that the division between nature and culture is possible and thinkable only from the perspective of language/culture. Kristeva argues that her analysis of the origin and economy of language in the subject "does not unfold without a share of *fiction*, the nucleus of which, drawn from actuality and the subjective experience of the one who writes, is projected upon data collected from the life of other cultures, less to justify itself than to throw light on them by means of an interpretation to which they obviously offer resistance" (Kristeva 1982, p. 68). Emphasizing the "fictional" status of its normative assumptions, Kristeva grounds her notion of abjection in a *necessarily* impossible real, for abjection describes the process whereby the criteria for determining "truth" and "falsity" are established.[8]

As the title of Kristeva's book suggests, abjection is a brand of horror or, more precisely, fear or phobia spawned by the emptiness and impossibility of any "truth" or "real." "It is anguish that causes us to speak . . . anguish in the face of nothing" (Ibid., p. 42). To "make the analysand see the void upon which rests the play with the signifier" is to produce "the truest equivalents of fear". Although it is common and reassuring to think of the origin of language in nature, and the origin of a sign in some signified which it "truthfully" and fully represents, language arises not from an originary plenitude, but from lack.[9] According to Kristeva, fundamental to the possibility of signification is the construction of the myth of the signified, the myth that behind the sign is a true, actual, existent reality available for representation – e.g., "use value" or the state of nature. Kristeva describes this gesture as a "hallucination" of origin or of the real brought on by the fear experienced in the face of the impossibility and lack made evident through abjection. Horrified that neither truth nor origin is pure and/or definable, the abject constructs for him or herself "indexing value, pointing to something else, some non-thing, something unknowable. The phobic object is in that sense the hallucination of nothing . . . [or] the impossible object" (Ibid., p. 41). This hallucination, then, is of the truth or origin of present experience in some immaterial, inscrutable, and most importantly, *normative* sphere, a state which in some fashion rationalizes and/or justifies existing social, political, and ideological structures. Since the hallucination is not just the misplacement, misidentification, or misjudgment of some existing phenomenon, but is in fact the *creation* of its object, Kristeva emphasizes that the object of this brand of hallucination is impossible – i.e., *nothing*.[10] Insofar as the "subject" undergoing the process of abjection "finds the impossible within; [. . .]it finds that *the impossible constitutes its very being*" (Ibid., p. 5; emphasis mine), it is evident that the idea of some pure, true, uncorrupted state is a myth – is an *impossibility*.

Kristeva uses the notion of abjection to demonstrate the fallacy of accounts which, like the psychoanalytic Oedipal narrative, claim to describe the transition from some pure, unmediated natural state to self-consciousness and civilization. "No sooner sketched out," argues Kristeva, "such a thesis is exploded by its contradictions and flimisiness" (Ibid., p. 32). Rather than a clearly demarcated boundary between nature and culture, Kristeva argues that we "find a whole gradation within modalities of separation . . . a gradation constituting, in Lacan's brilliant formulation, the object relations, insofar as it is always a means of masking, of parrying the fundamental fund of anguish". The boundary between nature and culture is a "gradation" because, as the ambiguity of abjection indicates, nature is the *effect* or *product* of various types and layers of work on and by the speaking civilization, meant to abscond the fact that nature is itself a fiction, a lack.

By demonstrating the impossibility of a pure, authentic, "whole" state free of alienation, Kristeva's theory of the abject argues that humans, as social, speaking beings, are always-already alienated, and that our subjectivity rests precisely upon this "lack" or self-exile. Thus, Marx's language of "objectification" cannot stand as a moral indictment of commodity economies, because, as Kristeva's theory makes clear, "objectification" is a condition of subjectivity. Displaying the fundamental role alienation and exile play in the inauguration of truth and value, Kristeva's theory of abjection demonstrates the "impossibility" of the pure, whole, unalienated state Marx's critique of commodified labor takes as its moral basis. A process of constitutive exclusion which sets the stage for subject/object distinctions, abjection is "a vortex of summons and repulsion [which] places the one haunted by it literally beside himself" (Ibid., p. 1). Primarily a process of self-exile, abjection is paradigmatically described via examples such as vomit and excrement – i.e., as substances formerly internal to a body or subject, but which now appear as objects independent of and external to it. This inside/outside or subject/object distinction is quite tenuous and ambiguous, for the "object" of abjection is the abjecting subject: "It is no longer I who expel, 'I' is expelled" (Ibid., p. 3). Like Marx's claim that commodified labor produces the laborer as commodity (i.e., object), Kristeva argues that this self-abjection produces the subject. However, Kristeva's version views this production as the condition, not the absence, of agency; abjection sets the scene for the production of subjectivity as such. As a sort of prerequisite preparation for acculturation to subjectivity and language, abjection "objectifies" parts of the soon-to-be self *as a means to* subjectivity. Insofar as "the subject of abjection is imminently productive of culture" (Ibid., p. 45), the "alienation" characteristic of abjection is not a passivization or disempowerment of some a priori "active" subject, but the very basis for *acquiring* the faculties which Marx thinks this process robs us of. Since "objectification" and self-exile are the conditions of subjectivity, Kristeva's theory of abjection renders ambiguous the strict subject/object dichotomy operative in Marx's theory of alienated labor and commodity fetishism. In order to be a subject, one must already be an "object" for "oneself"; in order to be a moral agent worthy of respect, one must first abject oneself, use oneself as a means toward this rather important end. Moreover, the abject's ambiguity demonstrates that "objectification" and "alienation" are not, as Marx would have it, states of domination, for in Kristeva's theory, they serve as the conditions for the possibility of agency, action, and resistance.

Although she does not adopt the language of abjection, Simone de Beauvoir's *Ethics of Ambiguity* assumes this same ambiguity as fundamental to individual, political, and moral agency. Having demonstrated via Kristeva's theory of the abject that alienation and objectification are not prohibitive of human agency and well-being, I turn now to Beauvoir's text to examine ways in which this "ambiguity" might offer positive foundations for ethics. Understanding that, how, and why alienation is not in and of itself morally problematic will point us towards what is really the problem with jobs such as those of sweatshop laborers.

Beauvoir: Ambiguity and Freedom

A specifically existentialist ethics, Beauvoir's (1997, p. 17) text is, unsurprisingly, in many ways a treatise on human freedom. Although she situates her project in the tradition of German Idealism (namely, in its commitment to view human free will as coinciding with moral value),[11] Beauvoir's main thesis is that a false dichotomy between subject and object has led the history of philosophy to misrepresent the relationship between freedom and determinism.

Beauvoir (1997, p. 7) begins her argument with the observation that the difficulty of reconciling ideals of independence and autonomy with the fact of human finitude and the consequent dependence of humans on nature and on one another has lead philosophers to overlook important aspects of human existence in order to preserve these impossible ideals.[12] For example, philosophers have assumed that physical and political concerns present insuperable impediments to individual autonomy, and have thus privileged metaphysical phenomena – thought, the soul – as the sites of genuine freedom. As an existentialist thinker in the wake of the Second World War, Beauvoir argues that ethics must necessarily include action in the world among things and people, and that notions of ethics which fail to account for concrete, material human relations are grossly unjust.

Consequently, ethics must begin from the premise of the fundamental ambiguity of the human condition: namely, that human beings are both objects in the world, used as means towards ends other than themselves, and also agents in the world, morally valuable subjects whose subjectivity arises from their distance from the world of things. As one is "still a part of this world of which [one] is a consciousness," one acts as "a pure internality against which no external power can take hold, and [one] also experiences [one]self as a thing crushed by the dark weight of other things" (Ibid., p. 7). Inhabiting an irreducibly contradictory place, the human being is simultaneously an agent and an object on which agency is exercised by oneself, by other humans, and by forces of nature. The language of contradiction is not entirely appropriate here, for subject- and object-positions are never exclusive: it is not the case that, in any one situation, one is either a subject or an object. Rather, humans occupy these seemingly opposing roles simultaneously: in each moment and in every situation, one is inextricably both subject and object. Thus, Beauvoir describes this condition in terms of ambiguity.

In the context of the means-ends discourse common to Western moral philosophy, the ambiguity of the subject-object distinction translates into an ethical ambiguity. As Beauvoir explains, humans "know themselves to be the supreme end to which all action should be subordinated, but the exigencies of action force them to treat one another as instruments or obstacles, as means" (Ibid., p. 9). If human existence is fundamentally ambiguous – i.e., if subject and object positions are necessarily interrelated – then it becomes impossible to treat someone purely as an end in him or herself. Insofar as one is both a subject and an object, for oneself and for others, it seems inevitable that one will become a means toward some external end. For example, Beauvoir argues that subjectivity, the "privilege... of being a sovereign and unique subject amidst a universe of objects, is what he shares with all his fellow-men" (Ibid., p. 7). Even though sociality seems to be elemental to human subjects, it is precisely this sociality which renders their autonomy ambiguous: "In turn an object for others, he is nothing more than an individual in the collectivity on which he depends" (Ibid., p. 7). To participate in a free society alongside other subjects it seems that one is necessarily and inevitably treated as an object, both by oneself and by others. Since traditional moral theory – particularly Kant's categorical imperative, but also Marxian notions of exploitation – does not account for this ambiguity, Beauvoir views her task as one of elaborating an ethical system which accommodates the fact "that separate existents can, at the same time, be bound to each other, [and] that their individual freedoms can forge laws valid for all" (Ibid., p. 18). Such an "ethics of ambiguity" is possible because, as Beauvoir argues, the possibility of individual freedom rests on the individual's dependence on and debt to others.

Beauvoir's notion of ambiguity, like Kristeva's theory of the abject, posits the origin of agency in its very failure or lack[13] as evidence for an indeterminate boundary between subject and object. Insofar as "man makes himself this lack of being in order that there might be being" (Ibid., p. 12), "ambiguity" seems to describe the self-exile which, in the discourse of abjection, serves as the origin of subjectivity. "[W]e have seen," explains Beauvoir, "that the original scheme of man is ambiguous: he wants to be, and to the extent that he coincides with this wish, he fails" (Ibid., p. 23). In this scheme, being is predicated on the lack of being, and subjectivity is possible to the extent that it is also a failure thereof. Again, the relationship between being and its lack, just like the relationship between subject and object, is, for Beauvoir, ambiguous. Beauvoir's claim that "being is lack of being, but this lack has a way of being which is precisely existence" (Ibid., p. 13), clearly illustrates that this failure of being is not opposed or external to subjectivity and agency, but their very core. Indeed, it is the lack of being (what Rousseau might call "perfectibility") which makes freedom an issue in the first place: if one was complete and sufficient in and of oneself, there would be no need to pursue projects, make choices, or act in the world among others. "For a being who, from the very start, would be an exact co-incidence with himself, in a perfect plenitude, the notion of having-to-be would have no meaning" (Ibid., p. 10). As Beauvoir argues, freedom, and thus ethics, is meaningless without the possibility of failure:[14] in other words, "[t]here is an ethics only if there is a problem to solve (Ibid., p. 18), or, "[o]ne does not offer an ethics to a God" (Ibid., p. 10).

Kantian ethics, with its emphasis on treating humans as "ends-in-themselves" does, according to Beauvoir, precisely this:

> Kantism defined man as a pure positivity, and it therefore recognized no other possibility in him than coincidence with himself... Unlike Kant, we do not see man as being essentially a positive will. On the contrary, he is first defined as a negativity. He is first at a distance from himself. He can coincide with himself only by agreeing never to rejoin himself. There is within him a perpetual playing with the negative... (EA 33).

According to Beauvoir, the Kantian project, in viewing humans only as ends-in-themselves, seeks to eliminate human ambiguity; in doing so, Kant also eliminates the possibility for agency, freedom, and ethics. Beauvoir's ethics, on the other hand, holds it practically and theoretically impossible to imagine a situation in which humans are not always also taken as means towards other ends, either by oneself or by others. "[W]ithout failure, no ethics (Ibid., p. 10): ethics is possible because humans are constantly confronted with the failure of their agency, the renunciation of their ambiguity in complete objectification.[15]

Now, it is important to note that neither Beauvoir nor I are advocating exploitation as a positive phenomenon. Indeed, a state of complete domination is just as unambiguous as Kant's notion of the subject as end-in-itself. Rather, my point in offering Kristeva's notion of the abject and Beauvoir's notion of ambiguity as critiques of conventional notions of alienation is to emphasize the role that "objectification" plays in the constitution of subjectivity in order to re-focus the way business ethics analyze problems of exploitation, so that ultimately domination is minimized and humans attain maximal empowerment. My claim here is generally akin to Foucault's theory of the role of power in the subjectivization of the subject: namely, that power is productive of agency, and that in order for one to be a subject *of* power, one must also be subject *to* power.[16] The theories of the subject and of agency presented by Kristeva and Beauvoir illustrate a justly-termed "ambiguous" relationship between empowerment and objectification, self-determination and alienation. This ambiguity is not adequately captured in either Marx's critiques of alienated labor and commodity fetishism, nor in Kantian or Kantian-inspired ethics. Thus, when examining the obvious problems with jobs such as those of third-world women of color working in sweatshops, we must be careful to attend to the genuine ambiguity of his situation, and avoid reducing it too much on the side of either the subject (as Kantian and Marxist analyses would) or on the side of the object. If we follow Beauvoir's claim that ambiguity – i.e., the potential for failure as well as for success – is precisely that which opens the possibility for human freedom, it would seem that attempts to think away alienation and objectification would be just as disempowering as those which would reduce one to nothing but thing-ness and lack.

Rather ironically, attempts to eliminate alienation and objectification would produce the same consequences as attempts to maximize them. Because it would "resolve" the "problem" from which questions of ethics arises, the elimination of ambiguity would, in both Beauvoir's and Kristeva's schemes, reduce any possibility of agency in the first place. Accordingly, the problem with sweatshop labor, as with the analyses which would label his problem "alienation" or "objectification," is that it provides these women with, in the words of the Sex Pistols, "no future." If we really want to address situations like those of third-world female sweatshop laborers, we should not be concerned with the supposed fact that they are removed from some "natural" or "complete" state that they inherently "are"; rather, we should attend to the ways in which their situation prevents them from realizing what they "could be". We would, as Beauvoir advises, "regar[d] as privileged situations those which permit it to realize itself as indefinite movement" (Ibid., p. 32). In other words, we would care for a subject who "wishes to pass beyond everything which limits its power; and yet [recognizes] this power is always limited" (Ibid., p. 32).

The discourses of alienated labor and commodity fetishism construct false active/passive and subject/object binaries which, in overlooking the "ambiguity" of concrete human situations, work to *decrease* human agency and well-being. Because it severely delimits what sorts of power relations constitute "real" or "meaningful" forms of subjectivity, choice, and agency, the Marxian-Kantian paradigm views as exploitative and ethically suspect situations which are in fact demonstrable occasions of human agency and liberty. In other words, if "alienation" and "objectification" are thought to be mutually exclusive of subjectivity, then most people in the world are rendered absolutely passive, and the very real agency and subjectivity they do exercise (albeit many times among severely limited choices and in overdetermined situations) counts for nil. Even sweatshop laborers and migrant workers, who most certainly have important aspects of choice and liberty foreclosed from them, are nevertheless quite capable individuals, not the passive, helpless, "things" in need of rescue by intellectually and economically privileged academics and activists. Indeed, as interviews in Pietra Rivoli's book *The Travels of a T-Shirt* (2005) indicate, many times sweatshop workers have actively chosen "alienating" industrial labor over the "natural" and "un-alienating" toil of subsistence farming. Certainly neither choice is particularly attractive, and these women's choices are undeniably circumscribed by a variety of factors – sexism, racism, global economic marginalization, to name a few; however, representing them as completely objectified and alienated fails to recognize the choices they do make and the agency they do have – it fails to recognize their ambiguity, the subjectivity exercised in the midst of internal and external objectification.

The notion of privilege brings me to my final point, one I have not yet addressed, but I believe to be highly significant. It seems that gender and race privilege are elemental to these various objections to "alienation" and "objectification," for a "pure" subject-position free from exploitation, objectification, and stereotyping seems genuinely available only to those who aren't, for one reason or another, systematically marginalized. For women and people of color (and other disadvantaged groups, such as queers and persons with disabilities), the world is always-already objectifying and alienating (e.g., double consciousness, viewing oneself in terms of the stereotypes about one's gender, race, etc.). In order to even "play the game" of business (or anything, really, in a culture so thoroughly marked by patriarchy and whiteness) they must participate in a system, capitalism, which rests both historically and concretely on the exploitation of unpaid "women's work," the slave trade, and undocumented workers. In other words, it would be impossible for women and people of color *not* to objectify and alienate themselves, because the system already does that for them. On the other hand, they can't not play the game if they seek to better their economic, social, and political circumstances. For example, in the women's movement, there has been a tension between the need to increase the economic independence of women – which many rightly view as preliminary to improving other aspects of women's rights – with the need to address the ways in which current economic practices and premises exploit women and devalue femininity. Linda Scott argues that the fashion industry, criticized for exploiting female sweatshop workers, models, and female bodies/body image, has been instrumental in providing well-paying jobs for women and unparalleled in its promotion of female executives. Even though the fashion industry in the U.S. may "exploit" women by treating them as objects, it was and is the industry in which women hold the greatest proportion of economic power. This economic power, developed from the 1850s onward, was instrumental in twentieth-century developments in the women's movement and women's rights. "Objectifying" jobs – modeling, sweatshop labor – gave women the concrete economic means to gain political influence and effect social change. Scott's analysis of the American fashion industry provides a clear case in which "objectification" – or participation in a "game" which is generally objectifying to women – directly led to greater autonomy, and eventually to concrete political power (suffrage).

Similarly, a reassessment of the situation of third-world women of color working in contemporary sweatshops reveals that, given their position in intersecting systems of gender, race, ethnic, and economic marginalization, their *choice* to work in factories rather than, say, on the farm or in the sex trade, indicates a degree of individual autonomy, and is far from a symptom of passive capitulation. This is not to say that these women aren't multiply marginalized in relation to various networks of power and privilege; however, the exploitative character of their employment arises not from alienation and/or objectification – as the classic Marxist and Kantian paradigms would conclude – but from something else. Insofar as third-world women of color already live in a society which objectifies, stereotypes, and misrepresents them, "alienation" is not, for them, an abnormal condition. The choices they make, the ideas, the actions have all arisen in the context of these multi-layered objectifications; the *privilege* of being "normal," having "equal" access and opportunity, is precisely what has been denied them. "As she encounters the difference and disparity between her working conditions and the opportunities of the normative U.S. citizen publicized around her," Lov (1997) argues,

> the working Asian immigrant woman may be less likely to *identify* with the model of the citizen than to *disidentify* with it. Her horizon is constituted by the material conditions of her female immigrant 'lifeworld': low wages for menial, repetitive labor, poor environmental health conditions in the workplace, capitalist penetration of the immigrant 'home,' gender discrimination, and racism exclude her from the equal citizenship promised by democratic inclusion" (Lov 1997, p. 271–272).

Like bell hooks's (1992) notion of the "oppositional gaze," wherein black female film spectators, due to the incongruence between their lived reality and the "reality" represented on screen, reject the narrative paradigm of Hollywood films, Asian immigrant women who work in sweatshops reject conventional American narratives of liberation and citizenship because these narratives do not accurately represent or make sense in terms of their experiences. As a working-class immigrant woman of color, she is always already multiply objectified: her "lifeworld" does not demonstrate the "reality" of free, equal subjectivity. Any choices she makes, any improvements in her situation have come in the face of many intersecting forms of objectification.[17] Indeed, alienation doesn't seem to be the source of her problems so much as racism, sexism, Eurocentrism, and other intersecting systems of social privilege which position her in this structurally disadvantaged – but not thereby passive or helpless – position.

Kristeva's notion of the abject and Beauvoir's ethics of ambiguity allow us to understand situations such as those described by Scott and Lov. Giving a more nuanced account of the relationship between subject and object, agency and "exploitation," these ideas provide a means for thinking about issues in business ethics that will prove to maximize individual autonomy. As my preceding examples demonstrate, it is essential to recognize that not all individuals are situated equally in respect to power and privilege; in order to treat them fairly and increase their liberty, it is necessary to acknowledge the ways in which the very possibility of their participation in mainstream culture requires a degree of self-objectification and exploitation. Furthermore, the ideas of abjection and ambiguity maintain that this "double consciousness" arising from self-objectification is foundational to human subjectivity in the first place. Accordingly, these ideas open ethical theory to a "real" rather than "ideal" world, one in which exploitation, alienation, and objectification are part of the human condition, facts which must be addressed, not merely dismissed as "anomalies."

Notes

1. The Marx Engels Reader (MER), 70–81; appears in Shari Collins-Chobanian's *Ethical Challenges To Business As Usual* (286–291), Thomas I. White's *Business Ethics: A Philosophical Reader* (144–148).
2. "Now laws determine ends as regards their universal validity; therefore, if one abstracts from the personal differences of rational beings and also from all content of their private ends, then it will be possible to think of a whole of all ends in systematic connection . . . " (Pojman 1993 p. 173).
3. "Labor produces not only commodities; it produces itself and the worker as a commodity" (MER, 71).
4. "The consciousness which man has of his species is thus transformed by estrangement in such a way that the species life becomes for him a means" (MER, 77).
5. "Estranged labor reverses this relationship, so that it is just because man is a conscious being that he makes his life-activity, his essential being, a mere means to his existence" (MER, 76).
6. Ignoring for now the heteronormativity of his comments, Marx explains that the heterosexual relationship, as the most "natural" relationship among humans, illustrates "the extent to which man's natural behavior has become human, or the extent to which the human essence in him has become a natural essence – the extent to which his human nature has come to be nature to him" (MER, 84). From this passage it is clear that Marx does not believe that "nature" is necessarily a given, determined "essence", and that it could be no more than, as Nietzsche might say, habit or "second nature". Regardless of the source of this "nature", Marx's conception of human inter- and intra-subjective relations is nevertheless essentialist: the best relations are those which conform to this "nature", and those which do not (e.g., alienated labor, commodity fetishism) are morally problematic.
7. "External labor, labor in which man alienates himself, is a labor of self-sacrifice, of mortification" (Marx 1978 p. 74).

8. Abjection is reworking of the psychoanalytic Oedipal narrative which, in shifting emphasis from *Oedipus Rex* to *Oedipus at Colonus*, also shifts the emphasis in the psychoanalytic account of the origin of the speaking being from disavowal to exclusion. While the first installment revolves around Oedipus' denial or disavowal of the truth of his parentage and the fact that *he* is the source of Thebes' contamination, in this second play, "there is, first of all, a spatial exclusion. Oedipus must *exile* himself" (Kristeva 1982 p. 84). Thus, while the first play ends with Oedipus ending his disavowal of the "facts" and blinding himself to symbolize the force of this enlightenment, the second one offers exile and excision of the abnormal and undisciplined as a solution to this situation. According to Kristeva, what Sophocles presents in *Oedipus at Colonus* is not a model of the disavowal and then recognition of castration (i.e., a model of fetishism), but the workings of a spatial model whereby the very boundary between what counts as actual and what counts as false/wrong is negotiated. In other words, *Oedipus at Colonus* illustrates that the transition into civil society and into language occurs through "building the wall, reinforcing the boundary that wards off opprobrium, which, because of this very fact, is not disavowed but shown to be alien" (PoH, 84). It is not fetishism, with its focus on the disavowal of castration, but abjection, which attends to the spacing between proper and improper, that best describes the subject's acquisition of and relation to language.
9. Kristeva's (1982 p. 37) discussion of the origin of language in the constitutive exclusion and/or loss she names abjection highlights several specific differences between abjection and fetishism. Even though language "is based on fetishist denial ('I know that, but just the same,' 'the sign is not the thing, but just the same')", fetishism already assumes the existence of a self-present subject for whom objects appear and are experienced as such. Indeed, the ability to calculate equivalences implied in the "just the same" – a judgment common to both psychoanalytic and Marxist notions of fetishism – requires two assumptions that the process of abjection does not: first, that there is a clear distinction between a subject and the objects to which it relates, and second, that there is some object and its supposed 'truth' or 'reality' available for misrecognition. At work in the claim that something is "just the same" as another is the assumption that there are at least two entities which are distinct from each other and from me; in order for one to deny the distinction between the fetish and that for which it substitutes, this distinction must first be in existence. Furthermore, in order for the fetishist to judge these objects to be equivalent, he or she is assuming that they contain content about which a truth claim can be made; what is denied is that the "truth" or "reality" or "use value" of these objects is, in fact, unique.
10. The privileged example of this impossible object is the maternal phallus, which symbolizes two related ideas: maternal phallus as the non-civilized state of nature (often described as a matriarchy, where either Mother Earth or human mothers rule), or maternal phallus the fetishized penis/phallus of the mother. Either as state of nature or gender equality/indifference, the impossible object is something which does not, empirically or ideologically, exist. The impossibility of the abject is tied to its association with the "enigma" or inscrutability of femininity. Though a slippery elision of the impossibility of nature/the real with the impossibility of comprehending the enigma of femininity, "the feminine body, the maternal body, in its most un-signifiable, un-symbolizible aspect, shores up, in the individual, the fantasy of the loss in which he is engulfed or becomes inebriated, for want of the ability to name an object of desire" (Ibid., 20). Nature is abjected, the constitutive exclusion whereby the boundaries of what is knowable and unknowable are founded. Thus, in a patriarchal system, things associated with femininity will fall into the category of the unknowable, for epistemic structures are not developed for this purpose (and indeed are meant to keep "femininity" out of the domain of knowledge proper). Further, in a system which privileges *logos*, things that are not subsumable under or controlled by it will either become threatening or intoxicating in the mystery they seem to present the thinker. Thus, we see how abjection allows us to account for the ways intersecting ideologies and systems of privilege influence the content which comes to be included or excluded from the spheres of "truth", "right", and "proper". While fetishism assumes an a priori normative state, abjection illustrates how and why *this* state comes to be valued as such.

11. "By affirming that the source of all values resides in the freedom of man, existentialism merely carries on the tradition of Kant, Fichte, and Hegel, who, in the words of Hegel himself, 'have taken for their point of departure the principle according to which the essence of right and duty and the essence of the thinking and willing subject are absolutely identical" (Beauvoir, 1997 p. 17).
12. "As long as there have been men and they have lived, they have all felt this tragic ambiguity of their condition, but as long as there have been philosophers and they have thought, most of them have tried to mask it".
13. According to Beauvoir, this lack of being or "failure is not surpassed, but assumed" (Beauvoir, p. 13).
14. "Value is this lacking-being of which freedom makes itself a lack; and it is because the latter makes itself a lack that value appears. It is desire which creates the desirable, and the project which sets up the end." (Beauvoir p. 14/5).
15. "[F]or a being who, from the very start, would be an exact co-incidence with himself, in a perfect plenitude, the notion of having-to-be would have no meaning" (Beauvoir, p. 10).
16. "I have always been somewhat suspicious of the notion of liberation, because if it is not treated with precautions and within certain limits, one runs the risk of falling back on the idea that there exists a human nature or base that, as a consequence of certain historical, economic, and social processes, has been concealed, alienated, or imprisoned in and by mechanisms of repression. According to this hypothesis, all that is required is to break these repressive deadlocks and man will be reconciled with himself, rediscover his nature or regain contact with his origin, and reestablish a full and positive relationship with himself. I think this idea should not be accepted without scrutiny. I am not trying to say that liberation as such, or this or that form of liberation, does not exist: when a colonized people attempts to liberate itself from its colonizers, this is indeed a practice of liberation in the strict sense. But we know very well, and moreover in this specific case, that this practice of liberation is not in itself sufficient to define the practices of freedom that will still be needed if this people, this society, and these individuals are to be able to define admissible and acceptable forms of existence or political society." (Foucault 1997 p. 282).
17. Her agency comes perhaps most effectively by exploiting her structurally disadvantaged position: the U.S. and global economy relies on the low-wage labor of female sweatshop workers, so they have the power to disrupt the system if it completely denies their agency.

References

Beauvoir, Simone de. 1997. *The Ethics of Ambiguity*. Trans. Bernard Frechtman. Secaucus, N.J.: Citadel Press: Carol Publishing Group.

Collins-Chobanian, Shari. 2005. *Ethical Challenges to Business as Usual*. Pearson/Prentice Hall, Upper Saddle River, N.J.

Foucault, Michel. 1997. "The Ethics of the Concern for Self as a Practice of Freedom" in *Ethics, Subjectivity, and Truth*. Ed. Paul Rabinow. New York: The New York Press.

hooks, bell. 1992. "The Oppositional Gaze" in *Black Looks*. Boston: South End Press.

Kristeva, Julia. 1982. *Powers of Horror* (PoH)*: An Essay on Abjection*. Trans. Leon Roudiez. New York: Columbia University Press.

Love, Lisa. 1997. "Work, Imigration, Gender: Asian 'American' Women". *Making More Waves: New Writing by Asian American Women*. Elaine Kim, Ed. Boston: Beacon Press.

Marx, Karl. 1978. *Capital, v.1* from *The Marx and Engels Reader*. (MER) Ed Robert C. Tucker. New York: Norton

Pojman, Louis. 1993. *Moral Philosophy: A Reader.* Indianapolis: Hackett.

Rivoli, Pietra. 2005. *Travels of a T-Shirt*. New Jersey: John Wiley & Sons

White, Thomas, I. 1993. *Business Ethics: A Philosophical Reader.* Prentice Hall, Upper Saddle River, N.J.

The Grameen Bank and Capitalist Challenges

Sokthan Yeng

Introduction

In 2006, the Nobel Peace Prize committee gave the honor to the Grameen Bank for its work in micro-lending. The success of the program, founded by Muhammad Yunus, is connected to the way in which he challenged discourses embedded within capitalism while not completely abandoning the capitalist structure. Though traditional business wisdom identifies poor women as risky and unworthy creditors, Yunus granted small loans (some as small as $20) almost exclusively to groups of impoverished women and has enjoyed a repayment rate that vastly exceeds those of typical lending practices. Because Dr. Yunus willingly ignored the biases within the lending system, I believe that his economic strategies show how business can both be negatively and positively linked to a network of power relations. I will use bell hooks and Michel Foucault as the philosophical cornerstones of the discussion because they have similar readings and critiques of power that highlight the uniqueness of the Grameen Bank enterprise. Although both hooks and Foucault argue that modern power should be thought in terms of an interconnected network of power, hooks' explicit exposition of the link between capitalism and the oppression of women relays just how different Grameen Bank's objective and method is from traditional capitalist transactions. The Grameen Bank does not attempt to sever the tie between capitalism and the role of women but rather uses capitalism as a means to empower women. Dr. Yunus' project, therefore, can serve as a concrete example of how resistance to long-standing power structures is possible—something that Foucault claims is achievable but is often faulted for not fully discussing the possibilities.[1]

On the one hand, my study of the Grameen Bank will show how traditional capitalist business paradigms are a part of the dominating force that bell hooks believes is connected to a philosophy of oppression. On the other, I will argue through the philosophy of Michel Foucault that this capitalist discourse can change precisely because power is dynamic and allows for interaction among players. What made Dr. Yunus' business practices so radical and innovative was that he understood the

S. Yeng
Assistant Professor, Department of Philosophy, DePaul University, Chicago, IL, USA
e-mail: syeng@depaul.edu

M. Painter-Morland, P. Werhane (eds.), *Cutting-edge issues in Business Ethics*,

shortcomings of traditional capitalist discourse and sought to find another way of doing business that created an alternate path between poor women and power. A capitalist system does not, as hooks suggests, necessarily have to contribute to female oppression. Though I believe hooks is right to point out that the present capitalist mode is entangled with the oppression of women, the Grameen Bank is a concrete example of how power within capitalism can be changed and redirected to affect a different outcome for women and help them see themselves and be seen by others as valuable members of the community.

The Grameen Bank also lends itself to an interesting discussion about community in the philosophies of both hooks and Foucault. Although hooks argues that capitalism moves away from the value placed on community, the Grameen Bank is an example that shows how capitalism can be compatible with resource sharing among members. Groups function as the core of the micro-lending process and encourage group members to be invested in the projects of others.[2] And because Foucault mostly insinuates that societal normalization results in negative consequences, the Grameen Bank also counter balances the negative examples of social normalization established by Foucault. In a sense, this proves both Foucault and hooks to be correct. Dr. Yunus' project concretely demonstrates how economic operations are part of a broader network of power that will inevitably have social implications. Power must be thought in terms of multi-directional relations, as Foucault suggested. But because power is multidirectional and functions as an interlocking system, we cannot think that a turn in the economic system can rid society of oppression. Yunus, echoing Foucault when he states that there is no heart of resistance, admits that micro-lending institutions are not a panacea for all of society's ills. They have helped many women raise themselves out of poverty but not all. Micro-lending has not been able to break down all barriers for women or the poor. As a solution stemming from economics, it cannot address every way in which women face oppression or give all women access to power. We must, as bell hooks suggests, be mindful of other ways in which to improve the quality of lives for the poor. Still, the Grameen Bank is a promising and creative institution, which shows that the gap between capitalism and community resource sharing can be bridged.

Traditional Capitalism and Power

Part of hooks' frustration is that many are willing to acknowledge that oppression exists in the form of racism and sexism but are resistant to the idea that capitalism contributes to the on-going oppression within society. She believes that there is an audience (even if they do not overlap) to hear the ways in which racism and sexism are connected to oppression. In her work, hooks (1994, p. 244) endeavors to show how one's position in society is determined by a multitude of factors. She laments the fact that many describe how they face either racism or sexism but do not recognize how class operates within the equation. Her warning is that "[u]ntil we are all able to accept the interlocking, interdependent nature of systems of domination and recognize specific ways each system is maintained, we will continue to act in ways that undermine our individual quest for freedom and collective liberation struggle". For her, this underlies the inability or reluctance to understand the full scope of oppression. Ignoring the role of class in oppression is tantamount to overlooking how sexism can compound racism. Because she argues that racism, sexism, and capitalism are rooted in domination, she believes that we must see them as interconnected. Race, sex, and class all play a role in determining what place we occupy in society. The challenge, often, is to see how bias is embedded within the structure of capitalism.

In their remarks, Chowdhury et al. reinforce hooks' idea that one cannot separate the economic factor from other social factors. It would be misguided to think that one's economic status is unaffected by one's race or gender. Chowdhury et al. state:

> With respect to the formal sector, bans and other financial institutions generally require significant collateral, have a preference for high-income and high-loan clients, and have lengthy and bureaucratic application procedures. With respect to the informal sector, money-lenders usually charge excessively high interest rates, tend to undervalue collateral, and often allow racist and/or sexist attitudes to guide lending decisions. The failure of the formal and informal financial sectors to provide affordable credit to the poor is often viewed as one of the main factors that reinforce the vicious circle of economic, social and demographic structures that ultimately cause poverty. (Chowdhury et al. 2005: 298)

Although they explicitly state that informal lending sectors make use of racism and/or sexism when deciding who deserves a loan, I believe that a case can be made that the practices of formal lending institutions are also influenced by race and sex. While some forms of discrimination might be obvious, institutionalized discrimination is less visible because it is not directly tied to the prejudices of one person. It might be clear to see how racist and sexist discrimination contribute to lending practices of informal lenders because decisions might be made by one person or a small group of people who are willing to admit that they do not want to lend to a woman, for example, for whatever reason.

For formal money-lenders, this process is obfuscated. Though there is not one person who decides who and why someone does or does not get a loan in formal lending institutions, this does not mean that there are not similar prejudices involved. I argue that the rules for granting credit in a formal bank have erected reasons to not lend to women and the poor. Because the poor, by definition, and women have not historically had the means to acquire collateral, they are automatically excluded from receiving credit. In Bangladesh and elsewhere, women are not in control of family finances. They are not able to get loans because social systems largely place wealth in the hands of men. Because men are sole caretakers of family funds, women must take care to please their husbands and put up with abuses so their husbands will not leave them. Banks, therefore, operate within a system of de facto discrimination and contribute to the oppression of women.

While it is easy to see that those who are in charge of informal lending institutions, since they are people, make use of particular biases in order to make decisions, Foucault is helpful in making sense of how institutions can also be directed by certain aims and objectives that also fall in line with racism and sexism. The need to recognize that power is both intentional and unintentional cuts to the core of how Foucault understands modern society.

He explains:

> Power relations are both intentional and nonsubjective... there is no power that is exercised without a sense of aims and objectives. But this does not mean that it results from a choice or decision of an individual subject; let us look for no headquarters that presides over its rationality; neither the caste which governs, nor the groups which control the state apparatus, nor those who make the most important economic decisions... (Foucault 1990, p. 95)

On one hand, Foucault recognizes that power works to accomplish certain directives. In this case, we see that power has helped to garner wealth for particular types of people. On the other hand, Foucault warns us against believing that there is a mastermind that constructs how power is deployed. Although one can see that a pattern of power develops, one cannot trace power to one source. Power is not wielded according to the demands and desires of one person. Therefore, one person, being, or institution cannot be the origin of oppression. Because power is found everywhere but cannot be pinned to any person or place, power can operate insidiously. For example, hints of racism and sexism can function in institutions without manifesting openly discriminatory practices.

While it is true that capitalism both in the formal and informal sector can be considered to be examples of institutionalized discrimination, it is precisely these seemingly intractable biases that identify women and the poor as unworthy creditors that Dr. Yunus has challenged. He is able to offer an alternative to the present form of capitalist power because it is dynamic and pliable. Yunus took a chance by lending them money, even though most lenders saw women and the poor as unacceptable creditors. His idea moves beyond just a gesture of good will. It worked to challenge the discourse behind capitalism that not only discriminates against women and the poor but also helped to maintain their status in the margins of society. Banks do not simply use a lack of material resources as justifications for not lending to those who have been historically disenfranchised. They also rely on certain tropes about those without wealth to reinforce their decisions. For instance, common stereotypes about the poor are that they are not intelligent and do not work hard. Therefore, it is unwise for banks to grant loans to the poor not only because they do not have any collateral to guarantee the loan but also because they do not have the character resources that would enable them to repay the loan. The myth, of course, extends to the conclusion that if one were intelligent and worked hard, then one would not be poor. Recognizing this vicious cycle where the poor are deprived of the resources which could lead them out of poverty, Dr. Yunus went against conventional lending structures that help make the rich richer and the poor poorer.[3]

Resistance to the Resistance Movement

But the complexities of power also make a simple solution difficult to find. Despite Foucault's argument that power models allow for change and resistance, this does not mean that everybody can be made equal within the playing field of power. His understanding of power makes change possible but he never said that it would come easily or quickly. Dr. Yunus' project shows that women can profit from micro-credit and positive changes in their lives can be made. However, the path of resistance is neither straight nor direct. Many twists, turns, and roadblocks are encountered. The example of the Grameen Bank is no exception. Not everyone is in favor of the changes brought to fruition through micro-lending. While there are some who welcome micro-credit, others resist it because they do not want their situation or place in society to be altered.

The small loans given mostly to women by the Grameen Bank[4] relay both the foundations of female oppression and how it can be changed. In other words, the financial situation of poor women is connected to the degradation of women in general. The controversy over the Grameen Bank shows that although micro-lending, in theory, is foremost concerned with financial objectives, it causes a ripple effect and becomes drawn into a debate about social order. On the one hand, the micro-lending process has helped in some cases to positively change the way women are treated in Bangladesh. Though it is not clear that there is a move away from the acceptance of male domination—even in terms of physical violence—over women, there is some evidence to suggest that spousal abuse has decreased either because women are now more visible to the community or are more valued because they contribute to family earnings. On the other hand, some are outright hostile to the innovations of the Grameen Bank. This is because the micro-credit firm challenges the patriarchal structure at work and it has not gone unnoticed by those who want to maintain the hierarchy of that system and the social customs that accompany it.

If one doubted that the role of women was connected to a larger social order, one need only examine how and why there is a resistance to the project of micro-credit. Dr. Yunus speaks to this situation specifically. In an interview with *Time* magazine, Yunus discusses the obstacles he encountered with the husbands of the women who wanted to apply for the loans.[5] Many of the regulations prescribed by the Grameen Bank go against traditional Bengali customs. Some husbands objected to their wives taking part in such a financial project because it directly contradicts the edicts of purdah, which states that women must remain in the confines of her home. But to take part in the enterprise, women are required to attend meetings that take them away from their home. The rules for obtaining micro-credit stipulate that people must join forces with others who are not family members and some of those people may be men, which is not socially acceptable. (Develtere & Huybrechts 2005, p. 175) Because women are expected to not have any contact with any male outside the family, the structure of micro-financing falls in direct conflict with the social traditions of the culture.

Although these guidelines were not designed expressly to destroy convention, it cannot be said that Yunus did not recognize that working within social norms would be bad for business. Hal Varian explains that it is crucial to the program that a loan candidate must form a group with four other people who are not family members. This regulation is put in place in order to ensure the quality of the group. (Varian 2001, p. 2–3) Because the group members are supposed to work as a check for each other, it is imperative for the success of all involved that a group is constructed in such a way that there is a high probability that the loan will be repaid.

The theory behind lending to a group is that group members would have the sufficient power to put pressure on other members and ensure that the loans can be recovered by the bank. It seems to me that, in a society where the male members have such a strong influence on the women in the family, the ban on family groupings negates the problem of heavy inequities among the group. That is, there is a struggle to maintain a certain level playing field of power. If husbands were allowed to join together with their wives and other family members, the women may not have the necessary power to exert pressure upon them to repay the loan. Develtere and Huybrecht report that, even with the regulations in play, it is difficult to combat the ways in which women suffer due to their position within society. In the case where the man is held responsible for the repayment of the loan, there seems to be little problem impressing upon the wife that she has an obligation to repay whatever amount she has used from the pool. However, the wife has substantially less power to pressure the husband to repay whatever amount he has used from the loan, even if she is the one who is responsible for paying back the lenders. (Develtere & Huybrechts 2005, p. 180) While the Grameen Bank has taken a chance by lending to poor women in the efforts to raise their social status, the traditional patriarchal system cannot be done away with so easily.

An argument can be made that what underlies the husbands' refusal to repay loans, especially if it belongs to their wives, is the struggle to keep the patriarchal system in place. The act of taking his wife's loan money without any intention of repaying it can be seen as acting out of the power dynamics that the husband wants to reiterate—namely, that she will be the one who must suffer the consequences because she has no power over him. Because she has no sway over whether he will repay the money he has taken from her loan, she and her credit worthiness is at his mercy. It is also possible that breaking the link between micro-creditors and women in the community is a goal. If there is a way to ensure that the loans are not repaid, then there is a greater chance that women are not extended the ability to acquire future loans. This, of course, would be a way to sabotage any attempts to challenge the patriarchal hierarchy. Although this is not a flattering portrait to paint of husbands, I believe it is plausible if one considers how Dr. Yunus describes the common reaction husbands have towards micro-financing. He reports that husbands often view the act of giving their wives loans as a personal insult. (Tharoor 2006, p. 8) Just as in any culture where the man is supposed to be the one who provides for the family, the husband most likely sees an attempt for the wife to earn money as a challenge to his masculinity. It is difficult to fight the perception that there is a need for the wife to work because the husband is not an adequate provider and, therefore, not sufficiently male. In order to restore his sense of masculinity and, ultimately, worthiness, the husband might take steps to ruin his wife's chances of financial independence.

The traditional power model between the husband and wife leaves the woman in a very vulnerable position. Because she is reliant upon him for everything, she must endure hardships from him so that he does not leave her and render her unable to take care of herself and the children. Unfortunately, reclaiming his masculinity may be tied up with keeping his wife dependent upon him for her survival. And, as hooks explains, if the motivation for such action is connected to the desire to dominate, it is not difficult to see how violence can be injected into the situation. A study of Grameen Bank participants shows that 70 percent of women report an increase of violence in the household. (Develtere & Huybrechts 2005, p. 180) If the objective is to maintain the status quo, the use of violence is a clear way to impose the pecking order, so to speak. Physical domination can help enforce the idea that the man is in control, no matter how wives try to seek or achieve power outside the home.

Yet what makes the Grameen Bank an interesting example is that it does show how change is possible. Foucault states theoretically that power allows for resistance; Dr. Yunus' project shows how it can come to pass in reality. And even more interestingly, the Grameen Bank is an example of how social pressures and norms can be beneficial, which is rarely a point of investigation for Foucault. Despite the fact that domestic abuse still continues, there is also evidence that husbands are afraid of a backlash from community members. Fearing that community members will disapprove of their actions and that they will lose standing in the greater community for mistreating their wives, some husbands refrain from treating their wives poorly. However, husbands have not necessarily reversed their opinion on the use of force to punish their wives. The cause of the cessation of domestic violence may, rather, be attributed to the increasing visibility of the women in the public sphere. (Schuler, et al., cited in D&H) For women who followed the tradition of purdah, their seclusion from the outside world allows their husbands to mistreat them without many knowing about her situation. Without the shield of female seclusion, there is a chance not only that others will know that husbands are abusive towards their wives but that they will also disapprove of that type of behavior. This brings us to the intersection of capitalism and community.

Capitalism Contra Community

In addition to contributing to the devaluation of women, hooks charges that capitalism has a hand in destroying community. She argues that capitalism depends on an ethic that runs contrary to distribution of wealth among community members. While it is clear that hooks believes that the inequities within capitalist structures must be rectified, she focuses her attention on how capitalism subordinates the communal sharing of resources to individualistic achievement. She uses the black community as a prime example. Whereas there had been a tradition of distributing monetary funds among less financially solvent members of the family or community, this ethic is giving way to the desire for individuals to spend their money on acquiring the trappings that would make them appear wealthier than they are. Attaining acceptance through economic standing, however, meant that they were turning away from an ethic of communalism that served as a survival strategy within black communities when there was not the possibility of earning the same salary of the white privileged classes. According to hooks (1994, p. 176) the equation of freedom with concrete rewards signaled the replacement of a sense of accountability to a collective body in favor of the satisfaction of individual desires. Unfortunately, this translates, for her, into an increase in poverty. Not only is there a lack of wealth sharing that once existed but those who might have pooled their resources to help out other community members are also going further into debt to purchase the accoutrements of a wealthier class while forgoing more basic needs. What this shows is that power, though often associated with oppression, can also work positively. That is, power which is generated through capitalist discourse can produce action. In this case, it is the act of buying material goods in order to fit in with capitalist norms.

Although it is difficult to dispute hooks' claims about how the capitalist ethic has affected the black community within America, it is heartening to see that the Grameen Bank has been successful in integrating a community ethic into its capitalist venture. Its model of micro-lending, in fact, depends upon the building of community. Dr. Yunus has devised a plan to link individual achievement to community success. Individuals are invested the success of others because their future loans also depend upon the initial repayment of others in their group. Therefore, compliance to standards comes from the stance of strengthening the community rather than sheer personal gain.

Muhammad Yunus uses the Grameen Bank as a vehicle to challenge the idea that greed must be the motivating force for capitalism. Instead, he seeks to prove that there is room for social-consciousness-driven entrepreneurs within capitalism. He admits that our traditional concept of the greedy, even bloodthirsty, capitalist is not only a product of our imagination. Greedy capitalists do exist and Yunus concedes that, to large extent, they have set the rules for the business sector. But he does not believe that the greed-driven capitalists should be allowed to dictate the rules for everyone else (http://www.gdrc.org/icm/grameen-keynote.html).

Social-Consciousness-Driven Capitalism

Although Yunus does not suggest that traditional capitalist business models will disappear and be completely replaced by one of self-sacrifice, he does believe that a new vision of capitalism that makes room for social consciousness can change the demographics in the business world. He understands that, realistically, those who are driven by greed will continue to do business. His hope is that others who do not follow that business model will enter the business sector as well. Yunus is also quick to point out that capitalist ventures should not be viewed in such Manichean terms. He thinks that turning away from greed as the only motivating factor for capitalism allows business models to mix greed and social consciousness to their own tastes. In his vision of capitalism, one could create a business strategy to aid social problems while still making a profit. But the profit is not the main point of the social-conscious-driven capitalist. Despite his claims that profit can be made, the reward is not the maximized accumulation of capital. The return, he suggests, is a new world. He states that, "the world we can build will be totally free from poverty and human indignity; it will be a world of friendship, cooperation and happiness rather than a world of aggression and destruction of human values and environment" (http://www.gdrc.org/icm/grameen-keynote.html).

What Yunus shows us is that social consciousness is not incompatible with capitalism. However, it does seem that it is incompatible with greed-based capitalism. Yunus believes that the Grameen Bank still operates within the capitalist structure because loans are given with the expectation that they are repaid with interest. The interest on the loans is 2% (Chowdhury et al. 2005, p. 299–300). This is much lower than the rates that Non-governmental agencies (NGO) can offer, which can run the gamut from 10% to 30%. Dr. Yunus' program does not, therefore, operate in order to make the largest profit possible. His goal is, rather, to help those in his community. While this objective means that he must refrain from charging the greatest amount of interest possible, there are economic successes to be noted along side the humanitarian achievements. Even with the low interest rates, the Grameen Bank made a profit of $15.21 million in 2005. It also enjoys a loan repayment rate of 98.85%.[6] More importantly for hooks, these figures show that profiles of the poor and disenfranchised need to be revised. The achievements of the Grameen Bank demonstrate that the poor do have the character resources of intelligence and industriousness, which most in the business world and beyond are not willing to recognize within them.

Sharing Resources Other than Capital

Included within hooks' critique of capitalist culture is the idea that wealth and money are the only things that matter. She laments the notion that financial wealth is seen as the primary means to increasing self-worth. Instead, she suggests that there are other resources in which to share with those who are disadvantaged. Among them are literacy programs. I will show that Dr. Yunus' program has given rise to this type of resource-sharing, which helped to address not only financial matters but also other circumstances that are connected to the plight of the poor. Bangladesh Rural Advancement Committee (BRAC) and community programs are an outgrowth of the innovations of the Grameen Bank. This organization seeks to serve the poor through both financial opportunities and social programs. Dr. Yunus recognized that micro-credit loans were not a cure-all despite the progress made through them. (Dugger 2006, p. 2) If the focus was going to remain on the improvement of society, aid for the poor needed to reach beyond financial matters. This assessment is consistent with the message that community members should recognize that money is only one among many resources that can be shared, which hooks tries to convey. In particular, she mentions the exciting prospect of literacy programs—which is included within BRAC.

The emphasis on social literacy programs is especially important, considering there is no unanimous consensus that micro-credit reaches the very poor, who Develtere and Huybrecht call the "bottom poor". They observe that micro-lenders themselves operate by loaning money to a certain strata of the poor. Those who are extremely poor do not have the same access even to micro-credit as the richer poor. The point Delvetere and Huybrecht are trying to make is that micro-credit does not reach everyone. Part of the problem in reaching the bottom poor is the issue of self-exclusion. The idea of taking on even more debt is especially odious for the very poor. But some have suggested that if this barrier is tied to a lack in confidence, programs which are targeted at social relations can be helpful. Because they have so little assets and fear losing them, the poorest of the poor tend to exclude themselves. What is needed in this case, Hashemi suggests is a way in which to boost their confidence. (Delvetere & Huybrechts 2005, p. 175)

This is the motivation of BRAC. Although this does not negate the positive function of the Grameen Bank or necessarily even lay blame on them, the reality is that other programs are needed to help those in extreme poverty. Yunus, however, seems to still channel his energies through capitalist enterprises. Although he believes that it is better for everyone to think of themselves as an entrepreneur and go into business for themselves, he also recognizes that not everyone is quite at that level yet (http://www.grameen-info.org/bank/GBGlance.htm). Again, part of this problem comes from a lack of self-confidence. Dr. Yunus tries to lend them a helping hand, cultivate initiative and self-worth by setting up businesses in textiles, fisheries, agriculture, telecommunications, etc. This investment, like his others, does not completely break from the capitalist mold. Instead, he tries to rework it.

Conclusion

That the Grameen Bank received the Nobel Peace Prize rather than the Nobel Prize in Economics is telling. Muhammad Yunus was not given the Nobel Prize in Economics because his project was recognized more as an innovative approach to lessen the suffering of people around the world than as an economic advance. It shows that economics is connected to the larger schema of society. On the one hand, I endeavored to relay the ways in which the traditional capitalist model has far-reaching negative effects and is connected to a philosophy of dominance by a few. We can no longer ignore the ways in which capitalism manifests itself as and contributes to inequities in the social order. In particular, I have argued with bell hooks that there is a kinship between the oppression of women and the conventional capitalist model. The domination of women further shows that the widely-accepted version of capitalism devalues community. Although women are not the only marginalized group within capitalism, their position within capitalism demonstrates how this economic system has not historically been linked to the prosperity of the entirety of the community but rather the success of a few.

On the other hand, I also tried to show that the capitalist structure is susceptible to reconstruction and renovation. The Grameen Bank serves as an example of how capitalism can operate in a different mode; its goal does not have to be achieving the greatest possible profit. Yunus found a way to develop capitalism in accord with the ideals of community growth. Although he admits that he did not have any particular ideology that pushed him to lend mainly to women, this outcome helped to lift women out of poverty and the social ranks that often kept them there. It is difficult to deny the impact his program had in creating social capital as well as financial capital for women, even if it was not his original intent. (Varian 2001: 4) Of course, there is much more work to be done before poverty is extinguished[7] but the Grameen Bank and other programs that follow its model are an interesting beginning.

Notes

1. Campbell Jones evokes Fournier and Grey's widespread criticism of Foucault in organization studies. That is, his work denies or tends to neglect the possibility of resistance (Jones 2002, p. 225).
2. The Grameen Bank is named to reflect the importance of group work. Bengalis refer to their village as "gram".
3. http://www.gdrc.org/icm/grameen-keynote.html
4. The Grameen Bank reports that 97% of its loans go to women.
5. I should also mention that challenges came from various directions. He did not only face resistance from those who are traditionally considered to be in favor of maintaining a patriarchal system: husbands and religious leaders. Yunus also encountered problems from those who considered themselves to be progressive. He noted that he believed this last group to be one of the strongest impediments to his project because they believed that his venture would continue to grow the host of problems with which capitalism has historically been linked. While husbands and mullahs might object to his lending practices because it disrupts the social order and goes against proper social convention, those from the left also work against his project because they believe that capitalism is an inherently poor economic model.
6. Data obtained from "Grameen Bank at a Glance": http://www.grameen-info.org/bank/GBGlance.htm
7. In an interview with *Time* magazine, Yunus claims that our grandchildren will have to go to a museum to see poverty because it will be eradicated elsewhere. (Tharoor 2006: 8)

References

Chowdhury, M. Jahangir Alam; Ghosh, Dipak & Wright, Robert E. 2005. "The Impact of Microcredit on Poverty: Evidence from Bangladesh," *Progress in Development Studies*, Vol. 5(4): 298–309.

Develtere, Patrick & Huybrechts, An. 2005. "The Impact of Microcredit on the Poor in Bangladesh," *Alternatives*, Vol. 30 : 165–189.

Dugger, Celia. 2006. "Peace Prize to Pioneer of Loans to Poor No Bank Would Touch," *New York Times*, 10/14/06.

Foucault, Michel. 1990.*The History of Sexuality: an Introduction*. New York: Vintage Books.

hooks, bell. 1994.*Outlaw Culture*. New York: Routledge.

Jones, Campbell. 2002. "Foucault's Inheritance/Inheriting Foucault," *Culture and Organization*, Vol. 8(3): 225–238.

Tharoor, Ishaan. 2006. "Muhammad Yunus," *Time*, Vol. 168(17): 8.

Varian, Hal. 2001. "In a Model for Lending in Developing Nations, a Bangladesh Bank Relies on Peer Pressure for Collateral," *New York Times*, 11/22/01.

Yunus, Muhammad. http://www.gdrc.org/icm/grameen-keynote.html. This is taken from a keynote speech he gave at 85th Rotary International Convention held in Taipei, Taiwan, on June 12–15, 1994.

Building an Ethics of Visual Representation: Contesting Epistemic Closure in Marketing Communication

Janet L. Borgerson and Jonathan E. Schroeder

This chapter veers away from simplified versions of ethical systems that dominate business ethics texts, and turns to existential-phenomenology, feminist ethics and critical race theory. Such fertile conceptual foundations provide novel approaches to critical analysis of *representational conventions* – customary ways of depicting products, people, and identities – and insights into the potential impact of marketing communication on identity and attribution. In an image economy, evaluations of 'image appropriateness' – a category invoked in some ethics codes' checklists – must be informed by an awareness of the ethical relationship between marketing communication, including advertising representations, and ontology. Ours is not a naïve claim that consumers believe marketing communications' artificial, stereotypical, or idealized realms do or can exist; or that consumers consume advertising images from a single unitary, or predetermined (so-called "structuralist") perspective. Rather, we contend that marketing images are part of lived experience: they contribute to the realities into which contemporary consumers are socialized, influencing lives and relationships with friends, loved ones, and strangers, as well. We argue that such images, moreover, often evade apparent possibilities for creative interpretation and critical resistance touted by image apologists.

Our work here emerges not only in response to issues in philosophical business ethics, but also from an engagement with business school-based research, including the areas of advertising, marketing communication, and consumer behavior – and with the sometimes dubious, if inexplicit, goals of such research. Continental and poststructural philosophical notions, theories, and models of identity, subject formation, and individual agency have had some impact on developing directions in these, and other, business school disciplines (e.g., Brown 1995; Firat and Venkatesh 1993; Borgerson and Schroeder 2002; Jones and Munro 2005). However, work has for the most part neglected to evoke related ethical innovations and insights (Jones, Parker, and ten Bos 2005). For example, in consumer research drawing upon an existential-phenomenological notion of the subject applied to research methodology (Thompson, Locander, and Pollio, 1989), extended

J.L. Borgerson
Department of Management at the University of Exeter, England
e-mail: J.L.Borgenson@exeter.ac.uk

M. Painter-Morland, P. Werhane (eds.), *Cutting-edge issues in Business Ethics*,

possibilities for understanding ethical implications of co-creation, identity and agency remain obscured. Theoretical contributions invoking these concepts have fueled, rather, not only marketing strategy (Holt 2002), but a particular form of 'phenomenological interview' that elicits consumers' intimate life details as interpretative raw material for data collection, corporate strategy, and academic publication (e.g., Thompson 1997).

Moreover within business and management research, ethically motivated criticisms of marketing communication are often simplistically understood as generalized criticisms of capitalism and related excessive consumption (Crane and Matten 2007; Thompson 2004). In contrast, our work engaging ethical concerns does not include criticism of consumption *per se*, nor do we take a moralistic stance against materialism – or marketing's possible role in promoting materialistic desires. Instead, we elaborate on representations of identity, concerned that represented identities profess to express something true or essential about those represented. This chapter joins a growing body of work on ethical concerns in marketing's visual representation that shares a broad historical framework and a complex array of analytical tools (e.g., Bordo 1997; Desmond 1999; Goldman and Papson 1996; O'Barr 1994; Schroeder and Borgerson 2005).

Our ethical analysis attends not only to the implications, or consequences, of representational conventions within marketing communication, but also emphasizes the ethical context from which such representational conventions emerge. Demonstrating an encounter with business research and marketing communication practices, we draw upon resources from an existential-phenomenological tradition that could guide studies with ethical relevance and ground an *ethics of representation* (Borgerson and Schroeder 2005).

Legitimating the Need for an Ethics of Representation

From certain perspectives – including those developed in marketing communication and consumer research – damaging representations often fail to qualify as ethical or moral problems (Drumwright and Murphy 2004; Walker 1998). This chapter affords complementary, yet distinct existential-phenomenological investigations, marking crucial opportunities frequently overlooked in business ethics, and moreover in the wake of more established phenomenological methods in marketing and consumer research (e.g., Thompson 1997).

As Margaret Urban Walker contends, the assumption that people are a *kind* or *type* is propagated and created by *representational practices*, which "are among those that construct socially salient identities for people" (1998, p.178). Moreover, she argues that if practices of representation "affect some people's morally significant perceptions of and interactions with other people, and if they can contribute to those perceptions or interactions going seriously wrong, these activities have bearing on fundamental ethical questions" (Walker 1998, p.179). In short, Walker implies that a person influenced by such images may treat members of the represented group as less than human and undeserving of moral recognition.

The Ethics of Epistemic Closure in Visual Representation

A process of *epistemic closure* invokes an essentializing of being that tends toward creation of a recognizable "authentic" identity while knowing next to nothing "about the typical Other beyond her or his typicality" (Gordon 1997, p.81). Typified representations, especially those that are racist or sexist, for example, may undermine a group's dignity and historical integrity and cast a demeaning light upon their physical and intellectual habits and ontological status as human beings (cf. Miller 1994). Nevertheless, from Walker's point of view, traditional philosophical approaches lack sufficient conceptual strength to handle representations that characteristically manipulate and damage the identity of subordinate groups.

Philosophers concerned with ethical norms and behavior have traditionally proceeded as though all problematic situations of moral recognition could be countered in the following three ways: through constructive definitions of personhood, through formal requirements of universality or universalizability, and through substantive demands for impartial or equal consideration (Walker 1998). Unfortunately, argues Walker, these three prescriptions fail to provide sufficiently complex considerations to deal with problems of representation, and worse, damaging representations often fail to even qualify as ethical or moral problems.

Robert Solomon exemplifies this debate in his discussion of 'consumer intelligence and responsibility,' which includes advertising-based concerns (Solomon 1993). The use of "sex" – he apparently refers in this case to a displayed or evocative sexuality – to lend appeal to products, and "the offensive portrayals of women and minorities," manifests what he calls a "lack of taste": But, asks Solomon, is it "an ethical issue"? (Solomon 1993, p.362). What Solomon utterly neglects is advertising's role beyond appeal, information, and persuasion – its perpetual representation of an entire vision of life and the world around us, often provoking responses and consequences equivalent to, and as 'serious' as, "outright lying in advertising" (cf. Borgerson and Schroeder 2002, Borgerson 2007; Schroeder and Borgerson 2005; Vaver 2008).

In other words, reliance on preconceived or stereotypical characteristics and images to create a successful marketing communication presents an area of ethical concern. Presumably, representations of racial, gender, and ethnic identities are often most easily recognized and comprehended when they correspond to a preconceived typification of particular racial, gender, or ethnic identities. Furthermore,

> [a]dvertising is a particularly salient instance of a system of representation that draws on a stock of stereotypes and visual conventions. Advertisers construct "consumer-goods ads to maximize the likelihood of preferred interpretations. This requires them to overdetermine (to make redundant) the encoding process as a means of steering viewers in preferred directions . . . " (Goldman 1992, p.124).

In cases such as these, an intended or unintended audience reads or interprets the representation within a field broadly determined by cultural meanings and categories – what Linda Alcoff refers to as *common sense* (1999).

Marketing images are certainly read in different ways by different people, but creating a successful marketing communication of identity often relies upon typified representations. Further, consumers, or viewers generally, may have an "investment" in responding in certain predictable ways: "what makes one take up a position in a certain discourse rather than another is an 'investment', something between an emotional commitment and a vested interest in the relative power (satisfaction, reward, pay-off) which that position promises (but does not necessarily fulfill)" (De Lauretis 1987, p.16). Epistemically closed representations of identity harnessed in the attempt to create brand images or corporate identity potentially undermine full human status of represented groups and individuals particularly – as discussed below – in light of sedimented contextual knowledges and bad faith.

Phenomenological Interviews and Decontextualization in Marketing Research

A phenomenologically-based hermeneutical approach to consumer understanding of marketing communication and practice, and moreover consumer culture, offers a description of the consumer's interpretive process (Thompson 1997), but not a grounding for investigating ethical concerns. Such methodologies depend upon the sense data and reported experience of individual agents, thus much relies upon who one interviews. That is to say, phenomenology is concerned with a description of what 'appears,' often failing to pursue critical questioning and investigation of what 'appears' to whom and why.

Phenomenological methods in marketing and consumer research often attenuate the level of reflective or critical contextual understanding on the part of individual agents (Borgerson and Schroeder 2002). Further, phenomenological data often underestimates contextual factors and overestimates individual agency or interpersonal skill when making attributions about causal implications of behavior (Ross and Nisbett 1991). Individuals living in a context of oppression, for example, may be unable to reliably articulate their own position in relation to a broader cultural matrix, and what results is individual interpretation of decontextualized experiences (Bartky 1991; Borgerson 2001).

Individual consumers cannot be relied upon to recognize and articulate points of ethical concern. Hermeneutical, or interpretative, frameworks that attend to consumers' personal perceptions provide useful information to those interested in psychological insights for target-marketing purposes, but such data does not facilitate an understanding of broader undesirable trends that can anchor much-needed ethical analysis. Moreover, phenomenological methodology, particularly within managerial based marketing research, often fails to capture ethical concerns within image discourse. Our work attempts to ground recognition – for practitioners, consumers, and the public in general – of how representations communicate damaging identities.

Marketing Makes Meaning: Visual Representation, Photography, and Advertising

Marketing communication, including advertising, employs photography as information technology – to produce meaning within a circuit of production and consumption. Indeed representation today depends on photographic imagery to accomplish its many tasks (e.g., Schroeder 2008). Visual perception of "lives and the social world" is intensified and magnified by information technologies of photography – which includes still photography, video, film, and digital imaging. Crucially then, sociologists Goldman and Papson point out the close interconnected relationship between advertising and photography:

> [t]he power of advertising lies in its ability to photographically frame and redefine our meaning and our experiences and then turn them into meanings that are consonant with corporate interests. This power to recontextualize and reframe photographic images has put advertising at the center of contemporary redefinitions of individuality, freedom, and democracy in relation to corporate symbols. (Goldman and Papson 1996, p.216)

Furthermore, as Richard Lippke writes, "the ways in which individuals habitually perceive and conceive their lives and the social world, the alternatives they see as open to them, and the standards they use to judge themselves and others are shaped by advertising, perhaps without their ever being consciously aware of it" (Lippke 1995, p.108). Indeed, one consumer theorist points out that, "[I]t is chiefly the visual aspect of the advertisement that conjoins the world and object between which a transfer of meaning is sought" (McCracken 1988, p.79). Yet, marketing research often treats visual issues solely as an information-processing variable.

Conventional views of representation hold that things, such as objects, persons, or consumers, exist in the material and natural world, and that their material characteristics define them in perfectly clear terms. Representation, according to this view, is of secondary importance in meaning making, and serves to communicate and manifest 'real' or natural characteristics. In contrast, if representation refers to meaning production through language systems (cf. Stern 1998), how that language is used is central to creating particular meaning. That is, the very process of representing objects or ideas shapes meaning.

In this way, representation enters into the very constitution of things. Some marketing scholarship has turned to the concept of representation for insight into diverse market-related phenomena, including advertising imagery (Pearce 1999), war propaganda posters (Hupfer 1997), research methods (Stern 1998), information technology (Schroeder and Borgerson 2002), and photography (Schroeder 2002). Indeed, using representation as an analytic tool, recent studies have emphasized how cultural practice, such as laws, rituals, norms, art, and advertising, all contribute to meaning production within marketing and consumer research (e.g., Fırat and Shultz 1997; Hirschman 1986; Messaris 1997; Schroeder 1998; Pracejus et al. 2006).

In short, meaning produced or constructed by social and cultural forces gives representation primary importance. Advertising, as a pervasive representational form, both reflects and creates social values. Photographic representations, harnessed by advertising, ripple through the culture, circulating information about the social world. As Cadava (1999) expresses it, even the world itself has taken on a "photographic face". Indeed, marketing communication and advertising itself have been called 'the face of capitalism' (Schroeder 2002). Research using this approach has been characterized as falling into two categories, semiotic and discursive (Hall 1997). Semiotic research, or the *poetics* of representation, is concerned with how representation produces meaning. Discursive research, or the *politics* of representation, stresses effects or consequences and connects representation to power and culture (Hall 1997). Both types of research – at times overlapping, at times discrete – are necessary for a full examination of representation as the core of the production of meaning.

Tendencies in Philosophy and Visual Representation

Linking marketing communication to ontological dilemmas, including recognizable categories of being, in visual representation enables researchers to engage a global communication system in which images provide resources for, and hence shape, our understandings of the world – including the identities of people and places. Additionally, an astonishing number of marketing communication scenarios gesture to the field of aesthetics as marketing images instruct the consumer in the philosophical quest for a good life (e.g., Crocker and Linden 1998). We contend that visual representations are central to aesthetic processes as well as ethical inquiry; thus our approach to visual representation research attempts to comprehend the ethical, aesthetic and cultural implications of representing, for example, geographical locations, individuals, or cultural identities – particularly the identities of marginalized or oppressed groups of people. After all, pictures of people – models, celebrity endorsers, spokespersons, "average" consumers, managers and employees – make up a large part of marketing imagery; and visual images constitute much corporate communication about products and services, economic performance, and organizational identity (e.g. King 2002; Schroeder 2008). Serving as stimuli, signs, or representations that drive cognition, interpretation, and preference, images influence what we know, believe, and crucially, what we do (e.g., McQuarrie and Mick 1999; Zaltman 2002; Borgerson and Schroeder 2005).

Philosophical Biases

In the history of Western philosophy, sensible, material things (*aisqhta*) have often been opposed, and subordinated, to immaterial, non-sensible, or 'thinkable' things *(nohta)*: the sensible, material world and experiences based upon its appearances and temptations have been thought in many ways inconsequential (e.g., Weston 1992, p.173). Nevertheless, philosophers have attempted to discover, understand, and articulate the relationship between human being and these apparently discrete and unequal domains. Explorations of the distinctions and interactions between body and mind, emotion and rationality, image and reality, the beautiful and the sublime, the false and the true have expanded the spectrum of philosophical aesthetics and complicated – not without anxiety – the boundaries between these categories.

For example, Immanuel Kant sought to articulate the *a priori* principles of knowledge gained by way of the senses (e.g., Deleuze 1984). To put this another way, experience in the material world underlies Kant's proposition – the necessary framing of time and space upon the organization of basic information and data toward human knowledge. Such a perspective would apparently grant the material context within which one finds oneself a certain importance.

> However – as suggested in Solomon's dismissal of advertising images' ethical import – conceptual binaries and related hierarchical dualisms founded upon basic philosophical distinctions continue to influence designations of value, creating blind spots concerning the impact of the undervalued, often overlooked sense-related material environments and elements; and moreover overestimating the role and influence of that which is associated with mind-related capacities and immaterial realms. Ethics in such a context must turn to discerning the multiple (aesthetic) processes, elaborated by Hegel, by which external things are made objects of desire and dominating agents are allowed to claim all that they see as their own (Hegel 1993).

Represented identities profess to express something true or essential about those represented and certain ontological assumptions emerge, often functioning in relation to culturally defined hierarchies and dominant semiotics – grounding what categories, characteristics, or individual signs might mean within the dominant culture. Semiotic meanings such as those drawn upon to frame marketing communications prescribe and structure the elements of identity and difference that will be readily rendered culturally intelligible. Moreover, visual representations in marketing communication can be considered socio-political artifacts; they create meaning within the circuit of culture that often extends beyond what may be intended by photographers, art directors, advertising agencies, and firms whose products are advertised.

For example, theorists and scholars interested in ethical and aesthetic dimensions of cultural production attempt to determine what aesthetic (and political) choices are made when a less powerful, subordinate, or colonized group is represented by a dominant group within the cultural realm of visual representation, including marketing communications on the World Wide Web, television, billboards, and in magazines, travel guides, and tourist brochures (Desmond 1999; Gross 1988).

Image Creation and Identity

If marketing communication depends upon images, including brand images, corporate images, product images, and images of identity, then an ethics of representation for marketing communications must be capable of addressing the concerns that such images evoke. Images and representations in marketing communications often 'stand in' for experience – especially when other sources have less prominence – and serve as a foundation for future attempts to comprehend and construct the world around us. Furthermore, information, sensibility, and attitudes gleaned from representations may influence thinking and understanding about people and cultures, affecting the way new experiences and information are interpreted. In other words, one feels that one has learned something in observing or examining a photographic image of a person or a geographic location. Yet the way that marketing representations stand in when experience is lacking, or function in conjunction with experience, has the power to make us believe that we know something of which we have no experience and to influence the experiences we have in the future.

At times, image creation in marketing communication draws upon and reinforces simplified, even subordinating, representations of cultural difference, group identity, and geographic specificity. That such representations, harnessed in the attempt to create a product image, potentially undermine the full human status of represented groups and individuals is of great concern (Cortese 1999; Davila, 1997; O'Barr 1994; Schroeder and Borgerson 1998; Stern 1993; Williamson 1978). Representations of identities that are exoticized, sexist, or racist, may damage the reputation of represented groups, and associated group members, and manipulate their being for consumption by others. The claim is not that some advertising, as well as other forms of marketing communication, might offend the damaged group or its members, but that semiotically and ontologically associated groups and individuals, and their opportunities for the future, may be damaged by certain forms of representation.

As an illustrative example, consider a recent advertisement for American Express "Red" – part of a campaign involving a number of major brands who have created iconic red versions of their products to express a "passion" for a solution to the AIDS crisis. The image features two tall, thin and leggy individuals: one, the white Western well-known model Gisele, the other, apparently a black African "Masaai Warrior" named Keseme. Whereas the Red campaign attempts to call attention to a globally recognized tragedy and does express a certain equality in the two people by capturing certain physiological similarities that seem to express essential qualities – their height, smiles, and long legs, for example – the advertisement figures a dynamic, 'colorful' man who comes to stand in for all of Africa, as the heart of the devastating crisis. His exoticized anonymity – although we are given his name – demonstrates the risk of repeating typicalities and epistemic closure even with ethically motivated and good intentions.

Discussions of marketing ethics rarely include visual issues – apart from largely atheoretical attention to shock advertising, sexual appeals, or stereotyping. Rather, discussions typically revolve around deception, the questionable accuracy of product claims, and the targeting of vulnerable consumers, such as children (Hackley 2005; Smith and Quelch 1993). Indeed, most marketing communication research focuses on persuasive effects of communication from a consumption orientation. In short, marketing communication depends largely on visual representation to produce meaning, brand images, and spectacular simulations that create associations in consumers' minds, yet despite their importance in creating meaning, a theoretical consideration of visual issues is rare in marketing ethics scholarship.

Essentialized Ontology and Bad Faith

Representations of subordinate groups, particularly marketing representations circulating within the dominant semiotics of media culture, rarely contradict and typically reproduce versions of subordination. The necessity for an ethics of representation grows out of the ethical significance of culturally circulating ontological divisions and hierarchies and the reality of epistemic closure. Ontological explorations center on notions of being or identity, who one is and who one is not, including how relationships form and function. Being is active, verbal, not simply in the sense of being a speaking out, or voicing of a subjectivity, but related to activity in general. To be is to be, as an activity, human.

Some philosophers have attempted to define the essential features of being, including basic notions of animate and human life; but such essentialism denies the contingent social and historical context and construction of being. Lewis Gordon, in rejecting essentialist ontology – here around notions of racial difference – writes:

> eventually, blackness and whiteness take on certain meanings that apply to certain groups of people in such a way that makes it difficult not to think of those people without certain affectively charged associations. Their blackness and their whiteness become regarded, by people who take their associations too seriously, as their essential features—as, in fact, material features of their being. (Gordon 1995, p.95).

Furthermore, Gordon argues, ontology should be study of "what is treated as being the case and what is realized as the contradiction of being the case" (Gordon 1995, p.133). This attitude avoids "taking our associations too seriously" and promotes interrogation of naturalized normative hierarchies – sedimented knowledge about stratified categories of being. Moreover, this perspective comprehends the role of interpretation and makes a semiotic link between being and culture (e.g., Miller 1994).

Following upon Merleau-Ponty's observation that "perception represents sedimented contextual knowledges," Alcoff argues in relation to racial embodiment that "there is no perception of the visible that is not already imbued with value" (Alcoff 1999, p.15). A kind of "common sense," formed by "past historical beliefs and practices of a given society or culture" influences and informs racial knowledge. Yet, unlike explicit manifestations of racist, or sexist, ideologies, this "common sense" as part of everyday consciousness feels 'natural' rather than as a site of reflective or contestable knowledge. "The process by which human bodies are differentiated and categorized by type," writes Alcoff (1999, p.16), "is a process preceded by racism". To put this another way, perceptions preceded by generally circulating "common sense" reflect and enact racist knowing. While appreciating the varieties of racial common sense, Alcoff (1999, p.23) notes that "there is a visual registry operating in social relations which is socially constructed, historically evolving, and culturally variegated but nonetheless powerfully determinant over individual experiences". Thus, marketing communication's visual representations of essentialized ontologies – in a context of perceptual 'common sense' – emerge as an important sight for investigation.

In related modes of semio-ontological interpretation around "sedimented contextual knowledges," Gordon's work on anti-black racism mobilizes Jean-Paul Sartre's mechanism of bad faith. *Bad faith* describes the attempt to flee responsibility for the open nature of human being and human projects, resulting in the diminishment of human being. In bad faith, the inability to face the openness of human existence fosters a lie of predetermined being and limited possibility (Sartre 1956; Gordon 1995). This diminishment marks a closing down upon the fullness, uniqueness, and potential of human being, Gordon argues, and helps to articulate anti black racism and other forms of Manichean essentializing. Working to avoid bad faith in marketing representations carries forward Alcoff's project of "reactivating racist perception and experience toward a process of reorienting, reconfiguring, and disrupting 'habitual perception'" (Alcoff 1999, p.23). Moreover, the use of demeaning or stereotypical images is especially misleading in the global marketplace, where kaleidoscopic cultural contexts already complicate communication.

Ontological Othering and Typicality

Contemporary philosophical theorists have written extensively on the relations between representation, identity, and ontological status (see e.g., Ahmed 2000; Bell 1993; Bartky 1991; Borgerson 2001; Butler 1987/1999; Gordon 1995; McNay 2000; Walker 1998; Young 1990). These studies reflect upon and theorize varieties of being deemed capable of ethical agency and responsibility. They are linked by a concern with how visual, and visualized, markers such as skin color and gendered gestures – which are mapped in and onto the body as a kind of trope – represent or partially determine the status of beings, particularly in the context of racism and sexism.

> As a result of dichotomous thinking, *being* has traditionally been divided in two. As observed in the realm of aesthetics, this binary mode has given rise to well recognized, hierarchically ordered dualisms: self/other, white/black, heaven/earth, civilized/primitive, rational/irrational, finite/infinite in what has been called a "logic of colonialism" (Hawkins 1998; Plumwood 1993). A basic dualism, self/not self, paves the way for an understanding of the self that is set against the not-self (Kant 1973/1790). The self, as subject, defines the not-self as other, evoking knowledge of the self that develops through a self-versus-other epistemology of difference (e.g., Coviello and Borgerson 1999; Oliver 2001). This ontological *othering* – setting one element against the other – has perpetuated and reinforced the dualistic hierarchical orderings that historically have favored the male, the white, and the rational (cf. Goldberg 1993).

Ontologically dualistic hierarchies carry semiotic relevance and express the interrelations of subordinated elements, such as the female, the black, and the emotional or sentimental. For example, Gordon's semiotic reading locates blackness at the subordinated pole in the hierarchical black/white dualism that operates as a sign of value within what he calls an antiblack world (Gordon 1995). As suggested earlier, these poles of the one and the other reveal themselves in Plato's distinction between material and immaterial and Kant's marking the superior mode of the "sublime" in contrast to the "beautiful" (Kant 1960).

To take this point a bit further, traditionally philosophers have granted ethical superiority to traits and behaviors arising from a stereotypically male way of being. Kant (1960, p.77) in his *Observations on the Feeling of the Beautiful and the Sublime* insists upon maintaining the 'charming distinction that nature has chosen to make between the two sorts of human beings', placing females in the realm of the beautiful and granting male conjunction with the sublime. In this context, males exemplify capacities for depth, abstract speculation, reason, universal rules and principles. Females are said to be modest, sympathetic, sensitive, and capable of particular judgments, but not principles. In Kant's philosophical universe, then, this 'charming distinction' leaves women unilaterally unable to attain full ethical agency. Feminist ethics in particular has attempted to confront the impact and implications of such sexist dualisms (See e.g. Card 1996, p.49–71; Borgerson 2007).

Representational conventions in marketing communication draw upon such deeply entrenched meaning systems that easily reinforce and reproduce damaging images of identity. In such a context – as Hegel's statement evoked earlier – those associated with the privileged elements stand in the position to claim knowledge of all that is important to know about those associated with the subordinated elements. That is, this type of semiotically dualistic relation engages with the potential for epistemic closure.

Attending to epistemic closure means recognizing the danger of typified representations of identity that increase the probability of human subjects interpreting what they experience, or have represented to them, as typical (Gordon 1997), as well as interpreting these experiences and representations through versions of familiar typicality (Natanson 1986). Knowing the other as *typical* refers to an abstracting and condensing of characteristics that create a familiar identity or pattern for beings and occurrences of a kind. Epistemic closure leads one to believe that he or she knows the other's being completely, and this assumption of knowledge denies the other status as human being and erases possibility for human relationships.

As we have argued, one of the most serious outcomes of representational practices is that people's perceptions, even "misinformed perceptions," often have "the weight of established facts" (Gordon 1995, p.203). Ontological categories presented by images in marketing communication are not confined to the context of being a particular case in a given society in a particular historical moment. Rather, they are presented as what *is* the case about particular individuals or groups. This concretizing of contingent ontological categories serves as a further instance of bad faith.

Ethics and ontology are linked by many concerns, including how visual markers – such as skin color, embodiment, and gendered attributes – represent, influence or determine the status of human beings, particularly in the context of sexism and racism, and how meaning and being are created, interrelated, and represented. Thus, what we think we know about others from representations of identity – including those within marketing communication – can affect how we see, treat, and understand them. Below we explore further implications in the context of advertising images and meaning making.

Advertising Images: Repetition and Identity

Much of the ideological power of the representations lies in their almost infinite repetition – similar images are presented over and over in a wide variety of marketing contexts and epochs (Schroeder and Borgerson 2003). In short, advertising that promotes typification, producing ontologies and identities also instructs and informs (Bristor, Lee and Hunt 1995; Butler 1993). For example, reflecting broader cultural stereotypes, many advertisements represent women as inferior to men and build on notions of women as product, woman as sexual object, and woman as threat renewing and perpetuating these images to each generation (see e.g. Cortese 1999; Goffman 1979; Stern 1993).

To elaborate, advertising – in not surprising coherence with Kant – influences the ontology of women in several ways. First, it links women with fashion and style, ephemeral concerns of the moment. Second, advertisers portray women in ways that underscore the body as the site of female identity. Third, advertising rhetoric reinforces the ontological status of women as subordinate, non-intellectual, child-like, and *other* (Schroeder and Borgerson 2005). Here, the American Express Red advertisement's context again provokes reflection: Gisele is a female model and clearly aligned with fashion and style. Of course, this subordination is countered by a highly paid career, her fame, her white Western status, and her role in contemporary consumer culture – the money and consumption practices of which are called upon to save the world. Nevertheless, Gisele's value remains focused on a body-based earning potential. In fact, in the ad, viewers are called upon to note her physical features' mirroring of Keseme's – including the beaming smiles. Thus, drawing upon semiotically informed dualisms, her visually represented identity remains understandable within a subordinated realm of value, and rather than evoking ontologically dominating meaning that might disrupt the desired reading of the advertising image, expresses instead an equality with Keseme's exoticized blackness.

In general, and particularly in comparison to female bodies, the male body in advertising remains ontologically related to forms of masculinity represented through material success, professional skill and economic power (e.g., Schroeder and Zwick 2004). Of course, the status of maleness and masculinity can be enhanced or reduced by the introduction of other semio-ontological elements – such as, blackness or child-like poses and expressions that operate in the case of Keseme. However, the meaning produced around male bodies in ads tends to recuperate "patriarchal ideology by making it more adaptable to contemporary social conditions and more able to accommodate counter-hegemonic forces" (Hanke 1992, p.197). Recall, visions such as these do not just exist "out there", but must be created and reiterated.

Moreover, particular dominant groups often hold decision-making power about what and who will be represented and, perhaps more significantly, how subordinate groups will be represented (see Davila 1997). People that have a stake in representing and reinforcing certain stereotypical gestures, characteristics, or styles do not necessarily operate in the best interests of those represented. The lure of familiarity, typification and cliches points out the necessity for ethical theory and business ethics to confront instances of damaging representation.

It is important to remember that marketing does not merely use a preexisting discourse but works to create, and then sell, its own visual rhetoric through the use of carefully designed marketing communication and promotions (Schroeder and Borgerson 2003). Marketing representations work in a broad context to influence the construction of the world through marketing images (Fırat and Venkatesh 1993), and as cultural theorist Richard Leppert points out:

> Images show us a world but not *the* world....When we look at images, whether photographs, films, videos, or paintings, what we see is the product of human consciousness, itself part and parcel of culture and history. That is, images are not mined like ore; they are constructed for the purpose of performing some function within a given sociocultural matrix. (Leppert 1997, p.3).

Marketing, the mastermind of representational images designed to sell elaborately positioned products, including geographical locations and cultures, created in the past, actively creates in the present, and will have to continue to create in the future, images and identities designed to maintain the desired impact.

As we explore in the following section, semio-ontological analysis of images draws upon a theoretical apparatus that takes representational histories and hegemonic semiotic coding into account and focuses on the capacity to de-ontologize images (see, for e.g., Alcoff 1999; Gordon 1999; Mirzoeff 1999; Ramamurthy 1997). Our discussion of a Benetton ad campaign investigates the problem of negative stereotypes in contexts with few competing representations. We argue that marketing communication, with its increasing presence and influence in the global marketplace, needs an ethics of representation.

Representation, Domination, and Benetton in Bad Faith

Ethical issues arise when representations of subordinate groups facilitate the erasure of identity and domination of that group (cf. Kaplan and Pease 1993). Some scholars have argued that representation in marketing images is an improvement over racist and sexist days gone by, when most marginalized groups were not represented at all (cf. Rabinowitz 1994). However, there exists a strange phenomenon of absence through presence that is manifested in an *anonymity* through which anyone might stand in for anyone else of a certain kind or an *invisibility* through typicality that will never be undone by bad faith marketing representations (Gordon 1997, p.80; Natanson 1986). Clearly the human other exceeds this typicality. Yet, through the ease of epistemic closure and the lie that allows the typical to stand in for the human, bad faith emerges within representational practices.

Bad faith visual representation is not limited to specific geographical or cultural areas. The Italian clothing company Benetton and its creative director Oliviero Toscani provide an example of marketing communications interaction with ethical concerns. Benetton has received much critical attention for the marketing campaign it refers to as "the United Colors of Benetton." A crucial criticism of Benetton's advertising strategy has been that the images chosen by the company de-historicize and de-contextualize the people and situations represented. For example, a recent campaign used photographs of death row inmates in the United States who have been sentenced to die in seven states that allow the death penalty (Berger 2001, p.249; New York Times 1999). In trademark fidelity, Benetton has consistently used socially provocative photographs, violent images, and racial representation in its marketing communications, and the "Sentenced to Death" campaign fit this pattern well. Of the many ways that Benetton might have selected to deliver their message, it chose to present close-up photographs, almost portraits, of death row inmates, the majority of which are black men.

Among the sites chosen for the Benetton campaign were several prominent billboards in downtown Stockholm, Sweden. Although recent immigration is changing Sweden's demographics, particularly in larger cities, relatively few faces of color are seen in Stockholm. Further, few images of black men appear in Swedish media. However, black musical forms of jazz, soul, and funk are conspicuous throughout Stockholm. Rap is particularly popular and ubiquitous on European MTV providing a plentitude of controversial stereotypes that continue to inform understandings of black ontologies (Goldman and Papson 1996, p.165). In this context and in a homogenous country, such as Sweden, the Benetton ads may do little more than reinforce vaguely present yet negative versions of black male typicality – in this case, with death row prisoners – associated with extreme criminal activity and guilt.

Benetton claims that their images protest the death penalty and focus attention on the plight of death row inmates and the use of the death penalty in the United States. It may be that in Sweden, in particular, Benetton's use of black men in the death penalty ads does indeed focus attention upon racism and injustice in the United States – marking a site of black male oppression. That is, if a black man is more likely to be sentenced to the death penalty than a white counterpart, and he also happens to be innocent, this effect of U. S. racism further bolsters concerns about the death penalty. Indeed, blackness here may function as much as a sign of victim status as of criminality. Nevertheless, the presence of these images serves to perpetuate the visual representation of blacks as the exotic, yet recognizable, other (see Williams 1987). Moreover, the representations in Benetton's death row campaign semiotically link black identity with murder and death.

Perhaps not intentionally racist, examples from Benetton and American Express Red nevertheless raise justifiable concern over how identity is represented in marketing campaigns (e.g., Giroux 1994). It is crucial to understand how blackness functions semiotically as an ontological and representational category, and how representations of blackness, mired in typicality and anonymity, may associate negative and damaging cultural images to those identities that are represented by concretizing contingent categories of being (Gordon 1995).

The semio-ontological focus presented here underscores the process by which representations link embodied human beings to identities that make a difference in lived world experience. Despite Benetton's success in generating publicity and market share for its brand, marketing's use of social and cultural controversy becomes controversial itself. The situations of the men in the Benetton ads are clearly negative and seem destined to reinforce racist stereotypes about blacks (cf. Collins 1990; Fanon 1967; Goldberg 1993; James 1997). In fact, many have criticized this campaign as celebrating murderers by representing them not as criminals in mug shots, but rather in humanizing portraits. Yet we point to other potential problems of Benetton's death row campaign. Indeed, attempts to justify these ads based on a tenuous notion that they promote, for example, pity in the viewer could be met with the observation that pity itself signals an ontological status differential.

Similarly, Benetton might claim that these socially relevant ads motivate viewers to take action against the death penalty or somehow become involved in political controversies around issues of race, crime, and corrections. However, many commentators raise concerns about the use of controversy to promote clothing (Giroux 1994; Goldman and Papson 1996; Ramamurthy 2004); and we may wonder whether these advertising representations do more than foster a negative typicality in contexts where few other competing representations circulate in the visual culture.

Furthermore, Ramamurthy (1997, p.192) points out that history reinforces and thus insures the effectiveness of advertising's created images: "images do change meaning according to their context; yet images, like everything else, are historically based and cannot avoid the meanings and symbolisms which the past puts upon them". This is why marketing researchers are mistaken when they claim that representations that are de-historicized and de-contextualized are completely open to interpretation. The death row campaign may perpetuate longstanding racist assumptions about who black people are, who they can be, and provides yet another example of how marketing communications holds blackness and other subordinated identities in a representational prison. We argue that Benetton is acting in bad faith (Borgerson and Schroeder 2002).

An Ethics of Representation

An ethics of representation, especially in global marketing, must be heeded if business sincerely wants to create "a genuine ... centerprise, a mode of activity that resolves society's crises, not causes them" (Guillet de Monthoux 1993). Furthermore, if disciplines grounded in business concerns, including marketing, consumer behavior, and organization studies, are to be part of the solution rather than part of the problem, emerging practices must not contribute to epistemic closure, typified images and representational bad faith. How can reflections and investigations emerging from an ethics of representation impact work, for instance, in marketing communication? An ethics of representation enables recognition of problematic representational sites and moreover maintains an openness to what Houston Wood – in his analysis of "the rhetorical production" of negative cultural identities – calls "poly-rhetoric." Poly-rhetoric is defined as the attempt to conceptualize how communication might function if marginalized groups had greater access to mass media's representational power (Wood 1999).

We have pointed out that "bad faith" marketing creates a paradox, for even as more diverse human subjects are being represented in marketing communication and advertising images, human identity suffers from racist, sexist, and colonialist erasure. One might think that simply including images of under-represented or marginalized cultural groups in marketing communication would help, but this strategy often leads to exoticized images, images informed by typicality, and 'token' images. Moreover, representation can lead to an invisibility, a strangely equivocal effect that reflects the difficult dialectic between identity and representation in a context of oppression. Representations of the exotic other continue to evoke a historical matrix of subordination: Pictures of women in subordinated roles have marked implications as well. Moreover, that Benetton's approach to cultural 'inclusion' has been widely criticized as perpetuating stereotypes of difference – an ironic result, not unlike that of the American Express Red campaign – illustrates the complex intertwining of identity, representation, and marketing within the global economy.

Visual Literacy and Global Relations

An ethics of representation demonstrates an existential-phenomenological approach with an emphasis on the impact of semiotic systems and mechanisms in embodied lived experience. Awareness is one step – avoiding bad faith depends on an awareness of potential negative communication. Access to understandings of potential meaning is increased by visual and semiotic literacy – important components of societal marketing. Such understanding and literacy may be supported by a stakeholder approach to management – one that acknowledges multiple constituents for corporate activities, including marketing communication (e.g., Sirgy and Su 2000).

Most firms have been reluctant to offend targeted consumers, but recent trends in advertising show that shocking images gain attention. Sometimes these attention-grabbing images are shocking because they draw upon subordinating and oppressive typicalities. We believe that brilliant marketing campaigns need not rely on damaging representation, and we call on the industry to pay more attention to their message's complex and far-reaching meanings.

When marketing campaigns represent identities of groups or individuals so that the representations themselves purport to express something true or essential about those represented, aesthetic questions intersect with ethical questions and allow certain ontological assumptions to emerge. Identities are "performed" through images, especially images that enter the cultural landscape through popular mass media (Goffman 1979). In addition to damaging the reputation of members of represented groups, some forms of representation that are exoticized, stereotypical, sexist, or racist actually manipulate these groups for consumption by others. Given power inequalities and lack of access to mass media forms of representation, subordinated or oppressed individuals or groups often do not have control over how they are represented, nor how they are seen in broader cultural realms, particularly within the discourse of advertising.

An ethics of visual representation promotes visual literacy through training and education in visual communication. Furthermore, whereas photography is the most pervasive form of communication in the world, most people have had little formal training in the historical background of photography, the processes of photographic production, or the function of pictorial conventions. Advertising, like photography, seems to present a world *that just is*, even though photographic images are cropped, selected, and edited for consumption. Linking advertising to representation enables researchers to recognize advertising as a global communication system, based on visual images, that impacts upon human being and human relations in lived experience. Informed by an ethics of representation's existential-phenomenological approach, future research locating and identifying specific ontological themes in advertising will add to the gathering literature in this field. Suggesting further implications for ignoring these concerns, the concluding section opens the notion of 'grey zones' in marketing communications.

Harm and 'grey zones' in Marketing Communication

Claudia Card argues that institutions that create 'grey zones,' sometimes intentionally, are particularly culpable (Card 2002). In her discussion of 'the grey zone,' Card elaborates on the complex situations of 'some who are simultaneously victims and perpetrators.' Such a scenario might be seen arising in a rural community adjusting, for example, to the presence of new outsourced factory work in which some people come to hold the means of survival for others, perhaps suddenly, perhaps with nearly impossible demands from those farther up the supply chain; or impacting upon those whose identities are bought, sold, and consumed regularly in contemporary consumer culture. Thus, issues of responsibility and accountability reemerge in complex contexts; and the realm of advertising representation and business research is no different.

Card defines 'evil' most basically as 'foreseeable intolerable harms produced by culpable wrongdoing' (Card 2002, p.3). She writes,

> One reason that many evils go unrecognized is that the source of harm is an institution, not just the intentions or choices of individuals (many of whom may not share the goals of the institution, even when their conduct is governed by its norms). Another is that the harm is the product of many acts, some of which might have been individually harmless in other contexts. Victims are more likely than perpetrators to appreciate the harm. But when the source is an institution, even victims can be hard-pressed to know whom to hold accountable (Card 2002, p.24–25).

Particularly in situations in which privilege meets disadvantage, wealth meets poverty, or power meets constraint – constantly emerging for example in globalized labor, international health research practices, and cross-cultural or sub-cultural marketing (Borgerson 2005b) – decision making processes to avoid real harms in the face of apparent benefits become ever more opaque.

What Card argues is that, "evils may be prevented from perpetuating themselves in a potentially unending chain as long as victims who face grim alternatives continue to distinguish between bad and worse and refuse, insofar as possible, to abdicate responsibility for one another" (Card 2002, p.26). Some of her analysis specifically addresses social institutions; and clearly discussions of 'institutions' might as well suggest the organization, corporation, or various representational practices. Representations play a role in constructing reality and are part of the lived experience. To put this another way, every representation has the potential to influence the way cultures and communities see each other. Visual connotations of interpersonal relations are so familiar that an entire range of race relations and political power can be summoned with a single image of, for example, a hula dancer (cf. Leiss, Kline and Jhally1990). Those who create marketing communications must be encouraged to think critically about their responsibilities in this act of creation. As such, reflection upon these images is crucial to ethical concerns around ontological attributions, including those that effect global relations.

Surely, philosophers in business ethics and corporate social responsibility must take up what tools we can to recognize and reveal grey zones. Moreover, understanding these potential outcomes, business ethicists must call upon those in marketing communications in good-faith to reject the dubious tradition of drawing upon typicalities of ethnicity, race, and gender – especially those versions of typicality constructed from colonialist, racist, and sexist positions – to accept responsibility for the reverberations of their representations at home and abroad, and to assure that business practices engage with an ethics of visual representation.

References

Ahmed, S. 2000. *Strange Encounters: Embodied Others in Post-Coloniality*, Routledge, London.

Alcoff, L. M. 1999. "Towards a phenomenology of racial embodiment", *Radical Philosophy*, Vol. 95, May/June, pp. 15–26.

Bartky, S. 1991. *Femininity and Domination*, Routledge, New York.

Bell, L. 1993. *Rethinking Ethics in the Midst of Violence: A Feminist Approach to Freedom*, Rowman and Littlefield, Lanham, MD.

Berger, W. 2001. *Advertising Today*, Phaidon, London.

Bordo, S. 1997. *Twilight Zones: The Hidden Life of Cultural Images from Plato to O.J.*, University of California Press, Berkeley.

Borgerson, J. 2001. "Feminist ethical ontology: contesting 'the bare givenness of intersubjectivity'", *Feminist Theory*, Vol. 2, No. 2, pp. 173 187.

Borgerson, J. 2005a. "Judith Butler: Organizing Subjectivities", *Sociological Review*, Vol. 53, pp. 64–79.

Borgerson, J. 2005b. "Addressing the Global Basic Structure in the Ethics of International Biomedical Research Involving Human Subjects", *Journal of Philosophical Research*, special supplement: 235–249.

Borgerson, J. 2007. "On the Harmony of Feminist Ethics and Business Ethics", *Business and Society*, Vol. 112 No. 4, pp. 477–509.

Borgerson, J. L. and Schroeder, J. E. 2002. "Ethical Issues of Gobal Marketing: Avoiding Bad Faith in Visual Representation", *European Journal of Marketing*, Vol. 36 Nos. 5/6, pp. 570–94.

Borgerson, J. and Schroeder, J. 2005. "Identity in Marketing Communications: An Ethics of Visual Representation," in *Marketing Communication: Emerging Trends and Developments*, Allan J. Kimmel, (Ed), Oxford University Press, Oxford, 256–277.

Bristor, J., Lee, R. G. and Hunt, M. 1995. "Race and ideology: African American images in television advertising", *Journal of Public Policy and Marketing*, Vol. 14, pp. 1–24.

Brown, S. 1995. *Postmodern Marketing*, Routledge, London.

Butler, J. 1999/1987. *Subjects of Desire: Hegelian Reflections in Twentieth-Century France*, Columbia University Press, New York.

Butler, J. 1993. *Bodies That Matter: On the Discursive Limits of 'Sex'*, Routledge, New York.

Cadava, E. 1999. *Words of Light: Theses on the Photography of History*, Princeton University Press, Princeton, NJ.

Card, C. 1996. *The Unnatural Lottery: Character and Moral Luck*, Temple University Press, Philadelphia.

Card, C. 2002. *The Atrocity Paradigm: A Theory of Evil*, Oxford University Press, Oxford.

Collins, P. H. 1990. *Black Feminist Thought: Knowledge, Consciousness, and the Politics of Empowerment*, Routledge, New York.

Cortese, A. J. 1999. *Provocateur: Images of Women and Minorities in Advertising*, Rowman and Littlefield, Lanham, MD.

Coviello, J. and Borgerson, J. 1999. "Tracing parallel oppressions: a feminist ontology of women and animals", *Feminista!* Vol. 3, online: http://www.feminista.com/v3n4/coviello.html

Crane, A. and Matten, D. 2007. *Business Ethics: A European Perspective*, 2nd ed., Oxford University Press, Oxford.

Crocker, D. A, and Linden, T. (Eds.), 1998. *Ethics of Consumption: The Good Life, Justice and Global Stewardship*, Rowman and Littlefield, Lanham, MD.

Davila, A. 1997. *Sponsored Identities: Cultural Politics in Puerto Rico*, Temple University Press, Philadelphia, PA.

De Lauretis, T. 1987. "The technology of gender", in T. De Lauretis (ed.) *Technologies of Gender: Essays on Theory, Film and Fiction*, Indiana University Press, Bloomington, pp. 1–30.

Deleuze, G. 1984. *Kant's Critical Philosophy*, University of Minnesota Press, Minneapolis.

Desmond, J. C. 1999. *Staging Tourism: Bodies on Display From Waikiki to Sea World*, University of Chicago Press, Chicago.

Drumwright, M. E. and Murphy, P. E. 2004. "How advertising practitioners view ethics: moral muteness, moral myopia, and moral imagination", *Journal of Advertising*, Vol. 33 No. 2, pp. 7–24.

Fanon, F. 1967. *Black Skin, White Masks*, Grove Press, New York, trans. Markmann, C. L.

Fırat, A. F. and Shultz, C. J. II 1997. "From segmentation to fragmentation: markets and marketing strategy in the postmodern era", *European Journal of Marketing*, Vol. 31, pp. 183–207.

Fırat, A. F. and Venkatesh, A. 1993. "Postmodernity: the age of marketing", *International Journal of Research in Marketing*, Vol. 10, pp. 227–249.

Giroux, H. A. 1994. *Disturbing Pleasures: Learning Popular Culture*, Routledge, New York.

Goffman, E. 1979. *Gender Advertisements*, Harper and Row, New York.

Goldberg, D. T. 1993. *Racist Culture: Philosophy and the Politics of Meaning*, Blackwell, Oxford.

Goldman, R. 1992. *Reading Ads Socially*, Routledge, New York.

Goldman, R. and Papson, S. 1996. *Sign Wars: The Cluttered Landscape of Advertising*, Guilford, New York.

Gordon, L. 1995 .*Bad Faith and Antiblack Racism*, Humanities Press, New Jersey.

Gordon, L. 1997. *Her Majesty's Other Children: Sketches of Racism from a Neocolonial Age*, Rowman and Littlefield, Lanham, MD.

Gordon, L. 1999. "Philosophy of existence", in Glendenning, S. (Ed.), *Edinburgh Encyclopedia of Continental Philosophy*, Edinburgh University Press, Edinburgh, pp. 101–181.

Gross, L. 1988. "The ethics of (mis) representation", in Gross, L., Katz, J. S. and Ruby, J. (Eds.), *Image Ethics*, Oxford University Press, New York, pp. 188–202.

Guillet de Monthoux, P. 1993. *The Moral Philosophy of Management: From Quesnay to Keynes*. M. E. Sharpe, London.

Hackley, C. 2005. *Advertising and Promotion: Communicating Brands*. Sage, London.

Hall, S. (Ed.) 1997. *Representation: Cultural Representations and Signifying Practices*, Open University Press/Sage, London.
Hanke, R. 1992. "Redesigning men: Hegemonic masculinity in transition." In S. Craig , (Ed.), *Men, Masculinity and the Media*. Sage, London, pp. 185–198.
Hawkins, R. Z. 1998. "Ecofeminism and nonhumans: continuity, difference, dualism, and domination", *Hypatia*, Vol. 13, pp. 158–197.
Hegel, G. W. F. 1993. *Introductory Lectures on Aesthetics*, Penguin, London, trans.B. Bosanquet.
Hirschman, E. 1986. "Humanistic inquiry in marketing research: philosophy, method, and criteria", *Journal of Marketing Research*, Vol. 23, pp. 237–249.
Holt, D. 2002. "Why Do Brands Cause Trouble?", *Journal of Consumer Research*, Vol. 29, pp. 70–91.
Hupfer, M. 1997. "A pluralistic approach to visual communication: reviewing rhetoric and representation in World War I posters", *Advances in Consumer Research*, Vol. 24, pp. 322–327.
James, J. A. 1997. "Black feminism: liberation limbos and existence in gray" in Gordon, L. R. (Ed.), *Existence in Black*, Routledge, New York, pp. 215–225.
Jones, C. and Munro, R. (Eds.) 2005. *Contemporary Organization Theory*, Oxford, Blackwell.
Jones, C., Parker, M., and ten Bos, R. 2005. *For Business Ethics*, Routledge, London.
Kant, I. 1960. *Observations on the Feeling of the Beautiful and the Sublime*, University of California Press, Berkeley, trans, J. T. Goldthwait.
Kant, I. 1973/1790. *Critique of Judgment*, Oxford University Press, Oxford, trans. J. C. Meredith.
Kaplan, A. and Pease, D. E. (Eds.) 1993. *Cultures of United States Imperialism*, Duke University Press, Durham, NC.
King, J. M. 2002. "Photographic Images of Gender and Race in Fortune 500 Company Websites in the United States", *Business Research Yearbook*, Vol. 7, pp. 852–6.
Leiss, W., Kline, S. and Jhally, S. 1990. *Social Communication in Advertising, 2nd ed.* Routledge, New York.
Leppert, R. 1997. *Art and the Committed Eye: The Cultural Functions of Imagery*, Westview/HarperCollins, Boulder, CO.
Lippke, R. 1995. *Radical Business Ethics*, Rowman and Littlefield, Lanham, MD.
McCracken, G. 1988. *Culture and Consumption: New Approaches to the Symbolic Character of Consumer Goods and Activities*, Indiana University Press, Bloomington.
McNay, L. 2000. *Gender and Agency: Reconfiguring the Subject in Feminist and Social Theory*. Cambridge: Polity.
McQuarrie, E. F. and Mick, D. G. 1999. "Visual Rhetoric in Advertising: Text-Interpretive, Experimental, and Reader-Response Analyses", *Journal of Consumer Research,* Vol. 26, pp. 37–54.
Messaris, P. 1997. *Visual Persuasion: The Role of Images in Advertising*, Sage, Newbury Park, CA.
Miller, D. 1994. "Ontology and style", in Friedman, J. (Ed.), *Consumption and Identity*, Harwood, Amsterdam, pp. 71–96.
Mirzoeff, N. 1999. *An Introduction to Visual Culture*, Routledge, London.
Natanson, M. 1986. *Anonymity: A Study in the Philosophy of Alfred Schutz*, Indiana University Press, Bloomington.
New York Times News Service, 1999. "Benetton Peers into Death Row", *International Herald Tribune*, p. 15.
Oliver, K. 2001. *Witnessing: Beyond Recognition*, University of Minnesota Press Minneapolis, MN.
O'Barr, W. M., 1994. *Culture and the Ad: Exploring Otherness in the World of Advertising*, Westview, Boulder, CO.
Pearce, R. 1999. "Advertising: Critical Analysis of Images" in Parker, I. (Ed.), *Critical Textwork: An Introduction to Varieties of Discourse and Analysis*, Open University Press, Buckingham, pp. 78–91.
Plumwood, V. 1993. *Feminism and the Mastery of Nature*, Routledge, London.
Pracejus, J. W., Olson, D. C., and O'Guinn, T. C. 2006. "How Nothing Became Something: White Space, History, Meaning and Rhetoric", *Journal of Consumer Research*, Vol. 23, pp. 83–90.
Rabinowitz, P. 1994. *They Must Be Represented: The Politics of Documentary*, Verso, London.

Ramamurthy, A. 1997. "Constructions of Illusion: Photography and Commodity Culture", in Wells, L. (Ed.), *Photography: A Critical Introduction*, Routledge, London, pp. 151–199.

Ramamurthy, A. 2004. "Spectacles and Illusions: Photography and Commodity Culture", in Wells, L. (Ed.), *Photography: A Critical Introduction*, 3rd edition, Routledge, London, pp. 193–245.

Ross, L. and Nisbett, R. E. 1991., *The Person and the Situation: Perspectives of Social Psychology*, McGraw-Hill, New York.

Sartre, J. P. 1956. *Being and Nothingness: A Phenomenological Essay on Ontology*, Washington Square Press, New York, trans. H. Barnes.

Schroeder, J. E. 1998. "Consuming Representation: A Visual Approach to Consumer Research", in Stern, B. B. (Ed.), *Representing Consumers: Voices, Views and Visions*, Routledge, London, pp. 193–230.

Schroeder, J. E. 2002. *Visual Consumption*, Routledge, London and New York.

Schroeder, J. E. 2007. "Images in Brand Culture" in Phillips, B. J., and McQuarrie (Eds.) *Go Figure: New Directions in Advertising Rhetoric*, Armonk, NY, M.E. Sharp.

Schroeder, J. E. and Borgerson, J. L. 1998. "Marketing images of gender: a visual analysis", *Consumption, Markets, and Culture*, Vol. 2, pp. 161–201.

Schroeder, J. E. and Borgerson, J. L. 2002. "Innovations in information technology: insights from Italian Renaissance Art", *Consumption, Markets, and Culture*, 5(2), 153–169.

Schroeder, J. E. and Borgerson, J. L. 2003. "Dark desires: fetishism, ontology and representation in contemporary advertising", in Reichert, T. and Lambiase, J. (Eds.) *Sexual Appeals in Advertising: Multidisciplinary Perspectives on the Erotic Appeal*, Lawrence Erlbaum Associates, New York.

Schroeder, J. E. and Borgerson, J. L. 2004. "Judith Butler, Gender Theorist: Philosophical and Phenomenological Insights into Marketing and Consumer Behavior," in Thompson, C. J. and Scott, L. M. (Eds.) *Association for Consumer Research conference on Gender, Marketing and Consumer Behavior proceedings*.

Schroeder, J. E. and Borgerson, J. L. 2005. "An Ethics of Representation for International Marketing Communication", *International Marketing Review*, Vol. 22 No. 5, pp. 578–600.

Schroeder, J. E. and Zwick, D. 2004. "Mirrors of Masculinity: Representation and Identity in Advertising Images", *Consumption, Markets and Culture*, Vol. 7 No. 2, pp. 21–52.

Sirgy, M. J. and Su, C. 2000. "The ethics of consumer sovereignty in an age of high tech", *Journal of Business Ethics*, Vol. 28, pp. 1–14.

Smith, N. C. and Quelch, J. A. 1993. *Ethics in Marketing*, Irwin, Homewood, IL.

Solomon, R. 1993. "Business Ethics", in Singer, P. (Ed.), *A Companion to Ethics*, Blackwell, Cambridge, MA, pp. 354–365.

Stern, B. B. 1993. "Feminist literary criticism and the deconstruction of ads: a postmodern view of advertising and consumer research", *Journal of Consumer Research*, Vol. 19, pp. 556–566.

Stern, B. B. 1998. "Introduction: the problematics of representation", in Stern, B. B. (Ed.), *Representing Consumers: Voices, Views, and Visions*, Routledge, New York, pp. 1–23.

Thompson, C. J. 2004. "Dreams of Eden: A Critical Reader-Response Analysis of the Mytho-Ideologies encoded in Natural Health Advertisements", in Ekström, K. and Brembeck, H. (eds.), *Elusive Consumption*, Berg, Oxford, pp. 175–204.

Thompson, C. J. 1997. "Interpreting consumers: a hermeneutical framework for deriving marketing insights from the texts of consumers' consumption stories", *Journal of Marketing Research*, Vol. 34, pp. 438–455.

Thompson, C. J., Locander, W. B. and Pollio, H. R. 1989. "Putting the Consumer Back into Consumer Research: The Philosophy and Method of Existential-Phenomenology", *Journal of Consumer Research*, Vol. 17, pp. 133–47.

Walker, M. U. 1998. *Moral Understandings: Feminist Studies in Ethics*, Routledge, New York.

Wells, L. (Ed.) 1997; 2004. *Photography: A Critical Introduction*, Routledge, London.

Weston, A. 1992. *Toward Better Problems*, Philadelphia, PA, Temple UP

Williams, C. 1987. *The Destruction of Black Civilization*, Third World Press, Chicago.

Williamson, J. 1978. *Decoding Advertisements*, Marion Boyers, London.
Wood, H. 1999. *Displacing Natives: The Rhetorical Production of Hawai'i*, Rowman and Littlefield, Lanham, MD.
Young, I. M. 1990. *Justice and the Politics of Difference*, Princeton University Press, Princeton, NJ.
Zaltman, G. 2002. *How Customers Think*, Harvard Business School Press, Boston.

Of Dice and Men

Russell Ford

Introduction

Albert Carr's 1968 article, "Is Business Bluffing Ethical?" (Carr 1968) has provoked an enormous amount of critical response since its publication. This alone is a telling fact as to the perspicaciousness of the article's argument. Yet most of the literature fostered by the article – supportive as well as critical – has taken the argument to task for its structural weakness: pointing out that ultimately it amounts to little more than the assertion of an indeterminate, analogical relationship between "business" and "poker." The first task of these subsequent essays has therefore been to fill in the details of Carr's argument, showing its deficiencies or revealing its implicit strengths. Both of these approaches, however, leave unchallenged the very basis of Carr's claim: that bluffing in business is analogous to bluffing in poker because both behaviors are strategies adopted to manipulate the causative role of chance in situations that are formally equivalent as games. As with any analogy, the critical point is not one or both of the elements, but the common notion that facilitates the analogical relation: the game. Not only is this notion undefined in Carr's article, but, when an attempt is made to bring it into focus, the apparent diversity and heterodox character of games in general seems actually to reverse Carr's claim. Bluffing would be disallowed in business precisely because it is not just permitted but ubiquitous in everyday life.

Business is one game among many (the family, school, neighborhoods and cities, religious and civic organizations, etc.) that constitute, rather than exist alongside, everyday life. Each of these games is constituted by positions and rules that specify a structure of play permitting the specification and differentiation of one game from others. This play identifies both the constitutive activity of a single game, and the interrelation of these games necessitated by the assumption of different positions in different games by a single person. Play can therefore be differentiated into the structured activity of particular games as well as the unstructured interrelation of multiple, distinctly constituted games. Each type of play may be either lawful or

R. Ford
Assistant Professor in the Department of Philosophy, Elmhurst College
e-mail: fordr@elmhurst.edu

M. Painter-Morland, P. Werhane (eds.), *Cutting-edge issues in Business Ethics*,

unlawful. It is lawful when it adheres to the publicly recognized structure of the game, or of one game's relation to others; it is unlawful when its activity works against (deliberately or accidentally) the publicly recognized structure of an individual game, or against the equally recognized interrelation of different games. Bluffing, or self-interested misrepresentation (according to Carr's conception), is clearly lawful play in the game of poker and Carr's claim is that it is a lawful play in the game of business.

However even though Carr's analogy, as stated, might be shown to be incorrect, his insight that there is an analogical relation between bluffing in business and bluffing in poker may be accurate, but be facilitated by a notion more fundamental than that of the game. This more fundamental notion is that of play. An analysis of the concept of play therefore facilitates a categorization of the different types of games which, in turn, allows for the specification of the real difference between business and poker and a basis for the comparison of their respective types of bluffing. However, merely accepting the reduction of the analogy to the postulate that each activity is a game begs the question of how to differentiate a game from any other activity. Until the elements that make this differentiation possible are established, any debate as to the moral or ethical import of such bluffing is meaningless, the context has not been sufficiently specified to evaluate such questions. By tracing the apparent similarity of business and games back to its ground in the disposition to play, Carr's argument, rather than advocating a particular ethical stance, opens the way for the conceptualization of the very ground of business ethics as a domain of practiced values.

The centerpiece of Carr's essay is his argument that business interactions are analogous to interactions in the specific game of poker. Already this analogy has two distinct parts. On the one hand is the claim that the constitution or foundation of a particular game of poker is analogous to the constitution or formation of a transaction or a reasonably distinct subset of a market. On the other hand is the claim that within a particular market or market subset, the individual transactions occur according to rules that are analogous to the rules that govern the permissible activities in a game of poker. Carr makes his argument by tying these two aspects together and claiming that this combination is identical in business and in a game of poker. The two sides of the analogy are drawn together in three distinct ways: according to their distinctive constitution, according to the relation between their participants, and according to the relation of each side of the analogy to a third, ethically normative realm. In each case, it is poker that is described while the analogue of business is justified strictly by recourse to examples. Poker is constituted as a particular realm, according to Carr, through the disqualification of anyone who cheats. Such people are either excluded from the game at the outset, or their behavior reveals them as outside of the game in the midst of play, yielding a reorganization of the game itself. Within this distinctive exclusion, certain behaviors are permitted by the players in their relations with each other. These behaviors are rather crudely divided by Carr into "ethical" and "unethical" subtypes. Unethical behavior includes any behavior that is consistent with playing poker (and so does not jeopardize the fundamental constitution of the game) but that puts the "other players at an unfair disadvantage." From Carr's examples of such behavior one can infer that a player or players is placed at an unfair disadvantage when another player or players introduces a variable that is not regulated or acknowledged by the rules of the game. This is unfair because the rules of the game are meant to fix the apportionment of chance for each player equally, thereby constituting the game as a matter of skill, and the appropriation of an additional element causes the equal distribution of chance to become skewed if not decisively shifted to the advantage of those who import the variable. The consequence of this is that those who have entered the game find its parameters changed without the opportunity to remove their stakes from the now altered risk of loss. Ethical behavior would then be any and all behavior whereby a player or players employ strategies legitimated by the rules and recognized or acknowledged by other players in order to reduce their share of chance and engender a favorable result for themselves. Finally, Carr notes that the particular strategies available for the manipulation of chance differ from those available in the realm of everyday ethics, specifically in that "[t]he game [of poker] calls for distrust of the other fellow [sic]." (Carr 1968, p.146)

Carr's analogical argument works if and only if a game of poker is in fact constituted in the same way as a transaction or independent market segment. Specifically, both games and business transactions must have the same relationship to what Carr calls "the ethical ideals of civilized human relationships." Carr's claim that bluffing (the misleading or false representation of some aspect or aspects of one entity or group of entities to another entity or group of entities) is a feature common to both business and poker is accurate; however this alone is not enough to support the analogical claim. In his essay, "The Business of Ethics," Norman Gillespie summarizes Carr's full claim with the following argument: (1) business is a form of competition; and (2) the rules of this particular competition are different from the rules that obtain in society in general; such that (3) anyone who abides by the rules of society rather than the rules of business plays at a disadvantage in business; therefore (4) it is not unethical to abide by the rules of business, rather than those of society, in business practices. Three "rules" can then be derived from this argument: (1) if a business practice is not illegal (i.e. directly contrary to a societal rule), that practice is ethical because no one is required to seek their own disadvantage; (2) if one person does not take advantage of an opportunity in business, another will because resources are limited in a competitive environment, by definition; and, (3) if a business practice constitutes a norm, everyone who participates in business activity expects conformity because everyone is able to draw the same conclusion in the above argument. (Gillespie 1975) Gillespie's response to Carr's argument is among the most interesting and informative insofar as he gives Carr's argument a seriousness that some other critics implicitly (or explicitly) deny, and also because it formulates a clear and persuasive objection to Carr's conclusion. Gillespie's thesis is that Carr's analogy is unnecessary, that situations requiring difficult ethical choices are regular features of our everyday existence, and that business is only a particular set of such possible difficulties unified by the features that define a market or transaction. Business actions therefore do not require an appeal to a different set of standards of ethical valuation. They instead require a judicious application of values coupled with an apprehension of the risks and costs for performing or failing to perform different possible actions. On Gillespie's account, business ethics would then be a subject for the generalized practice of risk-benefit analysis which forms the substance of ethical decision-making (Gillespie 1975).

What is of particular interest in Gillespie's account is that even as he rejects Carr's claim that business constitutes a distinct ethical world with its own distinct standard, he achieves this rejection precisely by inscribing business ethics within a generalized system of ethical behavior that bears and accentuates a number of the characteristics of the "game" of business from Carr's analogy. When Gillespie makes the claim that business and everyday ethical life both require the same sort of risk-benefit analysis in order for an ethical subject to navigate meaningfully each sphere of relatively distinct objects, and argues this by explicitly accepting the formulation that Carr makes of the decision-making moves that the 'business gameplayer' engages in, Gillespie reveals that his disagreement with Carr is merely over the latter's compartmentalization of the business world, not the more substantive account of ethical decision-making. Like Carr, Gillespie understands an ethical decision to be one in which the values of the intentional actor are weighed against the possible and probable consequences – both ethical and nonethical – of their enactment. Ethical character is therefore the definition of a style of play, a series of decisions linked into a trajectory whose moments reflect the negotiation of one set of values with others. Gillespie's challenge to Carr is thus different but also far stronger than it initially seems since his critique of Carr's conventionalism exposes the extent to which everyday ethical action is in perpetual negotiation with established structures and norms. When this practice of negotiation is generalized, Gillespie's normative argument – that existing behavior in business ought to be progressively brought into accord with the norms of everyday ethics – loses its justification insofar as ethics is conceived as a mutual negotiation of an individual and a set of practices that are themselves the product of other, historical negotiations. Ethics, then, business or otherwise, is a particular type of play.

Purpose and Play

The concept of play has a surprisingly lengthy heritage in the Western philosophical tradition. According to one tradition, play is a moment of aesthetic experience which itself derives value from being instructive for ethical life. Although it arguably stretches back to Aristotle's conception of the educational function of dramatic tragedy, the key text in this tradition is Kant's *Critique of Judgment*. There, Kant argues that the subjective universal validity of judgments of taste – their ability to be both individual and possess an apparent claim to universal agreement – arises from the free play of the mental faculties of the imagination and the understanding. This free play is apprehended aesthetically when the judgment that would determine the intuition presented by imagination according to a concept instead apprehends the "purposiveness" of the object – its apparent ability to be conceptualized – and thereby defers subsuming the object under a determinate concept.

For Kant, this "free play" of the faculties has an immediate ethical component insofar as the indeterminate harmonization of the faculties is a symbol for the pure autonomy of the moral law. (Kant 1790; 1987) Friedrich Schiller seizes upon this connection and argues at length in his *Letters on the Aesthetic Education of Man* that the aesthetic is preparatory for the ethical insofar as the "play-drive"—that drive that is neither subjective nor objective—invigorates the subjective, particular, and worldly component of the free harmony of the faculties and makes the aesthetic experience an almost practical guide for reason's drive to incarnation. (Schiller 1794; 2004) The determination of this aesthetic play is more rigorously pursued by Marx for whom the aesthetic is almost completely eclipsed by the political insofar as the harmonization of human faculties is to be achieved only through the rational attainment of the concrete needs of individual human bodies. (Marx 1844)

Hans-Georg Gadamer's hermeneutics offers perhaps the most fully developed account of this moral coordination of the aesthetic. Although concerned principally with Kant, Gadamer refers to the Cartesian account of self-consciousness and free will as the most significant philosophical precedent that determines the way that we think about aesthetic experience today. According to this account, humans are distinguished and made superior to animals by their ability *to reflect* upon their own actions, to see themselves in the third person and thereby generalize and reason about the abilities and constitution of people in general. Gadamer notes that recent developments have done much to trouble this Cartesian understanding, an account that hit its high-water mark in the dialectical philosophies of German Idealism. Chief among these developments are Darwin's theory of evolution – which incorporates culture into nature – and Freud's theory of the unconscious – which claims that the origin of many human acts is in impulses or drives that not only are not but indeed cannot become conscious, and thereby intentional. The creative play of human beings might therefore be only a particular form of the play that we see in animals, and therefore not the product of a uniquely human "free will." Gadamer therefore poses the question: what is *distinctive* about play in aesthetic experience? (Gadamer 1975; 1986)

For Gadamer the key distinction of aesthetic experience is the "directedness" of human play. The organization that characterizes aesthetic activity gives to human play a particular "seriousness" perhaps most vivid in organized sports – that is not apparent in the play of other animals. This seriousness is a "free self-limitation of freedom," a description that remains staunchly within the Kantian tradition. As a free being, any human being can elect to limit their own freedom and this limitation is itself a free act. This "free self-limitation of freedom" moreover, appears to be constitutive of the difference that separates culture from nature insofar as the sort of "role-playing" where one acts "as if" the rules of a particular game were natural (for example, a soccer player acts "as if" he or she cannot touch the ball with their hands; a judge acts "as if" he or she has no personal opinion about a trial, etc.) defines the cultural and societal life of human beings.

However, further reflection shows that even animals are capable of acting "as if." For instance, Gadamer notes that the playful fighting of certain young animals seemingly has certain rules that allow the animals to fight without injuring one another, and also allows them to know, through the use of certain indicators, when the game is over. This seems to indicate that humans are not the only beings that possess freedom and an accompanying self-consciousness, and therefore the natural generation of playful activity is ascribed by Gadamer to a "universal constructive force" that one might compare with the "force" that animates and moves the progress of Darwin's evolution, or the psychic force that Freud labels "Eros." The distinctiveness of the aesthetic is to be found in the distinction between the play of human artistic production and the **universal constructive force** of "mere" nature. Gadamer accounts for this distinction by claiming that there is an additional aspect to human artistic production: human art is not produced insofar as something useful or "superfluously beautiful" is produced (art is not mere ornamentation), but rather insofar as there is an element of "free variability" that accompanies the production. For Gadamer, ***human*** *freedom* (as distinct from natural freedom) appears precisely in the play that incorporates this element of "free variability."

By "free variability," Gadamer highlights the *creative* aspect of playful intention. When one plays a game – soccer, for instance – although the rules are prescribed, the way that one acts within the rules is not. For instance, it is a rule that a player cannot contact the ball with their hands (except under certain conditions), however, this leaves open the possibility within the game of the player contacting the ball with their feet, their head, their knee, etc. And, the more specifically we determine the situation (a player in a game of soccer; a player at midfield in the middle of the game; a player in front of the opponent's goal at the end of the game; at the end of the game when the score is tied; etc.), the more this element of free variability, this element that marks the creative act as human, comes to the fore. In fact, this element of free variability is generally what we mean when we talk about the *style* of a player be they an athlete, an actor, a professional, or an artist.

Style is the object of aesthetic apprehension. Rather than merely facilitating the transmission of a meaning, style itself is displayed and constitutes the distinctiveness of an aesthetic encounter. Every instance of play belongs to a certain aesthetic "game," but what distinguishes one from another, and what constitutes them as specifically aesthetic experiences, is their appearance as 'styled'. Style, then, is the "free variability" of a work of art, but Gadamer also means for this term to bring out an aspect of the meaning of style that is often forgotten: as a distinct aspect of an aesthetic experience, *style is not just a way of expressing something, it also indicates the possible other ways of expressing something*. Style always indicates that something could be expressed otherwise – this is how an aesthetic object becomes distinctive as such. Precisely because of its "free variability," when we attend to style we are struck by the way that creativity is at play in the work, but we are also struck by the depiction of playfulness itself. We notice the distinctiveness of the experience, its style, at the same time as we imagine all of the other experiences that would indicate the same conceptual or normative structure, the fact of the game that is creativity itself. For instance, a game such as poker has very particular rules that constitute its distinctive structure, but this structure is not what we would consider the object of our aesthetic experience of the game. What we experience is the *activation* of the structure, the play of a participant in the game which must follow the rules (otherwise the player is not recognizable as such) but which is also always the stylistic expression of the structure, a stylized production that shows itself as other than both that determinate structure and other possible activations of it.

It is now possible to specify what constitutes specifically *human* artistry. In nature, play is the manifestation of a universal constructive force – it is the limitation of the creativity of nature to a particular form or task. The emphasis in natural play is on the product. Play means and indicates something determinate and other than the play itself. What is distinctive about human creativity – which is also, at least in part, concerned with the product – is that there is an *explicit* element of creativity in addition to the object produced: style. The emphasis in human play is on production. What distinguishes human creativity, human play, from the play of animals (or nature in general) is that human beings express not only their stylistic intention (their creativity), but also the distinction between this style and others. Gadamer writes: "Art begins precisely there, where we are able to do otherwise. ... It "intends" something, and yet it is not what it intends." Intending something while at the same time not being simply reducible to that thing is the nature of the symbol. Whereas an allegory merely substitutes one product for another, a symbol expresses a relation to something that cannot be a product at all – something that cannot be presented. What makes a work of art symbolic is not the indirect expression of a determinate meaning; aesthetic meaning exists as a symbol, as a meaning that is played at by those who experience it. This playing is an expression of the community of those who take it as a symbol insofar as this symbolic relation is only produced by a free harmonization of the faculties of each individual. Gadamer writes that "the experience of the beautiful ... is the invocation of a potentially whole and holy order of things, wherever it may be found."

The symbolic function of play through which the spectator is overwhelmed and swept up into the purposiveness of meaning makes play a remarkably concrete activity and not a way of escaping the world and worldly responsibilities. It is precisely as a symbol – because this symbol is always a symbol of the free creativity that marks the relation of human beings to their world – that art and aesthetic experience are always worldly. The experience of play is an aesthetic experience insofar as the object of play is a symbol, but it is also an aesthetic experience insofar as the symbol possesses a concrete orientation, an evaluative trajectory, that the player follows symbol. The accomplishment of this transition or transformation from spectator to participant is accomplished through the mimetic function of the symbol (Gadamer 1975).

As used by the Greeks (notably Aristotle), *mimesis* designates a specific kind of production, distinct from the production of physical objects (*poiesis*). It describes the production of a representation: an imitation. The concept of style (or "free variability") therefore isolates this notion of mimetic production as style understood as *the production of the appearance of play*. In other words, whereas natural production is the playful production of objects (either things or specific sorts of animals – and a play that proceeds according to the rules of natural laws) human play is both the production of objects (again according to natural laws – every game obeys physical laws, etc.) and the explicit showing (the dramatization) of this playful production. The purposiveness of mimetic imitation places a demand upon the spectator to apprehend it as imitation, and thereby to engage playfully with it. Style may then be re-expressed more completely as the *free imitation of the free self-limitation of freedom*. In the play that characterizes aesthetic experience, human beings indicate their inherence within the natural world (insofar as they play), and because human play emphasizes style, it distinguishes itself from mere natural creation (natural play) by showing itself as play. It is the mimetic aspect of playful creation that is uniquely human insofar as it opens onto ethical reflection. A justification for this thinking of play as a limit and link between aesthetics and ethics can also be found in the anthropological and psycho-analytical traditions. The psychoanalytical concern with play is solidly rooted in Freud's research—one thinks immediately of the importance of the observed game of "fort-da"—but achieved a new prominence with Melanie Klein's work on the development of children, (Klein 1932) and in the object relations school, notably in the work of D.W. Winnicott (Winnicott 2005).

Winnicott's theory and discussion of play arises through previous work he had done on what he termed "transitional objects." The transitional object is less an object proper than a structure or matrix that is generated in response to the particular needs of the infant. In order to make a successful transition from the pleasure principle to the reality principle, the infant requires that the shock of the initial awareness of its failure to control objective phenomena be ameliorated through the active intercession of another person (usually the infant's mother since the transitional object serves as a substitute for the internal object (the mother's breast)). This other person responds to the activity of the infant by helping to shape the objective world of real objects to fit the infant's desires. The transitional object is therefore neither internal/subjective nor external/objective since it is constituted by the mutual limit of the separate activities of the infant and the mother. The importance of play, and its meaning for Winnicott, arises from what he calls "the precariousness of the *interplay* of personal psychic reality and the experience of the control of actual objects." This "precariousness" reflects the fact that play must develop along a particular but individual trajectory in order for the infant to mature into an appropriately socialized individual. The parent must not only foster the "magic" feeling of omnipotence in the infant, but must also gradually recede into a position of reserve in relation to the infant's dealing with objects. The ultimate aim is not a fixed state but the ability of the infant to couple their play with the play of another which will be tolerated only if the infant has developed and retains a sense of assurance in its own power. Playing is therefore an exercise of the effective creativity of the infant, its ability to meaningfully interact and alter the real, objective world which has the capacity to block or hinder the infant's will, and it persists throughout the life of the individual as the greater or lesser degree of competence with which that individual can negotiate different and often conflicting structures of evaluation.

Value and Chance

"Le present est un coup de des." – Michael Foucault (Foucault 1970, p.906)

For Winnicott, play is the activity that founds and perpetuates not only the life of individuals but their communal and cultural life as well. As opposed to the rational determination of the purpose of play that characterizes the discussion of play by Gadamer and other representatives of the Kantian tradition, for Winnicott it is only in the concrete and aleatory process of play – a purposive process that extends across the entire life of the individual – that something like rationality, as a common set of cultural aims, comes to be. This reversal of the Kantian subordination of play to reason is characteristic of the Nietzschean tradition of the concept. The priority of play over any kind of constitutive, rational norm can arguably be traced back to the work of Heraclitus, one of whose fragments states: "The universe is a child playing with dice." However it is in Nietzsche's work and specifically through the reading of that work by thinkers such as Deleuze and Derrida that this idea attained much of its current philosophical importance.

For thinkers such as Deleuze and Derrida, the game is more than a useful analogue; it serves as the description of a style of thinking that attempts to take account of the historical contingency of values even as it recognizes their binding and obliging force. For Kant, the ultimate cause of the purposiveness of the rational will remained as unknowable as the ultimate cause of the world of experience. By historicizing the ultimate cause of morality, Nietzsche opens the ground or cause of morality to thought. The form of this thinking is genealogical. It is undertaken by a style of thought that Deleuze characterizes as "nomadic," using this term to indicate the implicit self-critique created by the genealogical thinker's own historical specificity. For Deleuze, whose reading of Nietzsche was decisive for a generation of French thinkers, the play that produces values is the work of the nomad; not the one who lives outside of the limits of ordered evaluation, but the one who freely crosses and re-crosses – who 'plays at' – those limits, creating new possibilities of evaluation. The moral legislation of the nomad is an art of purposiveness but not the creation of a new structure. The nomad creates a form that leaves frontiers open and welcoming to others, inviting incorporation into multiple structures. The pure formality of the categorical imperative is preserved as an aspect of moral distinctiveness, but this form is put into play amidst the individuals that it determines and enfolds. This generalized play constitutes the game that forms a properly critical thinking (Deleuze 2004).

Despite the apparent relativism of such a hermeneutics, in which the meaning of the moral law would seemingly be determined by the whim of the nomadic genealogist, the thought produced by the historicizing of morality possesses a sense. A genealogical aphorism is not concerned with providing an objective determination of an individual, and, in fact, emphasizes the lack of this determination by holding itself to its pure formality: "an aphorism is an amalgam of forces that are always held apart from one another." Genealogy, even as it gives content to the moral law, and so gives determinate value to a structured state of affairs, highlights the created rather than the absolute character of the values that constitute the ethical world. An amalgam of forces is shown to have a meaning, then, only insofar as its constituent forces are determined by exterior forces that function as principles of value and evaluation. The non-determinative presentation of historical values is an ethical expression of Nietzsche's eternal return. For Deleuze, the eternal return may be figured as a dicethrow (Deleuze 1983).

"With the dicethrow, the interpretation of the eternal return begins, but it only begins. It is still necessary to interpret the dicethrow itself, at the same time as it returns. . . . The game has two moments [*moments*] which are those of a dicethrow: the dice that are thrown [*lance*] and the dice that fall back [*retombent*]." The dice here are the figures of chance, where chance is understood as the multiplicity of concrete relations between forces. The dice that are cast, that are rolling and bouncing through the space of the game, form an image of chance in its pure state, chance without principle. Considered abstractly, the multiplicity of all concrete relations of forces forms the same scintillating virtuality as the flashing points of countless dice. The dice that fall back, that settle and stop, the actual dice, the dice actualized, are the figure of necessity. The virtual chaos of chance, all possible relations of forces, is actualized insofar as certain concrete relations of forces come to pass while others do not. Together, these two moments form the game in itself and, genealogically, they are inseparable.

In the *Logic of Sense*, Deleuze describes the form of a restricted, determinate game as the deployment of four requirements or moments. First, a game must be given a general form by a set or system of rules that differentiate the space of the game from what lies outside of the game, and which also determine the quality of actions as either falling within this space, or falling outside of it. Moreover, the rules remain categorical in regard to the playing of the game. They are never modified by its activity. The determination of the quality or qualities of the space of the game creates the various possibilities for the traversing of that space; for playing. These possible strategies, in turn, divide themselves into discrete moments insofar as each of these moments, as a moment of a determinant direction or strategy, is localized and given a place only in reference to the strategy of which it forms a part. Furthermore, whatever the particularities of the rules of a given game, these rules divide the game into discrete units of finite time. This is a third form, rather than a simple consequence of the second, insofar as this form determines the temporal aspect of the game while the rules of the game establish the quality or qualities of its space. Finally, in the form of a return, the fourth requirement of a game is the critical appraisal of particular strategies in terms of the rules of the game. This critical moment is the determination of a strategy as one that "wins" or one that "loses." In summary, the form of a restricted game is given by its rules that both ensure that all possible strategies conform to a particular, qualified space (the field of the game) by means of a determinate serialization of those strategies, and ensures that these strategies themselves conform to the rules as such through the critical evaluation which partitions these strategies into a ranking which ranges the between the extremes of defeat and victory (Deleuze 1990).

What is elided, for a moment, in this description of the game, occupies a place of particular prominence in Deleuze's account of the dicethrow as an image of genealogical thinking in *Nietzsche and Philosophy* (1983). The player, the "who" (*qui*) that plays at a game, there occupies the distinctive point insofar as it is the player, through the two times with which she is capable of encountering and to some extent determining or shaping the game, that creates the possibility of the circulation of the rules of the game as the subjection of the moments of the game to a particular mode of time. The dicethrow, the figure of the game, works in *Nietzsche and Philosophy* to constitute ethical determination as a problem of becoming, which is not a choice between structures. An instance of the dicethrow, an instantiating pictorial of becoming, betrays at its limit its reabsorption into a project of total critique precisely through the question of "who (*qui*) plays?" In other words, it is not by casting ethics as a game that one adequately conceives ethical evaluation, it is by casting oneself into play that thinking about ethical values becomes ethical thinking (Deleuze 1983).

Further Reading

Allhoff, Fritz. 2003. "Business Bluffing Reconsidered," *Journal of Business Ethics*, Vol. 45: 283–289.

Beach, John. 1985. "Bluffing: Its Demise as a Subject Unto Itself," *Journal of Business Ethics*, 4(3): 191–196.

Betz, Joseph. 1998. "Business Ethics and Politics," *Business Ethics Quarterly*, 8: 693–702.

Carson, Thomas. 1993. "Second Thoughts About Bluffing," *Business Ethics Quarterly*, 3(4): 317–341.

Heckman, Peter. 1992. "Business and Games," *Journal of Business Ethics*, 11(12) 933–938.

Hennessey, Jr., John W., & Gert, Bernard. 1985. "Moral Rules and Moral Ideals: A Useful Distinction in Business and Professional Practice," *Journal of Business Ethics*, 4(2): 105–115.

Koehn, Daryl. 1997. "Business and Game-Playing: The False Analogy," *Journal of Business Ethics*, 16(12–13): 1447–1452.

Piker, Andrew. 2002. "Ethical Immunity in Business: A Response to Two Arguments," *Journal of Business Ethics*, 36(4): 337–346.

Rosen, C. Martin, & Carr, Gabrielle M. 1997. "Fares and Free Riders on the Information Highway," *Journal of Business Ethics*, 16(12–13): 1439–1445.

Solomon, Robert C. 1999. "Game Theory as a Model for Business and Business Ethics," *Business Ethics Quarterly*, 9(1): 11–29.

Sullivan, Roger J. 1984. "A Response to "Is Business Bluffing Ethical?," *Business and Professional Ethics Journal*, 3: 1–18.

Van Wyk, Robert N., 1990. "When is Lying Morally Permissible?: Casuistical Reflections on the Game Analogy, Self-Defense, Social Contract Ethics, and Ideals, *Journal of Value Inquiry*, 24(2): 155–168.

References

Carr, Albert. 1968. "Is Business Bluffing Ethical?" *Harvard Business Review* 46, January–February: 143–53.

Deleuze, Gilles. 1983. *Nietzsche and Philosophy.* Trans. Hugh Tomlinson. London: Athlone Press.

Deleuze, Gilles. 1990. *The Logic of Sense.* Trans. Mark Lester, Charles J. Stivale. New York: Columbia University Press.

Deleuze, Gilles. 2004. "Nomadic Thought." *Desert Islands and Other Texts:* 1953-1974. Ed. David Lapoujade. Trans. Michael Taormina. New York: Semiotext(e). 252-261.

Foucault. Michael. 1970. "Theatrum Philisophicum" trans. D.F. Brouchard and Sherry Simon. *Critique* 282: 885–908.

Gadamer. Hans. 1975. *Truth and Method.* Trans. Garrett Barden and John Cumming. New York: Seabury Press.

Gadamer, Hans-Georg. 1986. "The Play of Art." *The Relevance of the Beautiful and Other Essays.* Ed. Robert Bernasconi. Cambridge: Cambridge University Press. 123-130.

Gillespie, Norman. 1975. "The Business of Ethics." *University of Michigan Business Review.* 27.

Kant, Immanuel. 1790; 1987; *Critique of Judgment.* Trans. Werner S. Pluhar. Indianapolis: Hackett Publishing.

Klein, Melanie. 1932. *The Psycho-Analysis of Children*: Trans. Alix Strachey. London: Hogarth Press and the Institute of Psycho-Analysis.

Marx, Karl. 1844; 1963. *Early Writings.* Trans. T. B. Bottomore. New York: McGraw-Hill Book Company.

Schiller. 1794; 2004. *Letters on the Aesthetic Education of Man.* Whitefish MT: Kessinger Publications.

Winnicott, D. W. 2005. *Playing and Reality.* London: Routledge, 2005.

Business, Ethics and the Hope of Society in Hannah Arendt: The Notion of Responsible Business Entrepreneurship

Angelo Carlo S. Carrascoso

Introduction

The portrayal by Hannah Arendt of business is admittedly bleak and stark, owing much to the activities that business entrepreneurs undertook in the latter part of the nineteenth century. Their desire to expand for expansion's sake adversely influenced and affected the political sphere, which assimilated this ideology and expressed it as imperialism and colonization. But is this interpretation the only possible understanding of business that we can get from Arendt? Are there other possible ways to construe the role of business in society?

In this chapter I argue that even from Arendt's historical perspective, business entrepreneurs can be the engines of progress and development that propel society forward in better, more sustainable ways. To achieve this, however, they need to adopt perspective drawing primarily on the Arendtian threefold distinction of human activity as Labor, Work and Action. Regarding themselves as entrepreneurs and seeing activities as Action, businessmen must return to the inception of their ventures when they reflected on those deep-seated values that inspired and guided their founding. They must also appreciate and provide for the long-term consequences of their actions through voluntary, endogenous contracts with those who affect and are affected by their decisions. Clearly, this Arendtian notion has much insight and value to provide to business practitioners as they navigate through the myriad of business issues that they face everyday.

Historical Arendtian View of Business

At first face, the views of Hannah Arendt on business are clear and explicit, and they are not at all favorable, to say the least. In her discussion of the Political Emancipation of the Bourgeoisie in *The Origins of Totalitarianism* (1976) she paints a rather stark picture of the phenomenon. To her, much of the confusion and chaos that

---

A.C.S. Carrascoso
Darden Business School, University of Virginia
e-mail: carrascosoAos@darden.virginia.edu

M. Painter-Morland, P. Werhane (eds.), *Cutting-edge issues in Business Ethics*,

ensued in the thirty-year period immediately preceding the First World War (and the subsequent upheavals thereafter) was brought about by a frenzied sense of expansion that found everyone as accomplices to the events that followed. Cecil Rhodes, the (in)famous British-born South African businessperson of this time, captured that spirit nicely when he said that "these stars . . . these vast worlds which we can never reach. I would annex the planets if I could" (Arendt 1976, p.124).

Business entrepreneurs played the key role in fomenting this expansive streak. In fact, to Arendt (1976, p.125), the whole idea of expansion is not really a political concept as much as it is a business concept, having "its origin in the real of business speculation, where expansion meant the permanent broadening of industrial production and economic transactions characteristic of the nineteenth century". Armed with a vast amount of resources at their disposal and an ideology that saw virtually no limits to what was possible and permissible, business entrepreneurs not only created empires that dominated national economies and ensured them enormous personal fortunes. They also wanted to constantly perpetuate this cycle of economic growth, embracing an ideology of expansion for expansion's sake[1] (Ibid., p.126) that set in motion a seemingly unstoppable cycle of consumption unto itself. Individuals such as John D. Rockefeller, Andrew Carnegie, James Duke, and Cornelius Vanderbilt are but a few of the people (in)famous for their very aggressive business practices. Collectively, these individuals controlled the American economy during the late nineteenth century – from railroads, to oil, to shipping and finance.

Only when national limits to their economic expansion emerged did business entrepreneurs turn to politics to expand this horizon. She (Ibid., p.126) notes that they "did not want to give up the capitalist system whose inherent law is constant economic growth; it had to impose this law upon its home governments and to proclaim expansion to be the ultimate political goal of foreign policy" Governments, initially resistant to the idea of expanding its political reach, eventually accepted the need for political expansion when it realized that "given the choice between greater losses than the economic body of any country could sustain,[2] and greater gains than any people left to its own devices would have dreamed of, it could only choose the latter." This is because new markets provided the conduits that made capital allocation and use efficient. New, attractive business opportunities suddenly emerged that promised significant returns to those who were bold and patient enough to make the investment.[3]

Of course there are many adverse effects of these actions of business on society. Hannah Arendt notes that the rise of imperialism and colonialism came about when about the boundaries separating business from political realm became significantly blurred, and this blurring clearly threatened the fabric of society. Statesmen "knew by instinct . . . that this new expansion movement in which patriotism . . . is best expressed in money-making, could only destroy the political body of the nation-state" (Arendt 1976, p.125) because nation-states "cannot be expanded indefinitely . . . and no nation state could with a clear conscience ever try to conquer foreign peoples, since such a conscience comes only from the conviction of the conquering nation that it is imposing a superior law upon barbarians"[4] (Ibid., p.126). Of course, business entrepreneurs would have nothing of this argument. Old-fashioned cowboy capitalism continued to reign supreme and there were no two ways about this.

Towards a New Perspective

This rather negative view of business entrepreneurship by Hannah Arendt is understandable if we appreciate the historical milieu that she was very much a part of. Indeed, her analysis offers such a profound insight on the role of business entrepreneurship in society, so much so that there is scarcely any serious academic who would doubt the integrity of the analysis that she had so carefully laid down. However, one must ask the question: is this the only way to understand and appreciate Arendt's reading? Can Hannah Arendt provide any useful insight that academics and managers can actually use to better inform this discussion, especially given that business entrepreneurs are increasingly being called to fulfill a broader set of responsibilities to society and other stakeholders (Phillips 2003, pp.1–2)? More importantly, are entrepreneurs suited to act as socially responsible agents? Is there anything substantive and non-trivially value-additive that they can contribute to this conversation?

I believe that her writings offer us a way to better understand the role of business entrepreneurship in society. Specifically, they contain the very seeds that allow such an alternative understanding to grow and develop. But to be able to undertake this step successfully, we need to go back to her understanding of work and action in *The Human Condition.*

Vita Activa and the Human Condition

A significant portion of *The Human Condition* (1958) is given to distinguishing the three forms of activity that are central to humans. The first, Labor corresponds to the "biological processes of the human body..bound to the vital necessities produced and fed into the life process by labor" (Arendt 1958, p.7). Labor activities include searching for means of sustenance (food), and its actual consumption. Work, on the other hand, corresponds to the "unnaturalness of the human existence... [It] provides an "artificial" world of things, distinctly different from all natural surroundings". Work activities include creating tools and machines – anything that is an 'artifice' of our hands. These two activities, however, are not what characterize human beings. According to Arendt (Ibid., p.13), "Neither labor nor work was considered to possess sufficient dignity to constitute a *bios* at all, an autonomous and authentically human way of life; since they served and produced what was necessary and useful, they could not be free, independent of human needs and wants."

Action is set apart from both labor and work because it corresponds to our higher human faculties. The characteristic trait of action that sets it apart from Labor and Work is the capacity of those engaged in it to create something 'new' or "to begin something anew" (Ibid., p.9) – that moment of natality that is borne about by the "human condition of plurality, to the fact that men, not Man, live on the earth and inhabit the world" (Ibid., p.7). and by the fact that we disclose ourselves as agents in the act under consideration. Because of our humanity (as opposed to our being mere animals) we are capable of undertaking Actions that are independent of our lower, vegetative functions. For the purposes of our discussion, we will focus on work and action.

Business Entrepreneurship as Action

Using the language of Hannah Arendt, are the activities of business entrepreneurs more like work, or are they more like action? It could be argued that they engage in "Work" in the Arendtian sense. They operate businesses on an ongoing basis, and these businesses either manufacture goods or render services for a profit that are relatively generic and distinct from them. Likewise, the Kirznerian[5] notion of an entrepreneur (Kirzner 1997) alert to the opportunities that exist in the market place can make such an activity much like work. She who is successfully able to arbitrage a price differential cares not so much about the good or product in question, as much as the profit that she can realize from the successful exploitation of the opportunity, whether it involves selling cars, cellular phones, real estate or paintings.

However, closer analysis reveals a much more complex picture than what is initially apparent. Indeed it can be argued that business entrepreneurs also engage in Action in the Arendtian sense, particularly in the early stages of their respective business ventures, whether they are the single proprietors, or shareholders funded primarily by venture capitalists and angel investors, or employees in a large, high-technology firm. Also, to the extent that entrepreneurship is fundamentally concerned with understanding how, in the absence of current markets for future goods and services, these goods and services manage to come into existence (Venkataraman 1997), then entrepreneurship is Action.

There are other features that mark the activities of businessmen as Action. For one, who they are – their respective identities – is revealed in the creations they make. These bear the mark and the imprint of their identities – the shape of the bottle that holds a new beverage, the way a customer is pampered by a slew of health and beauty products (not to mention medical procedures) etc. Business entrepreneurs also can and do become quite attached to their business ventures because this represents something that is quite literally their creation. Something about them is definitively revealed in this process, so much so that there is scarcely any businessperson involved in the creation of the firm who is also not emotionally invested in the success of the business venture that she founded. The Parenthood metaphor introduced by Cardon (2005, p.33) makes this point quite well – "Entrepreneurs whose ventures respond well during startup, launch and infancy phases[6] are likely to develop strong attachment to ventures especially if those ventures provide cues that embrace the entrepreneur's identification with them ... [They] may sacrifice their own needs to meet the needs of their ventures ... to ensure its healthy functioning".

One of the most interesting cases to consider here is the example of Oliver Heaviside whose invention of the loaded line, which (?) made possible the development of long-distance communication, is virtually unknown, but whose pioneering contribution to the invention of the telephone is absolutely crucial. Heaviside discovered the loaded line by using engineering concepts that were relevant to the technology that was developing (Wiener 1994, p.70). However, he had no foresight to secure the property rights of his invention. Soon enough, others were exploiting this loophole to justify the use of the loaded line without proper recognition and compensation to Heaviside. One such individual, Michael Pupin, sought to find aspects in Heaviside's work that were either incomplete or just downright wrong (Ibid., p.73).[7] Those involved with Alexander Graham Bell, the recognized inventor of the telephone, wanted to compensate Heaviside for the use of his invention. However, "Heaviside turned the offer down flatly, declining to accept one cent unless the company [of Bell] were to give him recognition as the original and sole inventor of the loaded line. This the company could not do, for if it had, the whole investment of half a million dollars which it had made to Pupin [for his supposed invention] would have ceased to be of any use" (Ibid., p.74). The stubbornness displayed by Heaviside in insisting on his ownership of the technology despite the legal defects demonstrates the very strong emotional attachment that he had on his invention. Business entrepreneurs can display the same intensity of attachment to their businesses as was discussed earlier.

Most obviously, according to Schumpeter (1934) business entrepreneurs effect significant change in society. Through sporadic and sometimes unpredictable outbursts, they undertake one (or more) of five possible actions that have been referred to as 'creative destruction.' Either they introduce new goods or services, develop a new method of production, opening a new market for their products and services, source a new supply of raw materials, or carry out and implement new organizational structures in industry (Ibid., p.66). This sense of action as defined by Arendt is very clear in the development of the light bulb, the calculator, the personal computer and a countless host of other inventions since they represented something radically new, unexpected and disruptive of the status quo.

Action as Double-Edged

Of course, the fact that businesses create something new and novel does not of itself guarantee that their results are always going to be beneficial to society. In fact, much of the criticism that Hannah Arendt levels against business entrepreneurs who have most likely been involved in some type of entrepreneurial venture in the past in a variety of settings lies in their turning a blind eye on the other side of action – its dark side, or the negative externalities that arise from entrepreneurial activities. While Action does bring with itself endless possibilities of new beginnings, these beginnings are always fraught with uncertainty and unpredictability (Knight 1957 [1921]) which are effects of the plurality that distinguishes action from the rest of human activity. With the advent of new technologies and ways of doing things, "Promethean powers – releasing powers with unfathomable consequences (xv)" are being unleashed on society at such an unprecedented scale that they threaten much of what we hold dear. For example, the widespread use of hazardous chemicals and products, for example have untold negative consequences not only to those immediately using them, but to future generations as well. William McDonough and Michael Braunart (2002) call our attention to the unprecedented levels of dangerous substances that surround us but which we are not even slightly aware of. Many of our household products – products such as the chair we sit in, the carpets we use, the TVs we watch and the computers we use everything for "contain mutagenic materials, heavy metals, dangerous chemicals and other additives that are often labeled hazardous by regulator, except when they are presented and sold to a customer" (McDonough and Braunart 2002, p.3). To the two, this represents a design problem remnant of an older time – a 'cradle to grave' mentality – that business entrepreneurs have not paid enough close attention to. They argue that many of those who employ such dangerous substances in their products have not thought through the process of understanding the after-effects of their use. The collective results of such actions on our environment are seen everywhere.

What Now?

What can business entrepreneurs do to reverse these trends? How can they be the engines of progress and development that will help strengthen, and not weaken society? First of all, extending the thought of Arendt in this regard, business entrepreneurs need to be proactive thinkers. They need to go back to when they were beginning their venture and remember that initial entrepreneurial moment when they were actually involved in the creation of something new – the unmistakeable flash of inspiration that started it all. This enables them to appreciate the bigger picture of what it is that they do –what brought them to start their ventures in the first place, what they wanted to achieve personally in such an endeavor, and what legacy they would like to leave behind long after they and their ventures have gone. This reflective, values-based thinking will go a long way in making them appreciate their motivations for being in business to begin with. This is the rationale behind many of the annual 'retreats' that corporations provide their employees. By providing them an opportunity to come together and reflect on their mission and values on a regular basis, they are able to remember what continues to bring them together within a particular organization.

However, they also need to look forward, needing to be conscious of the long-term consequences of their actions on others. They cannot remain stuck in the rather narrow understanding of their actions as being strictly and exclusively private in nature, which quite interestingly, according to Arendt, is a phenomenon "whose beginnings we may be able to trace back to late Roman, though hardly to any period of Greek antiquity, but whose peculiar manifoldness and variety *were certainly unknown to any period prior to the modern age*"[8] (Arendt 1958, p.38).

This is quite reminiscent of what John Dewey said in *The Public and Its Problems* (1954). He wrote that "human acts have consequences upon others, that some of these consequences are perceived and that their perception leads to subsequent effort to control action so as to secure some consequences and avoid others" (Ibid., p.12). Business entrepreneurs, to the best of their abilities, need to recognize, at the very least, that the goods and services they provide to the public – even perhaps their very organizational structure they employ to deliver these – might have adverse affects at some distant point in the future on people they do not expect to be affected by them. One of the most controversial examples that can help us understand this point well is the internet search giant Google. From its modest beginnings the company has emerged as the most popular internet search company in the last ten years, penetrating all of cyberspace and raising over $20 billion in its recent initial public offering. The actions of the company have been primarily guided by its "Don't be evil" motto which includes "making sure that our core values inform our conduct in all aspects of our lives as Google employees."[9] Recently however, this motto is being challenged from many sides. For example, Google introduced a Chinese version of their famous internet search engine. However, under pressure from Chinese authorities, they were forced to restrict access to sites that the government deemed politically dangerous and subversive.[10] International human rights groups heavily protested this action by Google, accusing the company of being 'evil' by acting as an accomplice to the abusive actions of the Chinese government. Google has recently allowed a limited amount of pictures of the 1989 massacre to be posted on its Chinese website, although it is still much less than the number of pictures posted on the general site. Very clearly, top executives in the company are only starting to come to terms with the emerging realities that are facing them. Have they really explored the proverbial "rabbit hole" to see what the far-reaching consequences are of "not doing evil"? Is that even possible?

Of course, it is recognized that business entrepreneurs cannot fully account for all of the consequences of their actions in the future. Psychologists and behavioral economists have systematically shown us for the past twenty years the limits to our rationality. In light of this, the Arendtian notion of promise-making (Arendt 1958, p.238) in the face of uncertainty becomes extremely important. But some qualifications need to be made at this point. The solution that Arendt proposes does not contemplate a singular promise that is binding for all time. Because of the ever-present unpredictability in the events and in the people involved in such events, no such eternal promises can be made. Rather, only temporary, renegotiable ones can be made. Freeman and Evan (1990) dealt with this issue when they discussed voluntary, endogenous contracts that firms can enter with their respective stakeholders. Under these kinds of arrangement, parties involved in the venture voluntarily enter into an agreement with one another for a particular undertaking. These 'promises to abide by the rules and cooperate' are in force for the most part except when certain internal or external factors necessitate a renegotiation of the terms of the agreement. Under the framework proposed by Freeman and Evan, instead of seeking an external, third party arbiter to settle the competing claims (who will also bear the cost of the renegotiation), the concerned parties will instead undertake to renegotiate the terms themselves, in effect endogenizing the process of 'promise-making and renewing.' Freeman and Evan argue that this arrangement is far more effective, and indeed there is some weight to it. If parties do bear the costs of the process, they are far more likely to take the process more seriously and deliberately. If, on the other hand, some external third party agency (such as the government most commonly) were to bear the costs, then compliance would be a much greater problem. In environmental issues, this is very much the case. Arrangements that required government intervention (such as messy environmental cleanups), while inevitable in many cases, are suboptimal compared to arrangements where parties stipulate to voluntarily undertake clean-up efforts if dangerous toxic spills took place in the environment. Not only will resources have been set aside and provided for to cover for these contingencies, but these adverse effects will also be handled with greater care and efficacy. Imagine if an arrangement was made by Exxon where it voluntarily undertook to clean-up any site that suffered an oil spill? How much less adverse public reaction would they have experienced, and how many less resources would have been needlessly wasted (lawyer's fees, etc) if Exxon actually did this?

Conclusion

In this paper, I have argued that the works of Hannah Arendt provide us with a way of understanding the positive role that businesses can play in society. Despite her historically grim view of entrepreneurs engaged in business during her historical milieu, there is hope for society. Using the threefold distinction of business activities as Labor, Work and Action, we remember that aspect of Business entrepreneurship as Action – the imaginative and inventive and identity-revealing activity that offers to us not only the promises, but also the often unforeseen perils that lay in such a creative activity. Cognizant of the latter, business entrepreneurs must learn to both look back at the beginning of their ventures, while at the same time "looking forward into the future" and trying to anticipate and manage whatever negative consequences might arise from their actions.

In essence what Arendt recommends to us as the source of hope is an ethical business entrepreneur – one who puts ethical considerations at the forefront of her decision-making, who is conscious of and owns up to the consequences of her actions on others. Only such an individual engaged in business can propel society forward.

Notes

1. This whole expansive ideological movement was borne out by advances in science and technology that, while it brought about economic prosperity and advancement, also created problems of alienation in people. They began to see themselves primarily as consumers of products, and valued only having more of more of what they already had.

2. To Arendt (1976, p.136), this period was marked by "wild speculations with superfluous capital, who had provoked gambling of all savings".
3. According to Arendt (1976, p.148), "The capitalists themselves realized that the only way that they could temper any future crisis and depressions was through a 'supply and demand that from now on must come from "outside the capitalist society".
4. Of course many of those who colonized at that time did not think that they were imposing a superior law on an inferior people, as much as they were providing such individuals with the proper education needed to unleash their rationality. Berlin (1969) says this eloquently in the following: "I may declare that they are actually aiming at what in their benighted state they consciously resist, because there exists within them an occult entity – their latent rational will, or their 'true' purpose – and that this entity, although it is belied by all that they overtly feel and do and say, is their 'real' self, of which the poor empirical self in space and time may know nothing or little; and that this inner spirit is the only self that deserves to have its wishes taken into account. Once I take this view, I am in a position to ignore the actual wishes of men or societies, to bully, oppress, torture them in the name, and on behalf, of their 'real' selves, in the secure knowledge that whatever is the true goal of man (happiness, performance of duty, wisdom, a just society, self-fulfilment) must be identical with his freedom – the free choice of his 'true', albeit often submerged and inarticulate, self."
5. The Kirznerian notion of entrepreneurship is contrasted with the Schumpeterian notion, where such entrepreneurs operate to *change* price/output data. In this way, as we shall see, the entrepreneurial role drives the ever-changing process of the market. The daring, alert entrepreneur discovers these earlier errors, buys where prices are "too low" and sells where prices are "too high." In this way low prices are nudged higher, high prices are nudged lower; price discrepancies are narrowed in the equilibrative direction. Shortages are filled, surpluses are whittled away; quantity gaps tend to be eliminated in the equilibrative direction. (Kirzner 1997, p.70)
6. Quite clearly, such successful ventures become what we call ongoing 'businesses.'
7. Pupin developed something very close to what Heaviside discovered that the Bell Company paid half a million dollars for.
8. The idea of the 'privatization' of the self was prompted by a strong desire for personal, intimate space that was free from the pressures of the public sphere – "society's unbearable perversion of the human heart" (Arendt 1958, p.39) that Romanticism resisted.
9. http://investor.google.com/conduct.html.
10. Internet searches for the 1989 Tiannamen Square Massacre using google.com contained pictures of the massacre that google.cn initially refused to post for fear that they were politically destabilizing.

References

Arendt, Hannah. 1976. The Origins of Totalitarianism. San Diego: Harcourt, Inc.

Arendt, Hannah. 1958. The Human Condition. Chicago: University of Chicago Press.

Berlin, I. 1969. Two Concepts of Liberty. In *Four Essays on Liberty*. Oxford: Oxford University Press.

Cardon, et al. 2005. A Tale of Passion: New Insights into Entrepreneurship from a Parenthood Metaphor. *Journal of Business Venturing*. 20: 23–45.

Dewey, John. 1954. The Public and Its Problems. Athens: Ohio University Press/Swallow Press.

Freeman, R. E. and William Evan. 1990. Corporate Governance: A Stakeholder Interpretation. *Journal of Behavioral Economics*. 19(4): 337–359.

Kirzner, I., 1997. Entrepreneurial discovery and the competitive market process: An Austrian approach. *Journal of Economic Literature*, 35: 60–85.

Knight, F. H. 1957 [1921]. *Risk, Uncertainty, and Profit*. 8th edition. New York: Kelley and Millman, Inc.

McDonough, William and Michael Braunart. 2002. Cradle to Cradle: Remaking the Way We Make Things. New York: North Point Press.

Phillips, R. 2003. Stakeholder Theory and Organizational Ethics. San Francisco: Berrett-Koechler Publishers, Inc.

Schumpeter, J. A. 1934. The Theory of Economic Development. Cambridge: Harvard University Press.

Venkataraman, S. 1997. "The Distinctive Domain of Entrepreneurship Research. *Advances in Entrepreneurship, Firm Emergence and Growth.* J. Katz (ed.). Stamford: JAI Press, Vol. 3: 119–138.

Wiener, N. 1994. Invention: *The Care and Feeding of Ideas*. Cambridge, Massachusetts: MIT Press.

Continental Philosophy: A Grounded Theory Approach and the Emergence of Convenient and Inconvenient Ethics

David Bevan

Introduction and Overview

"Continental philosophy" – what is that? In the field of Business Ethics this particular term of art brackets and divides a distinct group of writers as somehow different from some notional mainstream. Anecdotal evidence suggests that mainstream Business Ethics is a parochial ghetto, intellectually dominated by a troika: of managerialism in the Business Schools (Parker 2002), of analytic philosophy and of law in the Universities (Ghoshal 2005; Preston 2002). Amongst such constituencies the influence, or even the contribution, of so-called ***continental*** authors may go unappreciated (Jones, Parker, & ten Bos 2005). Against this background and in the context of this volume, a fuller consideration of this categorically different literature is indicated. This chapter will first consider from different perspectives a range of discussions of this ***continental*** bracketing. These perspectives reveal that the ***continental*** adjudication is both exogenously derived – that is to say developed and perpetuated from outside the constituency it seeks to classify – and rationally inconsistent by normal epistemological criteria. A consideration of the mainstream or, as here, the classical approach to Business Ethics lends support to the symmetry of this potential dichotomy – ***continentals*** may not so-name themselves, but they clearly are not classical either. Dismissing any preconceived notions as a necessary precursor to innovating a Grounded Theory approach, I then consider and interpret an indicative range of ***continental*** writing pertinent to Business Ethics to what might account for this exaggerated and partial differentiation. Theoretical sampling of this work clearly diffuses particular dimensions of the ***continental*** distinction, some of which are inimical to classical Business Ethics practice. Consequent to this, I shall suggest that ***continental*** philosophy, so construed, might equally embrace strands of (for example) Kant, Berkeley, Paine and Adam Smith along with Levinas, Bauman, Derrida, Lyotard and Bourdieu. The chapter concludes that this renovated generic distinction would be more appropriately understood as any work inconvenient to, or critical of, classical (i.e. traditional), restrictive, instrumental determinism and

D. Bevan
Management Department of the Royal Holloway, University of London
e-mail: david.bevan@rhul.ac.uk

M. Painter-Morland, P. Werhane (eds.), *Cutting-edge issues in Business Ethics*,

the effectively unrestrained imperial progress of market capitalism. The closing discussion elaborates the emergent convenient and inconvenient ethics as a means of informing a clearer understanding of why the category of ***continental*** philosophy exists and (reflexively) what approach to ethical practice it informs.

The Continental Adjudication

I construct no straw man argument here. I agree that no single definition of ***continental*** philosophy yet exists. Philosophy is replete with multiply contested and complex denominations like modernism or philosophy itself. The importance of this complexity in relation to this chapter rests in the primacy afforded to positivism, since the enlightenment, as an epistemology which suggests one reductive means of investigating claims to truth for mainstream Business Ethics. I propose to confront the confusion brought on by this reductive process with the innovation of a Grounded Theory approach to reveal a potentially different theorisation of ***continental***.

When we speak of ***continental*** philosophy we suggest one branch of philosophy is distinct from another. This complex and multiply contested distinction is, first of all, a distinction; I am curious to understand that need to distinguish. The editors of a forthcoming volume, at the time of writing, suggest that continental philosophy is a distinct body of non-traditional philosophy – so what might non-traditional equate to? On simple definitional principles, the ***continental*** adjudication appears to refer broadly to the continent of Europe in a post-Kantian era (Sedgwick 2001), and specifically following on from "The Critique of Pure Reason" (Critchley & Schroeder 1999). By such a taxonomy ***continental*** generally embraces European philosophy – the work of European philosophers – written after 1782 (or 1790 perhaps, depending on which version of Kant has inspired the work) and responding to it in some way, directly or indirectly. So, in the interests of clarity here, the work of Descartes [1596–1650] or Rousseau [1712–1778], while essentially European, may be considered as categorically excluded from the ranks of ***continental*** on the basis of the post-Kantian chronology. While any European post-Kantian philosopher might thus adopt the tag of ***continental*** to distinguish their work, none of them seems to adopt it. Within the limited scope of a single individual's reading I have never seen the term ***continental*** employed to describe a writer so-considered. Perhaps somewhere Bourdieu claims for himself a place in the ***continental*** tradition? I have no recollection of seeing it. This label appears to be entirely exogenous – a label which no-one applies to himself, a label which is always applied, from outside, by some other constituency. Is it simply a European post-Kantian school of writing? Within the constraints of a single chapter any exhaustive examination is precluded, so I enjoin the distinguished commentaries of others.

The Oxford Dictionary of Philosophy (Blackburn 2005, p.77) first appears to confirm this classification by defining ***continental*** as including "the writings of philosophers such as Hegel, Marx or Heidegger". These authors are indeed from Europe and writing after 1790. But for Blackburn (2005) there is an additional contradictory nuance: ***continental*** philosophy is "an inaccurate term used, often polemically . . ./. . . (and) generally contrasted with analytical philosophy, thought to be more the preserve of Anglo-American and Australian philosophers" (Ibid.). Seeking to refine this potentially inaccurate differentiation, ***continental*** philosophy is also seen as "an *invention*, or more accurately a *projection* of the Anglo-American academy" (Critchley 2001, p.32; italics in original) onto a Continental Europe that simply does not recognise the legitimacy of such an appellation. We might analyse from this that analytic and Anglo-American or Australian (whatever these dimensions might be) have some overlapping qualitative similarities. In his critique of strategy, Whittington (2002) theorises such a characteristic, structural combination of positivism with egoism as a "classical" approach (to strategy). Here, classical is a useful terminological bracket – avoiding the terms mainstream or traditional, while simultaneously embracing them – to differentiate the ***continental*** from that which is not.

The ***continental*** distinction establishes a separation from the projective world of classical business management: a world dominated by the managerialism of projects. This re-establishes a long-running dichotomy (see for example ***Phaedrus*** (Plato 2002)) in the history of human thought. The basis of this dichotomy is generally accessible by understanding traditional/analytic philosophy as characterised by a concern with providing a conceptual analysis of language, referring to the natural world and showing how beliefs are justified (Sedgwick 2001). Analytic philosophers are considered to be "primarily interested in formulating theories about language which concentrate upon the problems of meaning and reference" (p.vii–viii): ***continental*** philosophers "take a more social and historical view of philosophical issues" (Ibid.). So it is potentially a simple matter of ontological preference on which basis classical business management seeks to ostracise the ***continentals***? A brief consideration of classical business management, including ***continental*** readings, may be revealing.

The Classical/Mainstream Context

Along with Whittington (2001), many distinguished, classical management authors (Drucker 1989; Friedman 1962/2002; Porter 2004; Taylor 2005) locate mainstream management and managerialism – the activities on which much of Business Ethics focuses its attention – in an evident epistemology of positivist egoism or individualism. The classical approach to Business Ethics operates from within the objective, ordered, conservative, rational preferences associated with, and qualitatively unchanged since, the enlightenment. One commentator sees the legacy of the enlightenment functioning adversely as "a set of nineteenth – or even seventeenth-century Euro-American blinkers" (Law 2004, p.143). Post-enlightenment classical management has a legacy relationship with positivism which provides a unitary scientific method, the object of which is to structurally establish general laws (Charmaz 2006). Classical management and classical Business Ethics are performative, which is to say they help to produce realities (as well as non-realities). The scientific principle of objectivity seems to offer a pathway to true knowledge about our world and these pristine scientific principles need not be contaminated by the high-minded principles of morality (Dholakia & Firat 2006). Through this objectivity, classical business management and Business Ethics continuously seems to re-legitimise itself by reference to a system of structural metadiscourses (Lyotard 1984), organised lying (Huxley 2004) or distinguishing paradigms (Kuhn 1996), such as capitalism, government, religion and the law.

It is further possible to ascribe to this diffuse epistemology of classical positivism-with-egoism the contingent dimensions of militarism, determinism, hierarchical structures and a bureaucracy focusing always on the interests of the individual (Whittington 2001). In a complementary ***continental*** conceptualisation of individual project management, the word project itself becomes a discursive instrument of sociological critique (Boltanski & Chiapello 2006) – the projectivity of classical management evolves as an aggressive viral mutation of Lyotard's earlier performativity (1984). Thus, (and interpolating extensively here from Boltanski & Chiapello 2006, p.110) in the classical project of Business Ethics, the aim of all Business Ethics activity will be to generate more Business Ethics projects, or to achieve integration of one's Business Ethics activity into the Business Ethics projects of others. The project of Business Ethics thus presents itself as an action always to be performed, rather than as something that is already present. Business Ethics activity is expressed in the multiplicity of Business Ethics projects pursued concurrently and which, despite what happens, can be elaborated in an endless succession of non-achievement. Modern lives are such a succession of projects; the important thing (in the classical project paradigm) is to develop activity – to never to be without a project; to always have something in one's mind, in the pipeline, on the drawing board or the back burner.

Project managerialism thus structurally realises a managerialist capture of classical Business Ethics in a way that palliates or atomises all – even the most impeccable – moral impulse. Careful reading does not occur – it is an encumbrance in the path of the profit. "It's a money thing" is the venal capitalist's Nuremberg defence: this simple claim generally overwhelms all careful reading and assures the declarer of a clearer passage through the latest confrontation with his or her evident moral myopia. Managerialism is the amber of commercial expedience flowing still warmly over the howsoever well-meaning practice of classical Business Ethics.

For Derrida (1997a), the paradigm or meta-narrative is a screen for non-concepts, political tricks and strategies. Business Ethics, sustainability and globalisation are all such metanarratives, each increasingly and effectively approving the political appropriation of knowledge and practice in the name of the free market. Might the term ***continental*** also screen or conceal something about the market? On the principle that abuse may be subjective, does the term ***continental*** reveal more about those who employ it?

The interpretive elaboration of projective management may be constructive in considering classical Business Ethics in this present context. In the course of teaching Business Ethics in business schools and universities in UK and France since 2003, I have become conversant with textbook presentations of Business Ethics for the benefit of future managers. From a range of multiple edition readings (Crane

& Matten 2007; DesJardins 2006; Fisher & Lovell 2006), I interpret that Business Ethics is a consensual field generally arranged for the benefit, and not for the effective repudiation, of classical managers. A brief discussion of the indicative assertions of classical Business Ethics will inform the remainder of the chapter.

There appears to be a clearly discernible framework which can be broadly characterised as the classical tenets of Business Ethics across or embracing (at least) Anglo-American practice (Jones et al. 2005; Parker 2002). The framework is made up of a number of elements, each of which is based on a partial reading of some claimed authority. For example: an element of ethical egoism based in Adam Smith and informing enlightened self-interest (Harrison 2005); an element of duty based in Kant – what is right for one is right for all, people may never be used as a means to an end (Crane and Mallen 2007); an element of rights – to life, freedom and property – based in Locke (Crane et al. 2007), an element of justice based in Rawls (Crane et al. 2007), elements of social contract theory (Donaldson & Dunfee 1999), an element of utilitarian ethics based in Bentham and Mill which seeks an optimum solution for the greatest number of people (DesJardins 2006). These elements appear as necessary and sufficient to the instruction of a traditional/classical Business Ethics framework, although many refinements are available. Again, only indicatively, these ethical optional extras include another version of the social contract, where in stakeholder theory (Freeman 1984) sustains a pluralist attack on the legitimacy of stockholder monopolies; a simplified version of discourse ethics which permits a talk-about-it approach to ethical decision making; and virtue ethics based in Aristotle's concern with human intuition. This is a summary and not a careful reading. But it is such careless, abbreviated speech acts – like the most (in)famous by Friedman (1970), which I choose not to further perpetuate by quoting here – that despite best efforts are evidently remembered and enacted in current commercial venturing: and it is this which is, or has been, the cause of so many Business Ethics failures.

While I do not suggest that the intention or effect of any of these indicated authors is to furnish apologias for commerce, at the same time this evidently prevalent, necessary and sufficient framework of classical Business Ethics performs a number of valuable conventions within the classical project of Business Ethics. Without limitation (and excluding any intertextual analysis of its claimed sources), this framework unquestioningly supports – or does not effectively critique – the tenets of capitalism, property ownership, non-proportional democracy and the law. The framework also supplies, or at least rationally informs, a range of supporting normative axioms. These axioms can be (and often are in practice) further reduced to codes of corporate conduct, corporate ethics or corporate governance. Such codes provide, *inter alia*, key performance indicators by which classical corporate Business Ethics achievements apparently can be measured or otherwise rendered susceptible to adjudication and audit by the proprietors of ethics (Fullerton, Kerch, & Dodge 2004), accountability (Blagescu & Lloyd 2006) and sustainability (Kolk 2003) indices.

The performativity of projective effectiveness among such arrangements is the point here: codes of ethics make companies ethical we are told (Webley & LeJeune 2002). While I waive the methodological questions I might otherwise have on grounds of relevance, such a suggestion is practical in that performatively, or by means of a classical positivist equivalence, something called "codes of ethics" can be so-arranged to make companies ethical. The quasi-natural ethicality of business becomes a scientific truth and in the paradigm of classical managerial practice we have no need to ask "How does it do that?" Nor "What do you mean by ethical?" Classical Business Ethics has the means to reassure us that business can be good without reference to tricky concepts like the naturalistic fallacy, nor difficult empirical questions about the inherent correctness of profiting from addiction.

A few paragraphs back it became apparent that ***continental*** voice may not be entirely in tune with the self-polarising classical approach to management. ***Continental*** remarks are not helpful or supportive to the classical project: this is consonant with earlier suggestions of a categorical difference. But is this externally-applied distinguishing classification of ***continental***, separating classical Anglo-American from ***continental***, a simple style claim? Or is it possible that there is more going on than this intellectual version of "You like tomăto and I like tomāto" (Gershwin & Gershwin 1936) conceals? A ***continental*** *breakfast* is distinct, even foreign, and clearly different(iated) from conventional (qua proper or real?) – American or full English – breakfast, but I am unsure of what post-Kantian characteristics may be attributed to coffee and a croissant. Maybe it is something specifically post-Kantian that attracts this attributed divergence? Let us now consider what ***continental*** philosophy has to say in the field of Business Ethics that is so different as to be worthy of this distinction? Does the taxonomy so-far revealed have some salience in the context of Business Ethics? What clearly discernible claims for Business Ethics do the ***continentals*** offer? The dimensions of this emergent dichotomy will now be the focus of the grounded theory approach which follows.

A Grounded Theory Approach

I have been careful to announce a Grounded Theory **approach**. I acknowledge that this is not a fully developed Grounded Theory. Nonetheless this may be the first attempt to understand Business Ethics by (such admittedly incomplete) reference to Glaser's (1998) exhortation to knowledge: that Grounded Theory is a practice of systematically generating theory from data in order to plausibly explain some substantive problem – it is a discovery and not an invention. The substantive problem here is that there is no complete account of the term ***continental***.

As to method, I rely on simple "explication de text" (Ibid., p.25) which assists the researcher "who is doing constant comparisons to generate concepts that closely fit without imputation as to what is going on in the substantive area, while at the same time being able to claim authorship of the concept he generated" (idem). The sample is chosen by reference to the convenience principle: "one that is simply available to the researcher by virtue of its accessibility" (Bryman & Bell 2003, p.105) This will be followed by a theory building exercise – most of which happens away from the narrative. It is on this basis that I will sample some ***continental*** authors on matters which I suggest illuminate a characteristic ***continental*** approach to Business Ethics.

In doing so I have followed Charmaz (2005, p.39) seeking to avoid bias by using these selected texts "as objects of scrutiny themselves rather than for corroborating evidence." I accept that I have only a limited reading of a few authors from which to choose my objects of potential revelation. I apologise for the paucity of examples and the narrow range I have chosen from. The range is however symmetrically commensurate with and broadly responds to the range of classical or traditional Business Ethics theories summarised above.

I begin with an orthodox definition of Business Ethics to assist me in discussing ***continental*** contributions: "Business ethics is the study of business situations and activities where issues of right and wrong are considered" (Crane et al. 2007, p.5). On the basis of business itself – commerce – there is a potentially positive insight from Levinas:

> Commerce is better than war, for in peace the Good has already reigned
> (Levinas 2004, p.5).

Indeed business or commerce is surely better than war? But, is this a strikingly post-Kantian claim? Analysing this fragment of ***continental*** thought by Crane and Matten's interpretation of categorical imperatives – such a stance must approach a deontological correctness surely? The maxims of universality, consistency and human dignity are not discordant with this ***continental*** assertion. The problem with Levinas arises if one tries to use his work to attempt to link an activity which is better than war with any notion of ethics. Then there is a potentially insuperable ethical problem. For Levinas, it is argued, business ethics is an impossible proposition and all the more so for corporations. In claiming that only humans have a moral capacity and institutions as non-humans have none, Levinas approaches a position subsequently and repeatedly confirmed, on somewhat different terms as the corporate fiction argument, by Milton Friedman who is however generally not regarded as ***continental:***

> The corporation is amoral[1], but the people who run the corporation are not amoral
> (Achbar & Abbott 2005a, p.2).

> Can a building have moral opinions? Or social responsibilities? If a building can't have social responsibilities what does it mean to say that a corporation can? A corporation is an artificial legal structure, neither moral nor immoral (Ibid., p.1).

Leaving aside this minor categorical conflation of Levinas and Friedman for a moment, Emmanuel Levinas is a significant, indeed exemplary, *continental* author whose work can usefully (so invoking utility) provide a means of introducing selected other ***continentals***. Perhaps more than simply post-Kantian, Levinas makes a complete break – an *éclat* (Derrida 1997b) – with the history of all previous philosophy by considering it as a programme of tautological reduction. He regards traditional mainstream philosophy as:

> an attempt at universal synthesis, a reduction of all experience, of all that is reasonable, to a totality wherein consciousness embraces the world leaving nothing outside of itself, and thus becomes absolute thought. The consciousness of the self is at the same time the consciousness of the whole (Levinas 1985, p.75).

This is a sweeping repudiation of all analytic philosophy as a project of similitude. Very simply interpolating here, Levinas (2005) suggests that the world may be understood as duality. In one part, Infinity, the continuous single moment of our lives is led in a non-ontological state of freedom in which individuals, "I's", encounter the Otherness of others in the presence of the present. Infinity is where we live, breathe, sweat, love; it is the somatic world – it should not be ontologised, thematised or in any way reduced to a record or a positive fact. The second part of this duality, Totality, is the ontological world; a (here, classical) world of known facts and written concepts – a world of religions, property ownership, share certificates, money, contracts and accounts. Totality is life reduced-to-ontology – a bloodless, inhuman world; lifeless and factual. To employ a metaphor suggested by the title[2] of a work by Claude Lévi-Strauss (1983), who elsewhere theorises dualist variations of Totality and Infinity: like the process of the poaching of an egg where the albumen goes from clear, slippery and alive, to a solid, stable, dead white – so (for Levinas) the moments of living are reduced irreversibly to lifeless (if digestible) ontology- and in this context the subjectivity of ***convenient*** life is reduced to the objective boiled egg of positivism.

Again in the interests of conveying an elaborate notion in potentially over-simple terms, Levinas distinguishes along similar lines to such Infinity and Totality a difference between the vital action of 'the Saying', with the reported, reduced lifelessness of 'the Said'; for human relationships positions are identified and understood by references to the Self and the Other, but there is a further complication which arises in respect of the ever present Third (an individual, many individuals or a concept such as justice). This subjectivity is elaborated and becomes a vulnerable, sensible subjectivity exposed to outrage, frankness, sincerity, veracity and wounding which compels each individual into a responsibility-laden encounter of proximity with the Other (Levinas 2004); and such subjectivity is essential to ethics (Critchley 1999).

This schema is elaborated into a moral philosophy in which ethics is itself pre-ontological and wholly subjectively experienced. This has been comprehensively argued to validate the impossibility of any corporate ethics (Bevan & Corvellec 2007). Elaborating subjectivity to sensibility in a parallel argument, Roberts drives home this bleak point:

> It is from Levinas's insistence that our ethical capabilities, such as they are, are grounded in our senses that I draw the term 'sensibility'. This insistence immediately clarifies the confusion that can arise from the designation of responsibility as corporate. The corporate body is devoid of sensibility and, in this sense, is incapable of responsibility; ethics in business will always be a personal matter... much of corporate ethics can be seen as no more than an empty, if productive construction of ethical appearances (Roberts 2003, p.251).

Roberts reiterates the explicit occlusion of ethics by economic discipline. The reduction of everything to the same, economic rationale rather as suggested in the profit-maximising axiom of Jensen (2002), as clear in the mathematical fiction of formidable abstraction from Bourdieu (1998), the systemic, efficient terror from Lyotard (1984) – a point emphasised extensively by Teri Shearer (2002) and alternately by Dag Aasland (2004) again relying on Levinas. Roberts, too, appears to find Business Ethics ethically eviscerated by the dominance of classical financial interests. Business Ethics reduced to a regime of corporate social responsibility, operating insidiously in trans-national organisations only as a manufactured, cynical form of public relations supporting business as usual with neither reference to, nor influence on, what is actually practiced.

The work of Levinas differs from most traditional ethical theories (including those sampled in the previous section above) in that the ethical develops in a personal meeting of one (person) with another, rather than residing in any rational, internalised deliberation of the moral subject – such as that which may (or rather not) be discovered by measuring one's conduct against some code of governance or ethics in convenient Business Ethics. Levinas further emphasises an infinite personal ethical responsibility arising for each of us in the face of others.

Some ***continental*** philosophy sees the reductive bureaucratic processes of large businesses as structurally interrupting the moral impulse: Bauman's (1993) work is extensively claimed as grounded in Levinas. Bauman holistically informs multiple ***continental*** strands: he inscribes the multiple fractures, the effective atomisation, of any rule of responsibility of an institutional /organisational project. In bureaucratic organisations:

> all social organization consists therefore in neutralizing the disruptive and deregulating impact of moral impulse. This is achieved through a number of complementary arrangements: (1) assuring that there is a distance, not proximity between two poles of action – the 'doing' and the 'suffering' one; by the same token those on the receiving end are held beyond the reach of the actor's moral impulse; (2) exempting some 'others' from the class of potential objects of moral responsibility, of potential 'faces'; (3) dissembling other human objects of action into aggregates of functionally specific traits, and holding such traits separate – such that the occasion for reassembling the 'face' out of disparate 'items' does not arise, and the task set for each action can be exempt from moral evaluation (Bauman 1993, p.125).

Here – from this ***continental*** perspective we might consider that the exogenous term ***continental*** tends to add distance, exemption and dissimulation. Bauman's "complementary arrangements" are an inherent structural feature in other fields in which the normalisation of the unthinkable occurs (Arendt 1999; Herman 1995). This agentic structure of bureaucracy is potentially problematic for classical Business Ethics. The potential for a similar, palliative disruption of the moral impulse is experienced across the classical management field:

> Bureaucratic work shapes people's consciousness in decisive ways. Among other things, it regularizes people's experiences of time and indeed routinizes their lives by engaging them on a daily basis in rational, socially approved, purposive action; it brings them into daily proximity with and subordination to authority, creating in the process of upward-looking stances that have decisive social and psychological consequences; it places a premium on a functionally rational, pragmatic habit of mind that seeks specific goals (Jackall 2000, p.5).

Card (2005) meanwhile defines as evil anything which is foreseeable and contingent to the production of multiple and intolerable harms. Card offers a reconstruction of the evident bureaucratic disruption of the moral impulse, from Bauman and Jackall above, as a structural project of culpable wrongdoing:

> One reason that many evils go unrecognized is that the source of harm is an institution, not just the intentions or choices of individuals (many of whom may not share the goals

> of the institution, even when their conduct is governed by its norms). Another is that the harm is the product of many acts, some of which might have been individually harmless in other contexts. Victims are more likely than perpetrators to appreciate the harm. But when the source is an institution, even victims can be hard-pressed to know whom to hold accountable (Card 2005, p.24–25).

This last trio seems to somewhat radically encircle the classical projective institution with ***continental*** objections to its capacity to operate ethically.

In respect of the law, a cornerstone of classical business, Foucault sees the law in an oppositional ***continental*** stance as a means of calculation which merely maintains conformity with historically received norms or the avengement of a violation of such a norm (Hunt & Wickham 1994). Bourdieu offers an alternately denaturalised ***continental*** theorisation:

> (The) Law does no more than symbolically consecrate – by recording it in a form which renders it both eternal and universal – the structure of the power relation between groups and classes which is produced and guaranteed practically by the functioning of these mechanisms. For example, it records and legitimates the distinction between the position and the person, the power and its holder, together with the relationship obtaining at a particular moment between qualifications and jobs.... /... The law thus contributes to its own (specifically symbolic) force to the action of the various mechanisms which render it superfluous constantly to reassert power relations by overtly reverting to force (Bourdieu 2002, p.188).

As to the form and activities of the limited liability firm and capitalist project which dominate classical Business Ethics, Bourdieu analyses the neo-liberal free market consonantly as a utopia of endless exploitation:

> The neoliberal programme draws its social power from the political and economic power of those whose interests it expresses: stockholders, financial operators, industrialists, conservative or social-democratic politicians who have been converted to the reassuring layoffs of laisser-faire, high-level financial officials eager to impose policies advocating their own extinction because, unlike the managers of firms, they run no risk of having eventually to pay the consequences (1998, p.2).
>
> Hees (2006) too, sees the economic circuit as foreclosed by the processes of neo-liberalism in which the producer and consumer are mutually enslaved in a faire-faire (as opposed to orthodox laisser-faire) relation.

Other significant ethical nuances are established indicatively in Sartre and Lyotard. Sartre (1943) suggests an existential ethics centred on the reflexive and subjective notion that only by being true to ourselves can we act morally. Sartre is thus ***continental***:

> Most textbooks about business ethics do not mention existentialism. Indeed most texts on ethics – those written by Anglo-American philosophers at least – mention existentialism simply in passing, if at all, and then only to dismiss it as irrelevant or misguided (Ashman & Winstanley, 2006, p.218).

Lyotard must be mentioned again if only on account of his analysis of business from a ***continental*** perspective (1984) which shows the central importance of performativity to the classical project. Performativity in the classical project precludes reference to metaphysical discourse and requires the renunciation of fables[3]; it demands a clear mind and "brings the pragmatic functions of knowledge clearly to light, to the extent that they seem to relate to the criterion of efficiency" (Lyotard 1984, p.62) This emphasises the ***continental*** contrast versus the claims for classical concerns above. For Lyotard the traditional Business Ethics framework described above would sit well with his theorisation of scientific paradigms and their framework of power. He evidently responds to the element of rights and justice in somewhat severe terms:

> Rights do not flow from hardship, but from the fact that the alleviation of hardship improves the system's performance. The needs of the most underprivileged should not be used as a system regulator as a matter of principle: since the means of satisfying them is already known, their actual satisfaction will not improve the system's performance, but only increase its expenditures. The only counterindication is that not satisfying them can destabilise the whole. (Ibid., p.63).

Language games are a further strand of Lyotard's replete ***continental*** theorisation of classical commerce. Implicating the law in a manner anticipating Bourdieu (above) and creating the space for Derrida's subsequent development of aporias, even, to a certain degree, prefiguring deconstruction in his approach to literal truth and legitimacy, Lyotard demonstrates the transcendent, masking power of language pervasive in capitalist projects. This is also identified and extensively elaborated in the political work of contemporary authors, like Chomsky (2004, 2006) and Vidal (2002, 2004), or in the UK in the genuinely ***continental*** Pinter:

> Language is actually employed to keep thought at bay. The words 'the American people' provide a truly voluptuous cushion of reassurance. You don't need to think. Just lie back on the cushion. The cushion may be suffocating your intelligence and your critical faculties but it's very comfortable. This does not apply of course to the 40 million people living below the poverty line and the 2 million men and women imprisoned in the vast gulag of prisons, which extends across the US. (Pinter 2005, p.5).

And in natural language Serres ***continentally*** challenges what is elsewhere characterised as the crisis in legitimation (Lyotard 1984), the weatherworn divisions of the enlightenment between self and collective (Brown 2002), the mess in social science (Law 2004) and human disenchantment (Weber 1978):

> All around us language replaces experience. The sign, so soft, substitutes itself for the thing, which is hard. I cannot think of this substitution as an equivalence. It is more of an abuse and a violence. (Serres & Latour 1995, p.132).

There is even a ***continental*** perception of the effect of the enlightenment:

> Since the Enlightenment, thinkers have progressively differentiated humanity from the rest of nature and have separated objective truth from subjective morality. The greatest challenge of post-modern society may reside in their reintegration. (Gladwin, Kennelly, & Krause 1995, p.896).

Far from comprehensively, I have adduced an indicative range of ***continental*** positions broadly (cor)responding from a ***continental*** position, to the traditional classical framework of Business Ethics familiar from the mainstream approaches above. In the course of reading or deconstructing this chapter so far I believe it must be possible to at least discern the thrust of the conceptualisation of ***continental*** versus the traditional even if one or two curiosities remain.

Now taking these scripts as incomplete, but plausibly representative data, what grounded theory might one suggest or construct that will fit, work and be relevant to such a ***continental*** division? After a number of extensive readings of the traditional framework and the ***continental*** scripts along with the emergent confusion of the Friedman and Levinas issue, a pattern suggested by a reading of Foucault began to take shape. In his consideration of the archaeology of human sciences, Foucault (2002) [1966] contemplates the contribution of resemblance to the construction of knowledge in Western culture. How resemblance or similitude guided the interpretation of texts, organized the play of symbols, made possible knowledge of visible and invisible realms, and governed the art of how these matters were represented.

> The universe was folded in on itself: the earth echoing the sky, faces seeing themselves reflected in the stars, and plants holding within stems the secrets that were of use to man. Painting imitated space. And representation – whether in the service of pleasure or knowledge – was posited as a form of repetition (Ibid, p.19).

Based on Foucault's theorisation of convenientia – or adjacency – that here, opportunistically I abstract and neologise the simple notion of convenience for the purposes of this theory building exercise.

> Those things are 'convenient' which come sufficiently close to one another to be in juxtaposition, their edges touch and their fringes intermingle, the extremity of one denotes the beginning of the other (Ibid, p.20).

This is congruent with the convenient, or convenable, reductive notions here of tautology on the part of classical Business Ethics that is emphatically reiterated in the subsequent totalising refinement of this system of resemblance that condemns knowledge "to never knowing anything but the same thing" (Ibid, p.34).

Emergent Convenient and Inconvenient Business Ethics

In terms of the Grounded Theory advice to be fit and be relevant, this feels like good theorising. Enlightenment positions, classical analytic philosophy – duty, justice, utility, individualism can never seem to make business wrong in the way that ***continental*** writing can. And so the corollary for this emergent theory of convenient and inconvenient ethics really needs to be addressing the issue that ***continental*** philosophy is not adequately explained as being post-Kantian Europeans. The robustness of the theorisation will be a matter of argument, or contempt possibly, but let us at least try the idea out as I believe Barney Glaser would wish.

Convenient ethics: classical Business Ethics frameworks allow us to consider how (for example) the constituent firms of the Dow Jones Sustainability Index come to be considered as even sustainable. Or perhaps it tells us that sustainability, like the Corporate (Social) Responsibility it has recently displaced as the palliative for ethical concerns, is merely more, bigger, newer, window dressing?

Inconvenient ethics: ***continental*** writers are dismissed meanwhile as merely continental. They have nothing to say that is relevant to the concerns of commerce or, apparently, its cognate, government.

Classical Business Ethics are convenient for writing and realising codes of practice; theorising all sorts of twenty-first century invisible hand substitutes like the triple bottom line and socially responsible investing behind which normal business can carry on apparently as usual. Classical ethics are not only convenient, but essential to the concept of Business Ethics. ***Continental*** ethics are inconvenient – you cannot base a repeatable code on all that ***continental*** stuff, it is not so reducible, because it is ethical and ethics evades reduction. ***Continental*** positions on Business Ethics pose many subjective and qualitative questions, and inconveniently seem to have a far closer understanding of how business is conducted. ***Continental*** ethics are inconvenient for most of the basic activities of the entire Global 500 firms, and inimical to the parochial project of classical Business Ethics.

Continental philosophy may comprise the work of some post-Kantian European writers, but this emergent grounded theory presents some anomalies:

1. As to European: Milton Friedman is evidently a ***continental*** liberal, at least partially so. Adam Smith too was largely ***continental*** according to Ira Jackson in ***continental*** mode himself here:

   > (Adam Smith) has been expropriated as the poster boy for greed..../... And it is inappropriate and bemusing that he is so often invoked by Friedman and others as the papal invocation for corporations not engaging in public issues. Not engaging in any corporate philanthropy. And pooh-poohing generally the notion of civic engagement by the private corporation (Achbar & Abbott 2005b, p.1).

   Noam Chomsky, Gore Vidal and Michael Moore are also evidently ***continental.*** And what of Thomas Paine? This then brings us to the second dimension.
2. As to post-Kantian: Rousseau is a persuasive carrier of the evidently ***continental*** message:

   > The first man who, having enclosed a piece of land, thought of saying 'This is mine' and found people simple enough to believe him, was the true founder of civic society. How many crimes, wars, murders; how much misery and horror the human race would have been spared if someone had pulled up the stakes and filled in the ditch and cried out to his fellow men: "Beware of listening to this impostor. You are lost if you forget that the fruits of the earth belong to everyone and that the earth itself belongs to no one!" (Rousseau 1984, p.109).

But this was in 1755, perhaps a clearer counter-example for the chronology is from Ovid's account of Pythagoras who lived some 2500 years ago.

> [W]hat was before is put aside, and what was not comes into being: and every moment is renewed (Ovid: "*Metamorphoses Book XV*":176–198 Translation by author).

Continental philosophy is thus neither categorically European, nor is it uniquely post-Kantian. So what does this carefully maintained exogenous label mean? What are the implications in respect of the narrow field it has been possible to discuss in the course of this short chapter?

Continental is not in any sense an accurate term with regard to any continent – other than a notional continent of opposition – of contra-positivism. It appears, on the basis of this inexhaustive review, to be consistent only in being employed by classical-ists to dismiss the views of those writers who question the progress of imperial capitalism, when the weight of what they say cannot be overwhelmed by the propaganda of the market. This propaganda, or organised lying, expropriates the likes of Adam Smith and to a lesser extent Milton Friedman and Ira Jackson. This propaganda is itself a convenient project in the sense that it appears to be rational and regular but at the same time it operates in compliance with all corporate communication as theorised in the political economy of the mass media by Herman and Chomsky (1994)[4] and alternately in Huxley (2004).

Convenience thus tautologically convenes the status quo – it is the hallmark of classical Business Ethics. Smith (1998) presents in "The Wealth of Nations" the strands of an apologia for capitalism. He apparently presupposes the operation of late 18th century companies as a given to then explain the origin and development of a socio-economic structure characterised by the predominance of such companies. But companies and capitalism did not emerge from human prehistory (Bihr 2006) – this is merely a convenient contemporary tautology (indeed forced upon Smith by selective and incomplete reading). Such serial tautologies carry forward the imperial project of capitalism and the so-called free market economy. Such convenient tautological approaches are ontologically incongruent with the approaches characterised herein as inconvenient.

This classical Business Ethics framework is a convenient translation or realisation of the bureaucratic iron cage (DiMaggio & Powell 1983), which cannot be rationally evaded; the trans-organizational mimesis or isomorphic trends of neo institutionalist theories (DiMaggio & Powell 1991) is clearly evident in projective classical Business Ethics practice (Spence & Gray 2007). We do not have to trouble ourselves with whether big tobacco, banks, airlines and weapons manufacturers are actually fundamentally ethical, because they operate positively within the law. It is legal to sell noxious and addictive substances, as long as you are already making them. If you are not making them then it is likely to be illegal. Pragmatism – here in convenient, morally vacuous mode – asserts that we have to start from where we are. We can't stop something bad from continuing because we are making too much money at it. Such is the ethics of business together with inertia of the government, the morals of the free market and individual consumer choice according again to Freidman in another ***continental*** moment (Achbar & Abbott 2005a).

Indeed, on exactly this pretext of legitimacy, we are rationally pre-empted from asking any further questions such as why anything potentially so socially harmful is allowed to persist. All the same with issues of climate change, planetary overpopulation, the polarisation of poverty and excess, the decline of social cohesion (Sachs 2007); these externalities are all nothing to do with convenient Business Ethics.

The unique arbiter of this convenient Business Ethics, the guiding light of the *pax mercatoria* that I have sketchily inscribed above, is economics, capitalism, the business case. Whatever we may elect to name it, it embraces and governs all corporate commercial relations with whomsoever. Beyond the Business Ethics ghetto (Smith 2003) within which we operate, and without yet approaching the inconvenient ethics, let me foreclose any possible doubt about this single capital issue by reference to four elements, each of which suggests an inherent constraint on the ethical salience of convenient Business Ethics: an element from economics suggesting that the economics paradigm is totally unsuited for corporate social responsibility, sustainability or sustainable development (Korhonen 2002; Lazear 2000); an element from accounting that suggests that all business case arguments reduce any matter under consideration to a money sum (Shearer 2002) or more concisely:

> [B]usiness ethics has become an exercise in proclamation: the publishing of admonitions, inducements, seductions towards ethical conduct most evident in those who want to make the 'strong business case' for responsible corporate behaviour (Roberts 2003, p.250).

An element from Business Ethics itself which (after demonstrating the inherent logical fallacies of implementing stakeholder theory) demonstrates the non-viability of ethics as an agentic power in concepts of convenient Business Ethics because:

> It is logically impossible to maximize in more than one dimension at the same time unless the dimensions are monotone transformations of one another. Thus, telling a manager to maximize current profits, market share, future growth in profits, and anything else one pleases will leave that manager with no way to make a reasoned decision. In effect, it leaves the manager with no objective (Jensen 2002, p.237).

Finally an element from commercial practice – the object or activity reputedly at the centre of convenient Business Ethics' interests – in which the moral vacuity of the project of commerce is proclaimed and celebrated. Here, I quote Ira Jackson without further mediation:

> Capitalism is undeniably amoral[5], but it has emerged as a new global theology – a theology without morality, without a bible. It only offers a transaction manual for wealth creation and the efficient allocation of capital and it does that superbly well. No-one should question the benefits of capitalism . . ./. . . that is why it beat all the other 'isms' hands down: Communism, fascism, totalitarianism, socialism. Capitalism which is driven by competition has no competition of its own (Achbar et al. 2005b, p.1).

Each of these elements I have identified is singly sufficient to conveniently contain the ethical framework (explicated by reference to classical Business Ethics texts) earlier in this chapter. Like all convenient assertions, they simply repeat themselves in a network of analytic truths, each assuming and reproducing the validity of its own truth claims (Rosenau 1992) while at the same time supporting – or at least not successfully repudiating – all the other components in the epistemological network of *pax mercatoria*. So the convenient ethics of Business Ethics can be ethical to the extent that they reproduce themselves analytically and objectively to be congruent with the other actors in the network of commercial proposition. Anything which falls outside of this is inconvenient – or ***continental.***

Convenient Business Ethics is a monotone transformation of the needs of classical capitalism. Reflecting once more on the frankness of Jackson (above), the notional embrace of ethics can only be a convenient illusion. Ethics is rather in the apparent process of embrace, or capture, by capitalism in the same way to that in which authentic Christianity was rationally embraced and assimilated by capitalism (Tolstoy 1893/2001) in earlier times. Ira Jackson has previously shown the way to make the leap from the metanarrative of capitalism to the metanarrative of the Church. By way of clarification, for ***continental,*** in the following extract, the Sermon on the Mount is inconvenient but the Creed is convenient:

> The Sermon on the Mount, or the Creed. One cannot believe in both. And Churchmen have chosen the latter. The Creed is taught and is read as a prayer in the churches, but the Sermon on the Mount is excluded even from the Gospel passages read in the churches, so that the congregation never hears it in church, except on those days when the whole of the Gospel is read. Indeed, it could not be otherwise. People who believe in a wicked and senseless God – who has cursed the human race and devoted his own Son to sacrifice, and a part of mankind to eternal torment—cannot believe in the God of love. The man who believes in a God, in a Christ coming again in glory to judge and to punish the quick and the dead, cannot believe in the Christ who bade us turn the left cheek, judge not, forgive these that wrong us, and love our enemies. . . . /. . . The man who believes in the Church's doctrine of the compatibility of warfare and capital punishment with Christianity cannot believe in the brotherhood of all men.

In this theory building, ***continental*** philosophy has been shown to be a serious inconvenience in the sense that it generally obstructs, opposes or denaturalises the normative frameworks of classical Business Ethics. Classical Business Ethics is a rigid, rational framework of *shoulds* that may be seen, from the ***continental*** perspective, to serve as a deterministic iron cage (DiMaggio and Powell 1983). In more emergent terms the classical framework is a structure (Beck 1992, 2000; Giddens 1979, 1986, 1999) formulated from highly selective and partial readings of works whose ideas convene upon and support the *status quo* – ideas which support the framework of classical Business Ethics naturalised as perfectly normal business practice in the seductive, dominant discourses of management (Chomsky 2004).

To the extent that convenient Business Ethics and the entire project of capitalism relies on the classical ontology I have characterised above, for the achievement of *pax mercatoria*, it has been important for the understanding of inconvenient or ***continental*** ethics to contextualise them in a like manner.

Whereas classical Business Ethics requires the individual to rationalise objectively within the confines of convenient rules in order to justify a decision or choice, in the ***continental*** space subjective reflexivity is required. ***Continental*** philosophy takes as a compliment the humanizing charge that it is subjective (or not objective) as objectivity, or even neutrality, reside in a realm of impossible standards (Zinn 1997); such liberty does not fit well within the orthodoxy of classical positive ontology.

Discussion

It is perhaps adequate to invite the reader to take a moment to imagine how a corporation would frame a code of ethics based on unlimited responsibility to others – how would that work with competition and limited liability? How would a firm have a code of ethics when any code is a categorically unethical totalisation? How is a corporation able to respond to Roberts's location of accountability in subjectivity? And Bourdieu's concerns with the endless exploitation of the corporate form – how does a corporation cease to be exploitative? How would the CSR department reassemble the disruptions of institutional bureaucracy? How does a firm communicate without propagandising? How does it operate without complying with economic instrumentalism? And how would it be if corporations only spoke the truth?

It would not be convenient to rely on the tenets of existentialism when considering either the code of ethics of a company like GE or Anglo American for example, or how might British American Tobacco be more socially responsible because, under existentialism, such operations would be unlikely to persist, let alone feature prominently and with kudos in something called a sustainability index. In summary, convenient, classical, projective Business Ethics is a tautological regime of truth[6] (Foucault 1980). It is conventionally assembled from strands of originally rich, vital enlightenment theories – egoism, rights and justice, utility and duty – which have been reduced in the process to a morally vacuous but deterministically effective structure which essentially supports commerce doing whatever it wants. Milton Friedman is frequently quoted as saying that, in a free economy, "there is one and only one social responsibility of business – to use its resources and engage in activities designed to increase its profits" (1962/2002, p.133). In this single assertion, he manages to abduct an ethical notion and turn it not into a normative but a descriptive statement. Friedman is not saying what business should do; he is saying what it does. Over forty years ago a Nobel prize winning economist tells us what corporate (or rather, business) social responsibility is – this is a moment of truth to which the ghetto of classical Business Ethics is evidently oblivious. One problematisation articulated in Friedman's axiom is a blatant warning that the free economy is incapable or at least entirely disinterested in social responsibility.

These questions take us to an Alice-in-Wonder-land apparently. But still in the convenient world that is the problem with (inconvenient) ***continental*** thinking: it doesn't work. It is not performative. It does not translate easily into action. It is never a problem for the convenient world – which just pragmatically shrugs off such awkward interrogation in the manner suggested in both Herman and Chomsky, and Pinter. It is probably already clear that I favour the inconvenient ***continental*** ontology. I should also declare that 35 years of commercial experience leaves me disinclined to believe that Business Ethics is, currently, anything other than a commodity. A chattel with all the moral significance of an indulgence being sold to a venal merchant in a mediaeval basilica – I call on Ira Jackson to assist with understanding such a perspective. My impatience is not with business for not being ethical, but with the project of classical Business Ethics that seeks to make it so, because of the dangers that such capture entails.

I will set the conclusion here against a ***continental*** view of globalisation:

Today's major powers, driven by their overheated productive forces, are launched into a new Great Game to control not only energy resources but the globalized market... Citizens are required, not as producers but as consumers... and it remains unresolved how the citizens are to acquire the resources to function as consumers (Lingis 2007, p.xi).

This is a further *inconvenient,* or unhelpful and obstructive, way of presenting things to the establishment: it makes it look like no-one is in control. Instability is bad for capitalism and the markets when it goes beyond the limits of insurance policies. The precariousness this intimates becomes more evident when Pentagon computers are hacked into by highschool drop outs and the largest military apparatus on the planet finds itself under attack by a handful of determined individuals: all the great juggernauts of commerce are suddenly vulnerable to sabotage.

More worryingly, according to Professors Jeffrey Sachs (2007) and Sir Nicholas Stern (2006), the externalities of the Great Game referred to above have serious consequences for the biosphere. These externalities have moved us into an era called the Anthropocene (Crutzen 2006; Crutzen & Steffen 2003) – that is to say that man has reached the point where his convenient activities overwhelm the inconvenient power of nature. This inconvenient truth (pace Gore) is significant in our present context because, as Reason claims, the crisis of sustainability is a crisis of mind (2007). The scientific – convenient – worldview which has been established over 300–400 years leaves us as distinct from nature, not a part of it. Rocks and seas have no subjectivity or intelligence once they are objectified, along with us, by the positivist classical project.

This split between humanity and nature, and the arrogation of all mind to humans, is what Weber meant by the disenchantment of the world (Ibid, p.33).

The convenient – inconvenient polemic remains at the heart of this potential problem. There may be no objective ethical rules (MacIntyre 2002; Nietzsche 2003; Williams 1987), and in contemporary globalized modernity with all its precariousness and uncertainty (Bauman 2000, 2004) individuals can either adopt the convenient, if blatantly anachronistic, clockwork (i.e. Newtonian) classical morality, which promises certainties simultaneously known to be lies, or attempt inconveniently *continentally* and subjectively to emulate an individual level of integrity (Werhane 2006).

Good is not presented to freedom: it has chosen me before I have chosen it. No one is good voluntarily (Levinas 2004, p.11).

This is as closely as I may approach ethics – the good finds me and I (must) enact it. Convenient ethics will only suggest another code, or perhaps an audit by EthicAbility™ Inc., or another, new Business Ethics index. Inconvenient ethical practice will perhaps evolve to suggest that in the era of successful open resources like Linux and Wikipedia, we can have open source ethics. Resist the convenient, leave the classical Business Ethics project to extinguish. Be subjective and responsible: such (re)action is inconvenient and ***continental*** but there is no *otherwise than being* ethical.[7]

Notes

1. Ira Jackson and Milton Friedman both employ the term 'amoral' in connection with (variously) commerce, business and the corporation. I am unable to justify their use of this term which I know does not accord with many peoples' view of business, nor with some distinguished philosophers' understanding of (a)morality in connection with human activity. Perhaps this is a question for future research?
2. *"The Raw and the Cooked"*
3. Let us agree at this point that "the invisible hand" of neo-liberalism is a scientific reality and not in any way fabulous.
4. This contrastingly inconvenient theorisation, originally published in 1988 asserts a model of the so-called free market dominated by a cynical series of filters, by which the elite dominate the media and which I interpolate here in natural language in the interests of necessary brevity: The first filter is that all commerce is focussed on making a profit, the second filter is to be in business profitably you must use advertising media, the third filter requires that these advertising media also own and control broadcast news, the fourth stage is that if you disagree with the first three stages and try to rock the boat you are an idiot and you will either be ignored as unimportant, or you may be allowed to be an important idiot (like, with apologies for the locution of 'idiot', Michael Moore for example), the fifth stage is that if you really look like to could seriously disrupt the first three stages you will be called a communist and no one in the market will deal with you.
5. See first endnote
6. Each society has such a régime made up of the "types of discourse which it accepts and makes function as true, the mechanisms and instances which enable one to distinguish true and false statements, the means by which each is sanctioned; the techniques and procedures accorded value in the acquisition of truth; the status of those who are charged with saying what counts as true". (Foucault 1980 pp.109–133)
7. The author gratefully acknowledges the considerate persistence of the editors of this volume in assisting him with comments and suggestions to early drafts of this chapter.

References

Aasland, D. G. 2004. On the Ethics Behind "Business Ethics". *Journal of Business Ethics*, 53(1): 3–8.

Achbar, M. & Abbott, J. 2005a. The Corporation: the Pathological Pursuit of Profit and Power. Canada: Metrodome http://www.thecorporation.com/media/Friedman.pdf

Achbar, M. & Abbott, J. 2005b. The Corporation: the Pathological Pursuit of Profit and Power. Canada: Metrodome http://www.thecorporation.com/media/Jackson.pdf

Arendt, H. 1999. *The Human Condition* (2nd ed.). Chicago, IL: University of Chicago Press.

Ashman, I. & Winstanley, D. 2006. Business Ethics and Existentialism. *Business Ethics: a European Review*, 15(3): 218–233.

Bauman, Z. 1993. *Postmodern Ethics*. Oxford: Blackwell Publishers.

Bauman, Z. 2000. *Liquid Modernity*. Cambridge: Polity Press.

Bauman, Z. 2004. *Wasted Lives*. Cambridge: Polity Press.

Beck, U. 1992. *Risk Society: Towards a New Modernity* (M. Ritter, Trans.). London: Sage.

Beck, U. 2000. *World risk society*. Cambridge: Polity Press.

Bevan, D. & Corvellec, H. 2007. The Impossibility of Corporate Ethics: For a Levinasian Approach to Management Ethics. *Business Ethics: a European Review*, 16(3): 208–219.

Bihr, A. 2006. *La préhistoire du capital : Le devenir-monde du capitalisme, Tome 1*. Lausanne, HE: Page deux.

Blackburn, S. 2005. *The Oxford Dictionary of Philosophy*. Oxford: Oxford University Press.

Blagescu, M. & Lloyd, R. 2006. *Global Accountability Report*. London: One World Trust.
Boltanski, L. & Chiapello, E. 2006. *The New Spirit of Capitalism* (G. Elliot, Trans.). London: Verso.
Bourdieu, P. 1998. Utopia of Endless Exploitation: The Essence of Neoliberalism, *Le Monde Diplomatique*, Internet English Edition ed.: 8. Paris.
Bourdieu, P. 2002. *Outline of a Theory of Practice* (R. Nice, Trans.). Cambridge: Cambridge University Press.
Brown, S. D. 2002. Michel Serres: Science, Translation and the Logic of the Parasite. *Theory, Culture and Society*, 19(3): 1–27.
Bryman, A., & Bell, E. 2003. *Business Research Methods*. Oxford, UK: Oxford University Press.
Card, C. 2005. *The Atrocity Paradigm: A Theory of Evil*. Oxford, UK: Oxford University Press.
Charmaz, K. 2005. Grounded Theory in the 21st Century: Applications for Advancing Social Justice Studies. In N. K. Denzin & Y. S. Lincoln (Eds.), *The Sage Handbook of Qualitative Research*: 507–535. London: Sage Publications.
Charmaz, K. 2006. *Constructing Grounded Theory: A Practical Guide Through Qualitative Analysis*. London, UK: Sage Publications.
Chomsky, N. 2004. *Hegemony or Survival: America's Quest for Global Dominance*. Harlow: Penguin Books.
Chomsky, N. 2006. *Failed States: The abuse of power and the assault on democracy*. London Hamish Hamilton.
Crane, A. & Matten, D. 2007. *Business Ethics: Managing Corporate Citizenship and Sustainability in the Age of Globalization* (2 ed.). Oxford: Oxford University Press.
Critchley, S. 1999. *The Ethics of Deconstruction: Derrida and Levinas*. Edinburgh: Edinburgh University Press.
Critchley, S. & Schroeder, W. (Eds.). 1999. *A Companion to Continental Philosophy*. Oxford: Blackwell Publishers.
Critchley, S. 2001. *Continental Philosophy: A Very Short Introduction*. Oxford: Oxford University Press.
Crutzen, P. J. & Steffen, W. 2003. How Long Have We Been in the Anthropocene Era? *Climatic Change*, 61(3): 251–257.
Crutzen, P. J. 2006. Geoengineering Climate Change: Treating the Symptom Over the Cause. *Climatic Change*, 77(3–4): 227–228.
Derrida, J. 1997a. *Politics and Friendship: A Discussion with Jacques Derrida*. Paper Presented at the Centre for Modern French Thought, Brighton, UK.
Derrida, J. 1997b. *Adieu à Emmanuel Lévinas*. Paris: Galilée.
DesJardins, J. 2006. *An Introduction to Business Ethics*. New York, NY: McGraw-Hill.
Dholakia, N. & Firat, A. F. 2006. Global Business Beyond Modernity. *Critical Perspectives on International Business*, 2(2): 147–162.
DiMaggio, P. J. & Powell, W. W. 1983. The Iron Cage Revisited: Institutional Isomorphism and Collective Rationality in Organizational Fields. *American Sociological Review*, 48: 147–160.
DiMaggio, P. J. & Powell, W. W. (Eds.). 1991. *The New Institutionalism in Organizational Analysis*. Chicago IL: University of Chicago Press.
Donaldson, T. & Dunfee, T. W. 1999. *Ties That Bind: A Social Contracts Approach to Business Ethics*. Cambridge: Harvard Business School Press.
Drucker, P. 1989. *The Practise of Management*. London: Heinemann Professional.
Fisher, C. M. & Lovell, A. 2006. *Business Ethics and Values*. Harlow: FT Prentice Hall.
Foucault, M. 1980. Truth and Power. In C. Gordon (Ed.), *Power/Knowledge: Selected interviews and other writings* 1972–1977: 109–133. New York NY: Pantheon.
Foucault, M. 2002 (1966). *The Order of Things*. Cambridge: Routledge Classics.
Freeman, R. E. 1984. *Strategic Management: A Stakeholder Approach*. Boston: Pitman.
Friedman, M. 1962/2002. *Capitalism and Freedom* (paper ed.). London and Chicago: The University of Chicago Press.
Friedman, M. 1970. The Social Responsibility of Business is to Increase its Profits. *The New York Times Magazine*, No. 33, pp 122–126.

Fullerton, S., Kerch, K. B., & Dodge, H. R. 2004. Consumer Ethics: An Assessment of Individual Behavior in the Market Place. *Journal of Business Ethics*, 15(7): 805–814.

Gershwin, G. & Gershwin, I. 1936. Let's Call The Whole Thing Off: http://www.personal.umich.edu/~pfa/poemquot/calling.html.

Ghoshal, S. 2005. Bad Management Theories Are Destroying Good Management Practices. *Academy of Management Learning and Education*, 4(1): 75–91.

Giddens, A. 1979. *Central Problems in Social Theory: Action, Structure and Contradiction in Social Analysis*. London: Macmillan.

Giddens, A. 1986. *The Constitution of Society: Outline of the Theory of Structuration* Cambridge: Polity.

Giddens, A. 1999. *Runaway World: How Globalisation Is Shaping Our Lives*. London: Profile Books.

Gladwin, T. N., Kennelly, J., & Krause, T.-S. 1995. Shifting Paradigms for Sustainable Development: Implications for Management Theory and Research. *Academy of Management Review*, 20(4): 874–907.

Glaser, B. 1998. *Doing Grounded Theory*. Mill Valley CA: Sociology Press.

Harrison, M. R. 2005. *An Introduction to Business and Management Ethics*. Baisngstoke UK: Palgrave Macmillan.

Hees, M. 2006. *Des dieux, des héros et des managers: ou de quelques malentendus*. Bruxelles: Labor.

Herman, E. S. & Chomsky, N. 1994. *Manufacturing Consent: The Political Economy of the Mass Media*. London: Vintage Original.

Herman, E. S. 1995. *The Triumph of the Market*. Cambridge, MA: South End Press.

Hunt, A. & Wickham, G. 1994. *Foucault and Law: Towards a Sociology of Law as Governance*. London: Pluto Press.

Huxley, A. (2004). *Brave New World Revisited*. London: Vintage.

Jackall, R. 2000. *Moral Mazes: The World of Corporate Managers*. Oxford, UK: Oxford University Press.

Jensen, M. 2002. Value Maximization, Stakeholder Theory, and the Corporate Objective Function. *Business Ethics Quarterly*, 12(2): 235–256.

Jones, C., Parker, M., & ten Bos, R. 2005. *For Business Ethics*. London: Routledge.

Kolk, A. 2003. Trends in Sustainability Reporting by the Fortune Global 250. *Business Strategy and the Environment*, 12(5): 279–291.

Korhonen, J. 2002. The Dominant Economics Paradigm and Corporate Social Responsibility. *Corporate Social Responsibility and Environmental Management*, 9(1): 67–80.

Kuhn, T. S. 1996. *The Structure of Scientific Revolutions*. Chicago Il: University of Chicago Press.

Law, J. 2004. *After Method*. London: Routledge.

Lazear, E. P. 2000. Economic Imperialism. *The Quarterly Journal of Economics*, 115(1): 99–146.

Lévi-Strauss, C. 1983. *The Raw & the Cooked* Chicago IL: The University of Chicago Press.

Levinas, E. 1985. *Ethics and Infinity – Conversations with Philippe Nemo*. Pittsburgh PA: Duquesne University Press.

Levinas, E. 2004. *Otherwise than Being – or Beyond Essence* (A. Lingis, Trans.). Pittsburgh: Duquesne University Press.

Levinas, E. 2005. *Totality and infinity – an essay on exteriority* (A. Lingis, Trans.). Pittsburgh PA: Duquesne University Press.

Lingis, A. 2007. Why Bataille Now? Foreword. In S. Winnubst (Ed.), *Reading Bataille Now*: vii–xii. Bloomington, IN: The Indiana University Press.

Lyotard, J.-F. 1984. *The postmodern condition: A report on knowledge* (G. Bennington & B. Massumi, Trans.). Manchester: Manchester University Press.

MacIntyre, A. 2002. *A Short History of Ethics*. London: Routledge Classics.

Nietzsche, F. 2003. *The Genealogy of Morals*. Mineola NY: Dover Thrift Editions.

Parker, M. 2002. *Against Management*. Cambridge: Polity.

Pinter, H. 2005. *Art, Truth & Politics*. Stockholm: The Nobel Foundation.

Plato. (2002 (Ca.370BCE)). *Phaedrus*. Oxford: Oxford University Press.

Porter, M. E. 2004. *Competitive Advantage: Creating and Sustaining Superior Performance*. New York: Free Press.
Preston, D. S. 2002. Managerialism and the Post-Enlightenment Crisis of the British University. In D. S. Preston (Ed.), *The University of Crisis*. Amsterdam NL: Editions Rodopi B.V.
Reason, P. 2007. Education for Ecology: Science, Aesthetics, Spirit and Ceremony. *Management Learning*, 38(1): 27–44.
Roberts, J. 2003. The Manufacture of Corporate Social Responsibility: Constructing Corporate Sensibility. *Organization*, 10(2): 249–265.
Rosenau, P. M. 1992. *Post-Modernism and the Social Sciences: Insights, Inroads and Intrusions*. Princeton NJ: Princeton University Press.
Sachs, J. 2007. Bursting at the Seams: The 2007 BBC Reith Lectures, *The Reith Lectures*. London: British Broadcasting Corporation.
Sartre, J.-P. 1943. *L'Etre et le Neant*. Paris Librairie Gallimard.
Sedgwick, P. 2001. *Descartes to Derrida: An Introduction to European Philosophy*. Oxford, UK: Blackwell Publishing.
Serres, M. & Latour, B. 1995. *Conversations on Science, Culture, and Time: Michel Serres Interviewed by Bruno Latour*. (R. Lapidus, Trans.). Dearborn MI: University of Michigan Press.
Shearer, T. 2002. Ethics and Accountability: From the For-Itself to the For-The-Other. *Accounting, Organizations and Society*, 27: 541–573.
Smith, A. 1998. *The Wealth of Nations*. Oxford: Oxford Paperbacks.
Smith, C. 2003. Corporate Social Responsibility: Whither and How? *California Management Review*, 45(4): 52–76.
Spence, C. & Gray, R. H. 2007. *Social and Environmental Reporting: the Business Case*. London: Association of Chartered and Certified Accountants.
Stern, N. (2006). *The Economics of Climate Change*. London: H M Treasury.
Taylor, F. W. 2005. *The Principles of Scientific Management*. London: 1st World Library Ltd.
Tolstoy, L. 1893/2001. *The Kingdom of God Is Within You* (C. Garnett, Trans.): Project Gutenberg.
Vidal, G. 2002. *Perpetual War for Perpetual Peace: How we got to be so hated, causes of conflict in the last Empire*. Redhill: Clairview Books.
Vidal, G. 2004. *Imperial America: Reflections on the United States of Amnesia*. New York, NY: Clairview Books.
Weber, M. 1978. *Economy and Society*. London: The University of California Press Ltd.
Webley, S. & LeJeune, M. 2002. *Ethical Business – Corporate Use of Code of Conduct*. London: Institute of Business Ethics.
Werhane, P. H. 2006. A Place for Philosophy in Applied Ethics and the Role of Moral Reasoning in Moral Imagination. *Business Ethics Quarterly*, 16(3): 401–408.
Whittington, R. 2001. *What is Strategy – and does it matter?* London: Thompson Learning.
Williams, B. 1987. *Ethics and the limits of Philosophy*. London: Routledge.
Zinn, H. 1997. *The Zinn Reader: Writings on Disobedience and Democracy*. New York NY: Seven Stories Press.

Contribution Towards a Phenomenological Approach to Business Ethics

Stephen Meinster

There is a crisis in business ethics. In part, this crisis stems from the prevailing method of applying ethical theories to business issues. In most cases, applied business ethics extracts the basic principles from an ethical theory – usually Aristotle's virtue ethics, Kant's metaphysics of morals, or Mill's utilitarianism – and uses these concepts as so many tools with which to solve managerial problems. Instrumentalism is a valid approach to such problems, and it would be absurd to suggest that ethical theories from the history of philosophy should be used *only* by philosophers who have understood them within their historical, socioeconomic and cultural contexts. However, applied ethics takes it for granted that economic problems have emerged and are recognized by those who would apply these ethical theories to solve them. The preface to most major philosophical works is spent making the argument that such recognition has been lacking, and that a new philosophical method is required to find the solution to a moral, ethical, religious, scientific or political problem. In short, the crisis in business ethics is also caused by economic theories that distort economic experience and thereby hide phenomena that would otherwise demand ethical clarification.

Philosophy can mitigate this crisis by explaining the metaphysical, epistemological and methodological context for the theoretical tools business people use to make business decisions. The science responsible for manufacturing these tools is economics; and in this essay, I will apply the philosophy of Edmund Husserl to the economic theory of Joseph Schumpeter in order to explain how economic theory based on empiricist philosophical principles produces concepts that distort our experience of the economy. In particular, I will show that Schumpeter's empiricist epistemology causes him to mistake his own theoretical constructions for the real economy and its processes. In turn, I will illustrate how Alan Greenspan distorts economic realities when employing Schumpeter's concept of "creative destruction." The purpose of this analysis is to show how the science of economics can create a fundamental disconnect between the economy as it is *lived* by those within it and the economy as it *appears* to people whose experience is refined by economic theory.

S. Meinster
Doctoral candidate and Assistant Professor of Philosophy, DePaul University, Chicago, IL, USA
e-mail: smeinster@depaul.edu

M. Painter-Morland, P. Werhane (eds.), *Cutting-edge issues in Business Ethics*,

The underlying claim guiding this essay is that before we can apply ethics to issues in business, those issues must first appear *as* issues in need of ethical clarification.

The essay is divided into three parts. In the first part, I explain the basic tenets of Edmund Husserl's philosophical critique of modern science, and his account of why empiricist epistemology leads to logical contradictions that corrupt empirical science. In the second part, I apply Husserl's critique to the economic theory of Joseph Schumpeter in order to show that Schumpeter's empiricist model of science causes him to confuse his theoretical constructions for real economic processes. In the third part I will analyze a speech by Alan Greenspan where he employs Schumpeter's economic concepts to construct an image of the American economy favorable to his ideological position on minimum-wage legislation. I aim to show how these concepts can distort economic phenomena and hide economic conflicts that demand ethical clarification. I hope the essay will illustrate the need for a phenomenological approach to business ethics, an approach that can compliment prevailing methods of applied ethics in illuminating the ethical dimensions of business.

Part One: Husserlian Phenomenology and Critique of Modern Science

Edmund Husserl is considered the founder of contemporary phenomenology, a philosophical movement that emerged at the start of the 20th century in Germany. His ideas were influential in philosophy of science, particularly in the areas of logic and psychology, where phenomenology opened up new avenues of theoretical research. Husserl introduced his own phenomenology with a critique of empiricism because he thought empiricist epistemology unnecessarily restricted scientific inquiry. Rejecting the possibility of scientific inquiry into an entire class of essential being, empirical science ignored questions relevant to the human spirit, thereby detaching the progress of scientific and technological development from the elements of human life that first gave these projects meaning. The result was a crisis of the modern human spirit where technological and economic progress outstripped the ability of human sciences to understand their meaning for humanity. Husserl hoped phenomenology could remedy this crisis by studying the essential conditions for all meaningfulness shared by natural and human sciences.

The following treatment of Husserl's thought develops his critique of empiricist philosophy and the modern sciences that have their methodological grounds in logical positivism, a contemporary form of empiricism.[1] It is my intention to apply this critique to the economic theory of Joseph Schumpeter, who grounds economic analysis on the principles of logical positivism. Husserl's overriding criticism is that empiricism is fundamentally naturalistic, and that this naturalism bleeds into any science that defines its methods in accordance with empiricist epistemology. Naturalism, he argues, is a naïve philosophical position that cannot account for the ground of its own claims, and falls into various logical contradictions that destroy *all* science. Husserl believes that phenomenology is required to identify and correct the following errors in method: psychologism, skeptical relativism, and naturalistic misconstruction – each of which can be identified in the work of Joseph Schumpeter.

Empiricism, Naturalism and Psychologism

According to Husserl, the primary contribution of empiricism to philosophy and science is the doctrine of *naturalism*, which holds that all being is real, physical, and "exists as a unity of spatio-temporal being subject to exact laws of nature"(Husserl 1965, p.79). This principle is either ontological, where an empiricist posits a physical universe consisting *entirely* of bodies and their physical relations; or epistemological, where the empiricist claim that the human mind is an entirely physical process limits knowledge to physical beings that can produce motion in sentient. Husserl stresses that on the empiricist view, the laws of thought are equally laws of nature, since these govern the physical process of thinking (Husserl 2001, pp.48–51).

On the empiricist observational model of science, scientific knowledge is the product of physical causal relations between the mind of the scientist and the physical object of inquiry. Scientists indoctrinated into this model occupy "the natural standpoint," according to which they assert the "natural thesis" that the world consists of "the totality of objects that can be known through experience. Occupying the natural standpoint, positivism claims to be guided by the facts themselves" Husserl (1969, p.48); as such, logical positivism holds that the origin of all science is *sense-experience*, and that the *ground* of evidence must be found in immediate experience.[2] The positivists' obsession with "facts" leads them to conflate the ground of facts (sense-experience) with the ground of the *science* of facts (empirical intuition).[3]

When logical positivism attempts to account for its own logical foundations, a fundamental contradiction emerges. According to naturalism, this account is only possible if the origin of logic is a natural, physical process – human thinking. Empirical psychology treats logic as it would any other fact, as a physical object of sense-experience. As such it seeks to ground the necessity of logical relations in that which appears directly in experience – the causality of the psychophysical act of forming propositions and syllogisms. As a result, the laws of logic governing the *contents* of our thoughts are equated with the empirical laws governing physical *acts* of thinking, the judgments themselves (Husserl 2001, pp.48–50).

"Psychologism" is the error whereby a psychologist mistakes the act of judging that expresses the logical law for constitution of the law itself, as if real causal relations can produce ideal logical relations.[4] In accordance with empiricist logic, empirical psychology confuses "a law as a *term in causation with a law as the rule of causation*"(Ibid). Husserl grants that we come to *know* such laws only through the psychological act of thinking, but he warns that we do not thereby *constitute* the law as such. Because of their naturalism, "psychologistic logicians ignore the fundamental, essential, never-to-be bridged gulf between ideal and real laws, between normative and causal relation, between logical and real necessity, between logical and real grounds." (Ibid, p.50) Psychologism is a plague on natural science because it leads to skeptical relativism and naturalistic misconstruction – contradictions that destroy the validity of scientific method and the undermine universality of all knowledge.

Skeptical Relativism and the Destruction of Science

Psychologism leads to skeptical relativism because, in treating the ideal laws of logic as real laws of nature, it contradicts the "ideal conditions for the possibility of a theory as such" (Husserl 2001, p.73). That is, the content of psychologistic logic contradicts the very principles that would ground its validity. Each form of skeptical relativism stems from the fact that empirical research can only establish probabilities and not necessary laws.[5] This leads to the skeptical view that there are no necessary laws of logic, no universally valid principles of knowledge and no universal truth. Individual relativism (subjectivism), asserts the claim that "all truth (and knowledge) is relative to the contingently judging subject" (Ibid, p.77).[6] On this view there are no necessary truths because each individual defines truth according to his own personal experience. Species relativism is another form of relativism, one that correctly asserts that pure logical relations are *a priori*, and therefore absolute. Unfortunately, species relativism also makes the anthropological claim that the *a priori* conditions for logical truth are unique to the structure of human reason. This view is also called anthropologism because it holds that "all truth has its source in our common human constitution" and that "if there were no such constitution, there would be no truth" (Ibid, p.80). Husserl will not accept any epistemology that makes the conditions for truth contingent on an actually existing individual or a species.

Relativism in all its forms threatens science because it undermines the very idea of logically consistent theory, knowledge and truth. Individual and species relativisms are forms of psychologism because they argue that existence of truth is the *causal result* of an individual human consciousness, or human consciousness as such. Husserl's goal is ultimately to show that logical laws, which all forms of science take for granted – like the law of contradiction – cannot be established through positivist methods (Husserl 2001, pp. 56–78).[7] Induction can lead to probabilities and hypotheses, but it cannot generate the logical structure of universal, absolute and necessary laws.

Naturalistic misconstruction and the Husserlian Alternative

Without logical laws of the kind governing contradiction, a science like economics would be impossible. Husserl shows that the laws governing the meaningfulness of any concept or object are *a priori* and cannot be abstracted from sense-experience, as the empiricist tradition would have us believe. In opposition to empiricism, Husserl claims that laws of logic are not physical things. Although they do not have spatio-temporal existence, pure logical objects have constitutive meaning for consciousness, and therefore have *being*. Through acts of pure consciousness, such laws exert the normative power to constitute the logical structure of anything meaningful, including human thought. But the logic itself cannot have its ground in the contingent, empirical, psychophysical nature of human subjectivity; rather, its validity is grounded in an ideal, pure and phenomenological realm of essences.

While the historical, cultural, and natural sciences orient themselves toward empirical phenomena of the "real" world, pure phenomenology discloses the phenomenon *par excellence*, the phenomenological sphere of the world of essences. Husserl shows that before a thing can appear as an object of scientific inquiry, it must appear *as* something meaningful *for* consciousness. Phenomenological analysis of the structures of consciousness establishes the *a priori* logical conditions for all meaningfulness, from everyday experience to scientific knowledge. In doing so, phenomenology secures the pure, universal, and essential ground of all meaningfulness, the horizon within which all sciences find their respective objects of inquiry, no matter what their ontological region of study.

Husserl points out that before I can analyze the nature of the table on which I am writing, it must first appear to me *as* a table; that is, the table must already have meaning as a phenomenon *for* me. On the one hand, this table is an empirically real, physical existence that presents itself immediately through experience in a series of material sides. Husserl points out that no physical thing can present itself in all of its material sides at once. Instead, as I analyze the table its parts adumbrate through an inexhaustible number of sides or aspects. I can never see the entire physical table at once. On the other hand, however, the table first appears to me as a *whole* table, regardless of the impossibility of my observing all of its parts individually, let alone simultaneously.

Phenomenology discovers that every object is constituted by consciousness, which intends the object through two fundamentally distinct forms of intuition: eidetic (essential) and empirical. In the case of the table, eidetic intuition constitutes the universal, essential or ideal form of 'the whole table.' This act of consciousness intends the *idea* of a whole table, and without this act, the table could not appear to me as a meaningful whole. Meanwhile, empirical intuition is an act of consciousness that intends the individual, material form of the object in its spatio-temporal determinations. Empiricism, with its naturalistic principles, rejects the possibility of ideas (essences) and eidetic intuition, and accepts only one form of empirical intuition whose physical causality cannot account for our lived-experience of whole objects and the absolute unity of the world. Ironically, in its attempt to bring philosophy, logic and science entirely within the real world of spatio-temporal experience, empiricism has adopted principles that fail to account for experience.

This methodological failure has one particularly grave consequence for empirical science – a delusional disposition Husserl calls "naturalistic misconstruction." Naturalistic misconstruction is caused when a scientist treats ideal structures as if they are natural properties of real things. Since the positivist scientist ignores the work of eidetic intuition, he acts as if the ideal structure of the world is a real part of physical nature, and that laws are physical forces governing physical objects. Husserl argues that "natural science is naïve in regard to its point of departure" because it believes the "nature it is to investigate is simply *there*." (Husserl 1965, p.85) When the natural scientist gives a causal account of his experience, he pretends to "abstract" laws of nature from the physical things themselves through induction. Contrary to this naïve view, natural phenomena appear in accordance with laws because that is how consciousness constitutes them. Scientific consciousness also intends its objects in accordance with mathematical laws. To the scientist, nature *appears* to have a mathematical nature, but it is an error of naïve realism for the scientist to assume that this mathematical logic is a physical property of real nature. Naturalistic misconstruction causes the scientist to substitute a *theory* of nature and sense-experience for his lived-experience of the natural world.

Part Two: Skeptical Relativism and Naturalistic Misconstruction in Schumpeter

Joseph Schumpeter (1950, pp.81–87) is most famous for coining the phrase 'creative destruction,' the process of economic development unique to capitalism.[8] He is also known for his argument that the success of capitalist production will eventually create the conditions for its own demise, and lead the march into socialism. Drawing on the "sociology of science" movement led by Karl Manheim and Max Scheler, Schumpeter (1949, pp.347–348) proposed an "economic sociology" (Schumpeter 1954, pp.1–45)[9] that draws on natural and human sciences to guarantee analytic rigor without detaching economics from historically real economic processes. In his body of work, Schumpeter standardized economic analysis with positivist methods of induction and deduction, and invented a dynamic theory of economic development to address the real qualitative changes caused by capitalist expansion. But as we will see, each of these contributions leads to the kinds of skeptical relativism and naturalistic misconstruction that Husserl warned could follow from positivism and historicism.

Skeptical Relativism in Schumpeter's Positivism

Schumpeter believes that, to be considered an exact science, economics must employ rigorous scientific methods that have their basis in logical positivism. For Schumpeter (1954, p.8), empirical science establishes " 'facts verifiable by observation or experiment'; and reduce[s] the range of admissible methods to 'logical inference from the verifiable facts." From start to finish, economic science is based on the physical causal relation between a real economic process and an organic mind. It begins when this relation produces a copy or image of the economic process –

the real process is a *fact*, while the image produced is an economic *phenomenon*.[10] All science begins when phenomena and their relations are first observed in sense-experience.

From experience, theoretical models are built through induction, which unfolds as a series of "abstracting generalizations." (1954, pp.15–16) Scientific concepts are constructed by analyzing observed phenomena into parts, labeling these parts with names or numbers, and reformulating the phenomenal experience into propositions or theorems.[11] As the relations between phenomena persist, there is a recognition that "certain arguments and chains of reasoning tend to repeat themselves, and that certain concepts recur again and again." (Schumpeter 1982, p.1053) Eventually these concepts are isolated and generalized, classified according to subject, and refined into theories. Once a theory is induced from facts, its validity is deduced by applying it to new facts observed in experience.

In the case of economics, analysis is usually expressed though mathematical or symbolic logic. Schumpeter argues that economics did not establish itself as an exact science until equilibrium theory used calculus to bring into relief "the bare bones of the economic logic." (Schumpeter 1939, p.69) Equilibrium theory represents the economy mathematically, reformulating the real-world economic tendency toward equilibrium as a "pure logic of the interdependence between economic quantities." (Schumpeter 1936, p.794) This theoretical reconstruction of economic phenomena sets economic science apart from common sense understandings of economic phenomena.

From a Husserlian perspective, we can already identify the potential for skeptical relativism in Schumpeter's account of economic theory-building. In line with his positivist methods, Schumpeter tries to establish the objectivity of economics as a fact, like any other fact that can be observed in experience, induced into a theoretical framework, and deduced as valid when tested by further experience.[12] Economic sociology studies the behavior of economists to find behavioral regularities that can serve as standards in judging whether an economist truly derives his evidence from observed facts. (Schumpeter 1954, pp.1–45) But Husserl has shown that to ground the objectivity of scientific concepts in the physical *acts* of judgment that instantiate them is to mistake the physical causality of scientific *behavior* for the ideal laws governing the *content* of scientific judgments. Economic sociology uses an empirical observational method to furnish an objective test for other observational models of empirical science. This approach would lead to skepticism because for every objective test formulated by economic sociology, there must be a further objective test to establish the objectivity of the first. Instead of securing a foundation for economic science, Schumpeter has offered an infinite regress of inquiry tantamount to skepticism.

In recognition of this quandary, Schumpeter (Ibid) eventually seeks an objective principle in *instrumentalism*, according to which the success of a science is judged by its ability to make effective contributions to real economic problems, rather than by its capacity for formulating objectively valid concepts or objectively true claims about facts. Economic theory is nothing more than "refined common sense," an aptitude of the mind, developed over generations, that allows economists to find more efficient and rational methods for solving real economic problems.

The Unity of Economic Science: Statics and Dynamics

Schumpeter's theory of economic development is driven by his frustration with prevailing economic models that fail to account for the "organic process" which he considers "the essential fact about capitalism." (Schumpeter 1950, p.83) According to static economic models, like Keynes' *General Theory of Employment Interest and Money*, an economy has an ideal point at which all of its factors are in equilibrium. Keynes' static theory of economic development measures the 'tendency towards equilibrium' by taking snap-shots of the 'whole' economy, analyzing them mathematically, and comparing them to earlier snap-shots to determine whether there have been quantitative changes in total output. As Schumpeter (1934, p.61) puts it, equilibrium theory "describes economic life from the standpoint of a 'circular flow,' running on in channels essentially the same year after year – similar to the circulation of the blood in an animal organism."

Static equilibrium theories express the phenomenon of economic development as the *quantitative* progress of *qualitatively* identical economic structures. However, Schumpeter (1950, p.83) argues that the defining characteristic of capitalist development is the phenomenon of entrepreneurial activity. Entrepreneurship is a real motive force that creates *qualitative changes* internal to the economy, making production and distribution more efficient. The egotistical drive of the entrepreneur toward unbounded success displaces old firms, trusts and unproductive methods of production, replacing them with more efficient structures. The process through which entrepreneurs lead capital, labor and technology in revolutionary directions is called "creative destruction," the "fundamental impulse that sets and keeps the capitalist engine in motion..."

Schumpeter (1936, p.794.) calls creative destruction a "dynamic" phenomenon because it expresses a process of qualitative change immanent to the economy. The quantitative analysis of static theory ignores qualitative change and thereby "assumes away" the very phenomena and problems that arise as a result of capitalist progress. Ricardo and Keynes are both guilty of a "treacherous generality" that is "of another world and out of all contact with modern industrial fact."(Ibid) While the concept of creative destruction expresses a real-world process of economic development, equilibrium expresses an ideal state of being. Equilibrium theory constructs the concept by grasping "fragments of reality" and extending them into "conclusions about reality as a whole." (Schumpeter 1950, p.82) Equilibrium is never reached; rather, it is a theoretical construct that makes manageable the quantitative determination of price and quantity of goods. As a snap-shot of economic life, it is a partial reconstruction of the phenomenon of economic life; and as such, it cannot express real economic development.

Schumpeter's alternative to equilibrium theory does not abandon the concept of equilibrium. In *Theory of Economic Development*, Schumpeter argues for a synthetic economic model to bridge the gap between static and dynamic theory. His model synthesizes static and dynamic models into simultaneously interdependent *and* opposed parts of a unified economic theory. We recall that theoretical models are abstracted from static and dynamic phenomena, which in turn are mental copies of economic realities caused by the impact of real economic processes on the mind of the observer. Thus, Schumpeter's synthetic economic model is characterized by three pairs of opposites: 1) an opposition between two real processes – circular flow and creative destruction, 2) an opposition between two types of economic behavior – management of existing channels of economic routine and entrepreneurship, and 3) an opposition between two theoretical apparatuses – statics and dynamics. (Schumpeter 1934, pp.82–3)

Schumpeter's Naturalistic Misconstruction

Schumpeter's positivism demands a causal relation between real economic processes, economic phenomena, and theories of them. At first blush, his idea of science seems to fit neatly together with his synthetic theory of development. The real opposition between static and dynamic economic tendencies *causes* the opposition between static and dynamic phenomena in the mind of the scientist, an opposition that is then abstracted into a synthetic theory including statics and dynamics. As the economy changes, it produces new phenomena, and our scientific representation of them changes in kind. But is this a reasonable account of economics science and its relation to the world? Apart from the skeptical relativism implied in this view, are we beginning to see Schumpeter perform the naturalistic misconstruction, where his theoretical principles are projected into nature as real causes of phenomena? With Husserl as our guide, we see Schumpeter confuse theories of process for real processes, theoretical relations for real causal relations, and a theory of economic life for economic life itself.

Schumpeter's naturalistic misconstruction manifests itself in at least three ways. First, he treats economic data as if it is the cause *and* effect of economic life. He describes the tendency toward equilibrium as something akin to the biological concept of "adaptation," where the economy, like an organism, tends to adapt to changes caused by external factors like population growth and technology. (Schumpeter 1934, pp.62, 216) Schumpeter argues that the "ideal state of equilibrium in the economic system, never attained, continually "striven after" (of course not consciously), changes, because the data change." (Schumpeter 1934, p.62) Here, theoretical concepts and economic data act as part of a natural process that conditions economic behavior. Creative destruction, on the other hand, is a process "where economic life itself changes its own data by fits and starts." Ibid Here a real process changes economic data, and as the data change the phenomenon of economic life, economic theory also adapts. (Ibid, p.62) Schumpeter's naturalistic misconstruction conflates phenomena caused by real processes and phenomena reconstructed by theoretical methods. As a result, Schumpeter replaces economic life with a theory of economic life. But as Husserl has shown, the positivist *must* do this so that the effects of economic life can appear *as* data for the economist to collect, analyze and explain.

In his second naturalistic misconstruction, Schumpeter mistakes conceptual relations in his synthetic theory for real relations in nature. Equilibrium is an ideal economic state and is, by definition, purely theoretical. It cannot be derived from experience because it does not, and cannot exist. But Schumpeter describes it as a sort of natural *telos* toward which the economic system itself unconsciously tends. This impossible state of being has real effects because as creative destruction shifts the qualitative value of equilibrium, the economy adapts and tends toward it. In fact, this tendency is precisely what static theory is supposed to describe. Here Schumpeter fails to maintain a clear distinction between theoretical principles and real processes.

As Husserl has shown, it is impossible for an empiricist model of representation to derive ideals, pure laws, or objective principles from experience. The only way an empiricist can apply them is by smuggling them into his theory of nature as presuppositions. Schumpeter does this when he projects his theoretical principle of interdependence and opposition into nature as if it is an opposition between real economic processes. Projected as real causes, they seem to give rise to his scientific model through physical causality, by producing phenomena in the mind of the scientific observer. In turn, Schumpeter deduces the objectivity of his theory by comparing it to the phenomena from which it was abstracted. But creative destruction and the circular flow toward equilibrium are theoretically constructed phenomena. In a classic case of naturalistic misconstruction, Schumpeter is comparing his theory to itself by "discovering" it in experience, *qua* natural causes, through scientific observation.

The third example of Schumpeter's naturalistic misconstruction is the fact that he identifies the opposition between creative destruction and the tendency toward equilibrium as the engine for economic, intellectual *and* political development. Economic development is a relation of opposition and interdependence between the activity of entrepreneurs and traditional managers, and the economic theory that describes it manifests this same opposition. Analogically, the history of economics is fueled by the opposition between academic leaders who invent research models and schools that form around these leaders in an attempt to increase the quantity of research available on the basis of the same model. In Capitalism, Socialism and Democracy, Schumpeter argues that democracy functions best when citizens elect *leaders* who will act like entrepreneurs, competing for votes by creating new methods of governing that destroy ineffective methods and corrupt leaders. (Schumpeter 1950 p.269)

Is it possible that all layers of socio-economic reality operate in accordance with Schumpeter's synthetic principles? Or is it the case that this view is a theoretical distortion caused by Schumpeter's positivist conception of empirical science? His model of science requires ideals, principles and logical concepts that cannot be derived by positivism. Positivism can only construct models on the basis the physical relation between observer and real process. In an attempt to bring theoretical science closer to real economic processes, Schumpeter naturalizes his theoretical model, smuggles his theoretical principles into nature, history, politics and academia, and acts *as if* the ideal conditions for his science are physically real, natural conditions.

Part Three: Naturalistic Misconstruction in Alan Greenspan's Labor Economics

On Oct 10, 2005, Columbus Day, Alan Greenspan made one of his last public appearances as Chairman of the U.S. Federal Reserve, delivering a speech to the Italian American Institute that was meant to reflect and shape the terms of political debate over Senator Edward Kennedy's (D-MA) proposed amendment to the Fair Labor Standards Act of 1938. If signed into law, this amendment would increase the federal minimum wage to $6.25/hr. Despite the overwhelming popularity among Americans for an increase to the federal minimum wage, the Senate has rejected 11 attempts to raise the minimum wage since 1998, which is the year the last increase kicked in for the working poor. (Harwood 2006) Workers receiving the current minimum wage earn only $10,700 a year, almost $6,000 below the poverty line for a family of three. (Murray 2006) Members of congress who voted against these increases faced sharp criticism over the issue, in part because they have signed into law more than $27,000 in cost-of-living increases for *themselves* during the same span of time.

Greenspan did not mention the minimum wage legislation directly, but his speech was clearly designed to provide the philosophical justification for voting against any minimum wage increase that did not provide tax breaks and legislative changes to offset the rise in labor costs for firms. The argument underlying the positions of both Greenspan *and* most Republicans in congress was that an increase in the minimum wage would harm the economy by making the labor-force less flexible. Greenspan's thesis is that the American economy has been able to "absorb and recover from shocks such as stock market crashes, credit crunches, terrorism and hurricanes" because of "a remarkable increase in economic flexibility," caused by "deliberate economic policy and innovations in information technology.[13]"(Greenspan 2005)

The most effective economic policies, according to Greenspan, have been those which decrease government influence in managing aggregate demand, deregulate markets to make them more flexible and competitive, and "rely on markets do the heavy lifting of adjustment." (Ibid) Flexible labor-markets, he argues, foster an environment of maximum competition, and this economic environment is sustained by the market itself without – or rather despite – government regulation of labor-markets. Echoing Greenspan's sentiments, Senator Mike Enzi (R-WY) argued that increasing the minimum wage would ossify the labor market, since employers would be discouraged from hiring new employees, and minimum wage workers would lose motivation to gain experience, training and education to climb the ranks of the company payroll. Senator Enzi introduced an alternative amendment that would "balance a minimum-wage increase with economic relief for the small businesses."

Ibid The Enzi amendment would have exempted many small-businesses from the Fair Labor Standards Act entirely. It would also put an end to the 40-hour work-week by creating a "flextime" system where workers could work more in one week and take time off the next, making it legal for employers to avoid giving employees overtime pay.

In the second part of his speech Greenspan employs key economic concepts that describe economic phenomena in a way that reflects his theoretical principles, but ignores the lived-experience of those within the labor force – those who suffer the consequences of those principles. In the process, he hides the very ethical dilemma that should be the center of the debate on minimum wage. Here is a cross-section of his argument:

> "Flexibility is most readily achieved by fostering an environment of maximum competition. A key element in creating this environment is **flexible labor markets**. Many working people, regrettably, equate labor market flexibility with job insecurity ... Despite that perception, flexible labor policies appear to *promote* job creation, not destroy it. An increased capacity of management to discharge workers without excessive cost, for example, apparently increases companies' willingness to hire without fear of unremediable mistakes. The net effect, to the surprise of most, has been what appears to be a *decline* in the **structural unemployment** rate in the United States ... Protectionism in all its guises, both domestic and international, does not contribute to the welfare of American workers. At best, it is a short-term fix at a cost of lower standards of living for the nation as a whole. We need increased education and training for those displaced by **creative destruction**, not a stifling of competition ... A consequence of our highly competitive, rapidly growing economy is that the average American will hold many different jobs in a lifetime. Accordingly, education is no longer the sole province of the young. Significant numbers of workers continue their education well beyond their twenties. Millions enroll in community colleges in later life, for example, to upgrade their skills or get new ones. It is a measure of the dynamism of the U.S. economy that community colleges are one of the fastest growing segments of our educational system" (Ibid. Boldface mine).

The four economic concepts that tie this argument together are *labor-market flexibility*, *structural unemployment*, *creative destruction* and *human capital*. In short, Greenspan argues that **flexibility** is good for the labor market because it allows employers to invest capital more efficiently and more profitably. The economy develops through the process of **creative destruction**, where old technologies and financial instruments are ushered out in favor of newer, more efficient ones. As the capital migrates with the new technologies, unprofitable firms with their rigid labor forces are replaced by newer more profitable firms with more flexible labor. This raises the standard of living for all Americans, a claim that can be supported by the apparent decline in the **structural unemployment** rate. Naturally, workers displaced by creative destruction and those who fear such displacement associate flexible labor with job insecurity. But the problem is *not* that there are no jobs out there. The problem is that displaced workers are trained in old technologies and lack the tools required in the new labor-market. This is why displaced workers need to think of themselves as investments in **human capital**, and use community college to become the labor-force of tomorrow.

Through the lens of Husserl, we can see that Greenspan conflates the theoretical relation between his concepts with the causal relation between real economic processes. This leads him to substitute his theoretical construction of a labor-force for the lived-experience of the American labor-force. For example, Greenspan argues that workers are mistaken when they associate flexible labor with job insecurity, because when one considers the economy from the perspective of equilibrium theory, the number of jobs available is not decreasing. The quantitative measurement of structural unemployment ignores the qualitative changes laborers must undertake to remain a part of the labor-force. When a worker experiences job insecurity, the concept of structural unemployment does not ease the pain. The dynamic concept of creative destruction merely justifies the phenomenon by correlating job migration with economic growth. When Greenspan celebrates the fact that 'the average American will hold many jobs in a lifetime,' he clearly does not express the meaning of job security for the average worker. For the latter, job security means having the *same* job in the *same* place for as long as she wants it. As we have seen in Schumpeter, Greenspan seems to present an objectively valid theory of the American economy; but he deduces its validity by smuggling his theoretical principles into nature to appear *as if* they are real economic processes.

Greenspan's naturalistic misconstruction of the labor-market extends fragmentary theoretical elements into what *appears* to present the whole phenomenon of the U.S. labor-market. Meanwhile, he explains away the lived economic experience of the largest part of the economy: the U.S. labor force. He has also shifted the responsibility for rectifying the negative consequences of a flexible labor-market from the demand-side to the supply-side. On his model, workers must radically change their lives to remain flexible and employable. The responsibility for unemployment is placed on the very people who are hurt most by it, who have the least to gain from creative destruction, and the least influence on managerial decision-making. Greenspan does not address the paradoxical result that those who are unemployed and have little or no income must now *invest* in themselves to find work. The causality of creative destruction dictates that when capital migrates, it migrates on the demand-side of the labor-market, not the supply side.

Concluding Remarks

In the context of Husserlian phenomenology, the economic theory of Schumpeter and Greenspan illustrates the dangers of using concepts without the proper understanding of their origin, purpose and range of deployment. Economics is the science responsible for developing our collective understanding of the business world. If these theories are grounded on psychologistic logic, they will distort our understanding of the very phenomena they intend to describe. Schumpeter's methodological errors bleed into the political debate over minimum wage through the voice of Alan Greenspan. Meanwhile, the free-market ideology that arises from out of the empiricist tradition prevails among those who manage labor-markets for firms. As a result, the opposing sides of the minimum-wage debate seem to disagree on what it *means* to be a labor-force.

When the very science responsible for educating citizens and policy-makers about labor issues ignores economic phenomena as experienced by the vast majority of citizens, it hides the ethical issues most in need of clarification. With phenomenology as our guide, we have identified the cause of naturalistic misconstruction in Schumpeter and Greenspan. But as Husserl warned in *The Crisis of the European Sciences*, "Merely fact-minded sciences make merely fact-minded people." (Husserl, 1970 p.6). The longer phenomenology waits to explicate phenomenological structures underlying all scientific phenomena, and to secure the common ground needed for a genuine dialogue between economics, philosophy and all other sciences, the greater the risk that fewer and fewer issues will emerge as problems that demand a *business ethics*.

Notes

1. Husserl considers positivism a contemporary form of empiricism, and he understands them both as fundamentally naturalistic. For the purposes of the following discussion, their differences are negligible.
2. "The fundamental defect of the empiricist's argument lies in this, that the basic requirement of a return to the "facts themselves" is identified or confused with the requirement that all knowledge shall be grounded in experience" (Ibid, p.74.)
3. More on Husserl's distinction between experience and intuition below.
4. Husserl's distinction between real and ideal will discussed below.
5. No matter how many times I observe an apple falling to the earth, my experience does not establish the absolute validity of Newton's law of gravitation. The logical validity of the law has nothing to do with falling objects, but with the relations between the logical terms. Should the earth be knocked from its orbit by an asteroid, the apple could be propelled upward, in which case my experience will have changed. In this event, Newton's law of gravitation is still valid, but the conditions required for my experiencing the apple fall to earth have changed. Husserl's point is that the logical relations between concepts and terms within Newton's theory hold *a priori* and absolutely, regardless of whether the conditions for producing an empirical reality that expresses this law in space-time ever exist. This is what we *mean* by the word 'law.'
6. Husserl (2001, p.75–100) characterizes psychologism as a form of skeptical relativism in Chapter 7 of the "Prolegomena".
7. An empiricist would try to establish the logical law of contradiction on the basis of his observation that the mental state asserting "A" cannot exist simultaneously with the mental state asserting "∼A". In turn, the principle "A = not ∼A" can be induced from the factual mental state asserting "A". Husserl retorts that we can, in *fact*, make contradictory judgments, in which case the empiricist would either have to argue that the contradictory mental state does not actually exist, or that there is no necessary law of contradiction to be had. If the empiricist argues that the law should only be induced from *correct* thinking, he smuggles the normative principle "correct" into his argument as a presupposition, in order to "discover" it in his data.
8. "The Process of Creative Destruction" is the subject of Chapter VII of Schumpeter's *Capitalism, Socialism and Democracy*, New York, Harper and Brothers Publishers,1950, pp.81–87.
9. Schumpeter (1954, p.1–45) explicates the method of "Eonomic Sociology" [*Wirtschaftssoziologie*].
10. Schumpeter often uses his terminology loosely. At times he conflates phenomena and facts, at other times he conflates real processes and facts. But as I will argue below, this is precisely the

kind of confusion Husserl has told us to expect from a philosophy of science with naturalistic principles.

11. This empiricist description of theory-building appears in Schempeter (1954, p.45)
12. For example, Schumpeter (1949, p.348) claims that the objectivity of exact sciences are never questioned because "logic, mathematics, physics and so on deal with experience that is largely invariant to the observer's social location and practically invariant to historical change: for capitalist and proletarian, a falling stone looks alike."
13. A full transcription of this speech can be found at the Federal Reserve's website: http://www.federalreserve.gov/boarddocs/speeches/2005/20051012/default.htm. C-span aired the speech live.

References

Harwood, John 2006. "War-Weary Public Wants Congress to Lead." *The Wall Street Journal*, December 14, Page A4.

Husserl, Edmund 2001. *Logical Investigations*. Vol. I, Translated by J.N. Findlay. New York: Routledge.

Husserl, Edmund 1970. *The Crisis of European Sciences and Transcendental Phenomenology, an Introduction to Phenomenological Philosophy*. Translated by David Carr. Evanston: Northwestern University Press, p. 6.

Husserl, Edmund 1969. *Ideas: General Introduction to Pure Phenomenology. Translated by W. R. Boyce Gibson*. London: Collier Books.

Husserl, Edmund 1965. *Phenomenology and the Crisis of Philosophy: Philosophy as a Rigorous Science, and Philosophy and the Crisis of European Man*. Translated by Quentin Lauer. New York: Harper & Row.

Murray, Shailagh 2006. "Minimum-Wage Increase Fails." *The Washington Post*, Thursday, June 22, 2006 p. D02.

Schumpeter, Joseph A. 1950. *Capitalism, Socialism and Democracy*, New York, Harper and Brothers Publishers, pp. 81–87.

Schumpeter, Joseph A. 1949. "Science and Ideology," *The American Economic Review* Vol. 39, no. 2, March pp. 347–348.

Schumpeter, Joseph A. 1982. "The 'Crisis' in Economics – Fifty Years Ago," *Journal of Economic Literature*, Vol. XX (September 1982); p. 1053.

Schumpeter, Joseph A. 1954. History of Economic Analysis; edited from manuscript by Elizabeth Boody Schumpeter. New York: Oxford University Press.

Schumpeter, Joseph A. 1939. *Business Cycles: A Theoretical, Historical and Statistical Analysis of the Capitalist Process, 2 Vols*. New York and London: McGraw-Hill; p. 69.

Schumpeter, Joseph A. 1936. "Review of Keynes' General Theory," *Journal of the American Statistical Association* 31 (December); p. 794.

Schumpeter Joseph A. 1934. *The Theory of Economic Development; an Inquiry into Profits, Capital, Credit, Interest, and the Business Cycle*. Translated by Redvers Opie. Cambridge, Mass: Harvard University Press, p. 61.

Mental Models, Moral Imagination and System Thinking in the Age of Globalization: A Post-Colonial Proposal

Patricia H. Werhane

Introduction

After experiments with various economic systems, we appear to have conceded, to misquote Winston Churchill, that "free enterprise is the worst economic system, except all the others that have been tried."[1] Affirming that conclusion, I shall argue that in today's expanding global economy, we need to revisit our mind sets about corporate governance and leadership to fit what will be new kinds of free enterprise and to avoid past well-entrenched colonial habits that tended to appropriate and export resources and goods for the colonial power in question. The aim is to develop a values-based model for corporate governance that will be appropriate in a variety of challenging cultural and economic settings, contributing to, rather than extracting from, developing economies.

In what follows I shall begin with an analysis of mental models from a social constructivist perspective. I shall then develop the notion of moral imagination as one way to revisit traditional mind sets about values-based corporate governance and outline what I mean by systems thinking. I shall conclude with examples for modeling corporate governance in multi-cultural settings and draw tentative conclusions about globalization.

Mental Models, Mind Sets and Social Constructivism

Although the term is not always clearly defined, 'mental model' or 'mind set' connotes the idea that human beings have mental representations, cognitive frames, or

P.H. Werhane
DePaul University, Chicago, IL, USA,
e-mail: pwerhane@depaul.edu

A version of this paper was originally presented at the IESE Business School, University of Navarra, for the 14th International Symposium on Ethics, Business and Society: "Towards a Comprehensive Integration of Ethics Into Management: Problems and Prospects". May 18–19, 2006 and forthcoming in the *Journal of Business Ethics,* 2007.

mental pictures of their experiences, representations that model the stimuli or data with which they are interacting, and these are frameworks that set up parameters though which experience or a certain set of experiences, is organized or filtered (Senge 1990, Chapter 10; Gentner and Whitley, 1997, pp.210–11; Gorman 1992; Werhane 1999).

Mental models might be hypothetical constructs of the experience in question or scientific theories, they might be schema that frame the experience, through which individuals process information, conduct experiments, and formulate theories. Mental models function as selective mechanisms and filters for dealing with experience. In focusing, framing, organizing, and ordering what we experience, mental models bracket and leave out data, and emotional and motivational foci taint or color experience. Nevertheless, because schema we employ are socially learned and altered through religion, socialization, culture, educational upbringing, and other experiences, they are shared ways of perceiving, organizing, and learning. Because of the variety and diversity of mental models, none is complete, and "there are multiple possible framings of any given situation" (Johnson 1993; Werhane 1999). By that we mean that each of us can frame any situation, event, or phenomenon in more than one way, and that same phenomenon can also be socially constructed in a variety of ways. It will turn out that the way one frames a situation is critical to its outcome, because "[t]here are . . . different moral consequences depending on the way we frame the situation," (Johnson 1993).

Our views of the world, of ourselves, of our culture and traditions and even our values orientation are constructions – all experiences are framed, ordered and organized from particular points of view. These points of view or mental models are socially learned, they are incomplete, sometimes distorted, narrow, single-framed. Because they are learned they are changeable, revisable, etc. But all experience is modeled – whatever our experiences are about – their content – cannot be separated from the ways we frame that content.

Mental models, as Peter Senge carefully reminds us, (Senge 1990) function on the organizational and systemic levels as well as in individual cognition. Sometimes, then, we are trapped within an organizational culture that creates mental habits that preclude creative thinking. Similarly a political economy can be trapped in its vision of itself and the world in ways that preclude change on this more systemic level.[2] Let me illustrate.

Mental Models in the Age of Wal-Mart: "The Wal-Mart Paradox" (Waddock 2007)

Wal-Mart is the largest retailer in the world. Last year its revenues were over two billion dollars, and it employs 1.8 million people. Its stores are located across the United States and now in many parts of the world. Its mission is "Always low prices – ALWAYS." It has enormous stores many of which now include food supermarkets, it has extremely low prices, often forcing competition out of business, it has good quality merchandise and of course, there is the unparalleled customer convenience of finding almost everything at one location (Fishman 2006).

The company is a publicly-traded corporation. It has been very successful and almost every pension fund in America includes in its portfolio Wal-Mart stock. It is the ‘darling’ of Wall Street and conservatives, according to a recent article in *Business Week* (2004). Wal-Mart provides much-needed local jobs. In a recent store opening on the South side of Chicago, for example, 25 thousand applications vied for 325 positions (Smith 2006). It has recently instituted health care coverage for long-term part-time employees who can afford the $11/month. Unfortunately, however, most part-time employees cannot afford the health care, and many Wal-Mart employees, paid under the poverty level, are also on Medicaid. The new CEO, Lee Scott, has developed environmentally sustainable initiatives aimed at selling food that is organically grown, fish that are reproducible, and the company is focusing on selling a variety of products that are in various ways ‘green’.

Wal-Mart is well-known in other respects. Where there are Wal-Mart stores, often small shops, who ordinarily cannot compete with its low prices, are forced out of business. Moreover, none of Wal-Mart’s stores are unionized; Wal-Mart forbids unions in its stores, and works to prevent them in its supplier organizations. In the recent past it has had problems with the treatment of some of its employees, and in some locations employees have been denied bathroom and lunch breaks and worked over 80 hours per week. Most interesting, despite its new focus on environmental sustainability, much of Wal-Mart’s merchandise, and almost all its apparel, is manufactured off-shore, by companies under contract with *but not owned* by Wal-Mart, often under extremely horrifying sweatshop conditions. By the term ‘sweatshop’ I meant a factory that does not meet minimum working standards in the country in which it is operating, e.g., by working employees long hours without overtime pay, paying under minimum wage, not following minimum standards for ventilation, lunch rooms, restrooms, maternity leave, child care facilities, days off, etc. as mandated in the country in which the factory operates. (Arnold and Hartman 2005) (Fishman 2006; Waddock 2007). In Bangladesh, for example, where a number of factories produce clothing for Wal-Mart the law specifies minimum wages of $20/month, the law requires decent lunch and bathroom facilities, scheduled breaks, pay for overtime, child care facilities, and maternity leaves. Yet many factories in this country flout these regulations, and unfortunately there is no enforcement of these requirements. (National Labor Committee 2005)

Linking this description back to the analysis of mental models, the way one approaches Wal-Mart and measures it successes and/or failures frames one’s conclusions about its moral successes and failures. For example, if one concludes that customer satisfaction and shareholder value are primary then Wal-Mart is a great success. If one approaches Wal-Mart from an environmental point of view, its new push to become ‘green’ is clearly a very admirable initiative. Examining Wal-Mart using a standard stakeholder map (Fig. 1) one concludes that this company creates value-added for a number of its stakeholders, in fact, the majority: its executives, customers, shareholders, and those in the community worried about the environment. Fig. 1, as a model for dealing with ethical issues, places the corporation, in the middle of the graphic. Our mental model is partly constructed by the graphic, so that our focus is first on the company, only secondarily on its stakeholders, despite,

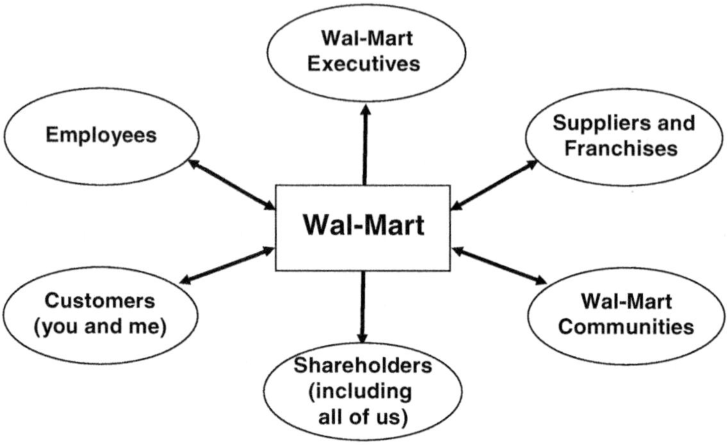

Fig. 1 "Standard" stakeholder map (Freeman, 2002)

from a stakeholder theory perspective, the claim that all critical stakeholders, those who most affect or are affected by the company, have, or should have, equal claims on value-added (Freeman 2002). Thus this focus – this attention to the center, the firm, marginalizes other stakeholders even when that is not the intent.

If one is interested in employees and the employees of Wal-Mart's suppliers, who after all are people as well, one becomes much more critical of Wal-Mart. If Wal-Mart is contributing to a culture of welfare, and/or if its goods are made under less than minimum working conditions, then moral questions arise. Is this company creating harms that are not counterbalanced by its value added in price, convenience, and shareholder returns? Is the preoccupation with "always low prices . . . ALWAYS" framing the company's decision-making in such as way that employment issues do not surface or surface sufficiently to be adequately addressed in all instances? And what happens to our mental models if we redraw the stakeholder map with employees in the middle, or, say, sweatshop workers in the middle? (Fig. 2) Now one cannot ignore the existence of these workers, they are no longer on the periphery of one's focus, even if there is still a preoccupation with low prices. Moreover, while it is hard to wrap one's mental images around 1.8 million workers, if I tweak the graphic further and place the picture of a Bangladeshi sweatshop worker in the middle, her concrete presence begins to affect our thinking about Wal-Mart's anti-union global practices. She now has a name and face; she is no longer a nameless other – merely a producer of goods. She is a real human person. (Fig. 2)

In the Wal-Mart case and others, how we look at this situation, how we draw the maps, where we focus our attention and preoccupations, our tradition and our assumptions frame these scenarios. If I tweak the maps, if I merely shift around the focus of the stakeholder map and add a picture of a real person, my frame is altered. I have broken an implicit model of exploitation that Fig. 1 intimates. Thus I have introduced an element of moral imagination – looking at a situation from a different and even more challenging perspective.

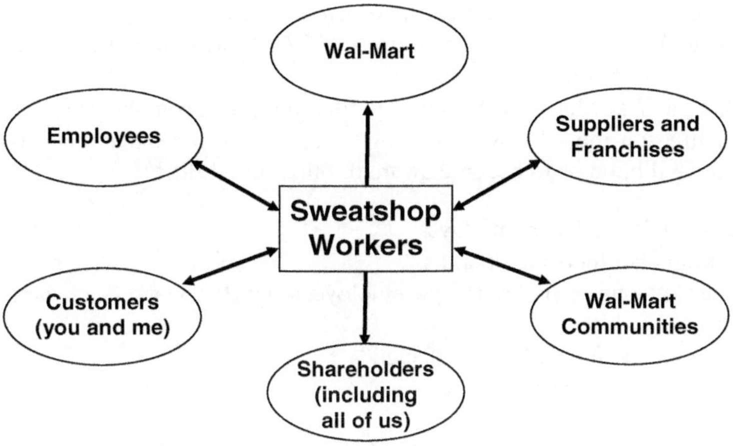

Fig. 2 Revised Stakeholder Map

Moral Imagination and Mental Models

Moral imagination can be defined as "...the ability to discover, evaluate and act upon possibilities not merely determined by a particular circumstance, or limited by a set of operating mental models, or merely framed by a set of rules" (Werhane 1999, p.93).

Thus moral imagination entails the ability to get out of a particular mind set or mental trap, and to evaluate both that mind set or mental model and, in some cases, its traps.

What, in detail does moral imagination include? On the individual level, being morally imaginative includes:

- Self-reflection about oneself and one's situation.
- Disengaging from and becoming aware of one's situation, understanding the mental model or script dominating that situation, and envisioning possible moral conflicts or dilemmas that might arise in that context or as outcomes of the dominating scheme. Secondly,
- Moral imagination entails the ability to imagine new possibilities. These possibilities include those that are not context-dependent and that might involve another mental model.
- Third, moral imagination requires that one evaluate from a moral point of view both the original context and its dominating mental models, and the new possibilities one has envisioned (Werhane 1999; Werhane 2002).

But how do we engage in this analysis while at the same time taking into account situational peculiarities, social context, and the system in which we are embedded? How do we act in a morally reasonable manner and trigger moral imagination? I think it is possible to get at, understand, revise and critique our operative mental models, but only from another perspective which itself is a set of mental models.

This shortcoming should not deter us, however, since a critical perspective is essential if we are to get out of our mental traps, in Wal-Mart's case, the driving force of its cost-driven mission.

Looking at Wal-Mart, one begins with that mission. Then one tries to disengage from that mission and ask, 'What's going on here?' How does that mission affect all that we do and blind us to become aware of other possibilities?

- What mental models are at play?
- What moral conflicts are operative?
- What is left out or ignored, e.g., employees and the workers in their supplier factories?
- What people, real people, are affected?
- What are other, new possibilities?

Then one engages the productive imagination: What are some alternatives that fit societal norms, corporate values and personal ethics? Why do employees matter? What is wrong with sweatshops in developing countries particularly in areas where there is massive unemployment? But WalMart does not own any of these factories. So how could we place responsibility for working conditions on them? What are some alternatives that challenge the *status quo*? Here again, redrawing one's stakeholder map is invaluable. What happens to one's thinking when I give a sweatshop worker a 'name and face?' (McVea and Freeman 2005; Benhabib 1992). Fig. 3 illustrates this kind of graphic. In the center is a picture of a 14-year old Bangladeshi sweatshop worker, whose average work week is 80–100 hours, under sub-human working conditions by Bangladesh legally mandated standards (National Labor Committee 2000, 2005).

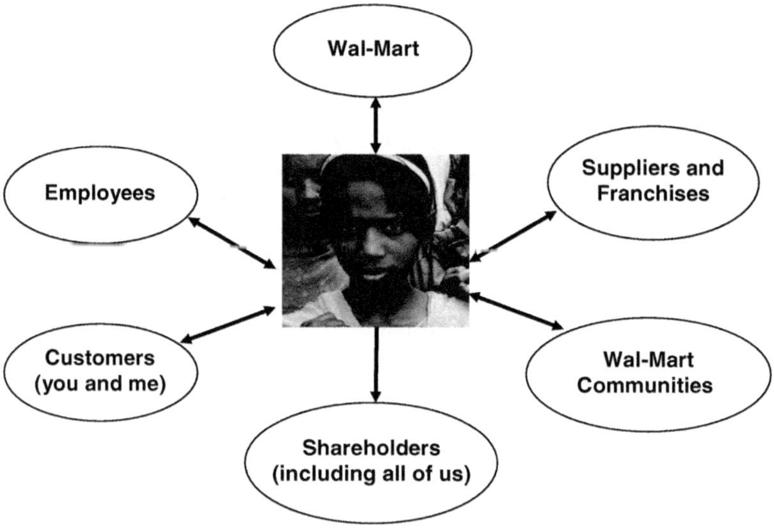

Fig. 3 "Names and faces (McVea and Freeman, 2005)

Continuing the process of moral imagination, one then engages in creative reflection and evaluation. What are some other possibilities? What are other values at stake besides low prices? How can we change the operative mental models without losing our focus on customer pricing and shareholder value?

While it is true that moral imagination often facilitates, rather than corrupts, moral judgment, the temptation is to focus primarily on individuals and individual moral judgments. But, I shall now suggest, this is an oversight. Before we can use this model to present an alternative to Wal-Mart thinking, we have to remind ourselves that all of these individuals and organizations engaged in the Wal-Mart phenomenon are in interlocking networked relationships. Taking the lead from Susan Wolf's (1999) and Linda Emanuel's (2000) work on systems thinking, and developing ideas from work on mental models and moral imagination, I shall argue that what is often missing in organizational decision-making is a systemic as well as a morally imaginative approach. Moral imagination is not merely a function of the individual imagination. Rather, moral imagination operates on organizational and systemic levels as well, again as a facilitative mechanism that may encourage sounder moral thinking and moral judgment and new models.

Moral Imagination and Systems Thinking[3]

> A system is a complex of interacting components together with the networks of relationships among them that identify an entity and/or a set of processes (Laszlo and Krippner 1998, p.51).
>
> A truly systemic view considers how a set of individuals, institutions and processes operates in a system involving a complex network of interrelationships, an array of individual and institutional actors with conflicting interests and goals, and a number of feedback loops (Wolf 1999).

A systems approach presupposes that most of our thinking, experiencing, practices and institutions are interrelated and interconnected. Almost everything we can experience or think about is in a network of interrelationships such that each element of a particular set of interrelationships affects some other components of that set and the system itself, and almost no phenomenon can be studied in isolation from other relationships with at least some other phenomenon.

Systems are connected in ways that may or may not enhance the fulfillment of one or more goals or purposes: they may be micro (small, self-contained with few interconnections), mezzo (within healthcare organizations and corporations), or macro (large, complex, consisting of a large number of interconnections). Corporations and healthcare organizations are mezzo-systems embedded in larger political, economic, legal, and cultural systems. Global corporations are embedded in many such systems. These are all examples of 'complex adaptive systems', a term used to describe open interactive systems that are able to change themselves and affect change in their interactions with other systems, and as a result are sometimes unpredictable (Plsek 2001). What is characteristic of all types of systems is that any phenomenon or set of phenomena that are defined as part of a system has properties or characteristics that are, altered, lost or at best, obscured, when the system is broken down into components. For example, in studying corporations, if one focuses simply on its organizational structure, or merely on its mission statement, or only on its employees or customers, one obscures if not distorts the interconnections and interrelationships that characterize and affect that organization in its internal and external relationships. Thus it is tempting to redraw the original stakeholder map (Fig. 1) to depict the embedded nature of global companies in communities that are seemingly peripheral to their mission and goals. (Fig. 4) However, again, despite our tweaking, the company is in the middle of this figure, attracting our priorities to the company and the to its primary and peripheral stakeholders.

Because a system consists of networks of relationships between individuals, groups, and institutions, how any system is construed and, how it operates, affects and is affected by individuals in various complex and interrelated configratuions. The character and operations of a particular system or set of systems affects those of us who come in contact with the system, whether we are individuals, the community, professionals, managers, companies, religious communities, or government agencies. An alteration of a particular system or corporate operations within a system (or globally, across systems) will often produce different kinds of outcomes. Thus part of moral responsibility is incurred by the nature and characteristics of the system in which a company operates (Emanuel 2000). For example, how Wal-Mart contracts with its suppliers affects those suppliers and their employees, as well as Wal-Mart's customers and shareholders.

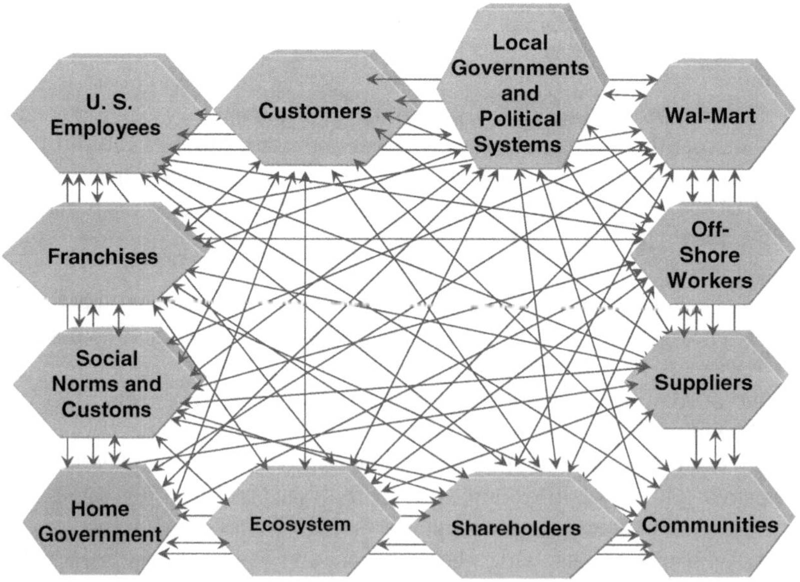

Fig. 4 Stakeholder Network

What companies and individuals functioning within these systems focus on, their power and influence, and the ways values and stakeholders are prioritized affect their goals, procedures, and outcomes as well as affecting the system in question. On every level, the way individuals and corporations frame the goals, the procedures and what networks they take into account makes a difference in what is discovered or neglected. These framing mechanisms will turn out to be important normative influences of systems and systems thinking (Werhane 2002).

Adopting a systems approach Mitroff and Linstone in their book, The Unbounded Mind, argue that any organizational action needs to be analyzed from what they call a Multiple Perspective method. Such a method postulates that any phenomenon, organization, or system of problems arising for or within that phenomenon of system should be dealt with from a variety of disparate perspectives, each of which involves different world views where each challenges the others in dynamic exchanges of questions and ideas (Mitroff and Linstone 1993, Chapter 6). A multiple perspectives approach takes into account the fact that each of us individually, or as groups, organizations, or systems creates and frames the world through a series of mental models, each of which, by itself, is incomplete. While it is probably never possible to take account all the networks of relationships involved in a particular system, and surely never so given these systems interact over time, a multiple perspectives approach forces us to think more broadly, and to look at particular systems or problems from different points of view. This is crucial in trying to address the Wal-Mart paradox. Because each perspective usually "reveals insights . . . that are not obtainable in principle from others" (Mitroff and Linstone 1993, p.98). It is also invaluable in trying to understand other points of view, even if, eventually one disagrees or takes another tactic (Werhane 2002). So a multiple perspectives approach is, in part, a multiple stakeholder approach, but with many configurations and accountability lines. It is also an attempt to shake up our traditional mind sets without at the same time ascribing too much in the way of obligation to a particular individual or organization.

A multiple perspectives approach also takes into account the fact that each of us individually, or as groups, organizations, or systems creates and frames the world through a series of mental models, each of which, by itself, is incomplete. While it is probably never possible to take account all the networks of relationships involved in a particular system, and surely never so given these systems interact over time, a multiple perspectives approach forces us to think more broadly, and to look at particular systems or problems from different points of view. This is crucial in trying to avoid problems such as those created by sweatshop labor, because each perspective usually "reveals insights . . . that are not obtainable in principle from others" (Mitroff and Linstone 1993, p.98). It is also invaluable in trying to understand other points of view, even if, eventually one disagrees or agrees to disagree. A Multiple Perspectives approach is essential if, for example, as Wal-Mart thinks about itself as a global company that affects and is affected by its suppliers and their employees and the various communities in which it contracts or operates. It is, then, part of a network as depicted in Fig. 5.

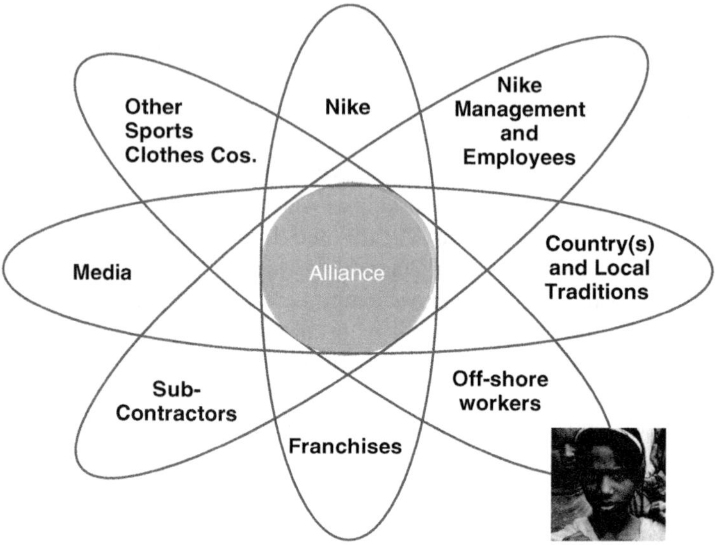

Fig. 5 Nike's alliance model (Model Courtesy of Mary Ann Leeper, COO, Female Health Company)

In every stakeholder map we draw, we prioritize our stakeholders, that is, we give them value. When Wal-Mart prioritizes low prices it is prioritizing its customers, particularly those who cannot afford fancy stores and high-priced goods. But this set of values, important as it is, needs to be put in a matrix with basic minimum moral standards for the treatment of every human being. If you sell goods that have been produced at under basic minimum human working conditions *in the country where these goods are produced,* by underpaid workers who at best, have two days leave a month (National Workers Committee 2005) one needs to rethink whether the positive value of low prices in developed countries preempts this human degradation where workers are frankly worse off than if they were unemployed.

There is one more consideration, that of individual responsibility, the responsibilities of the politicians, professionals, managers, and of individual citizens. A systems approach should not be confused with some form of abdication of individual responsibility. As individuals we are not merely the sum of, or identified with, these relationships and roles, we can evaluate and change our relationships, roles, and role obligations, and we are thus responsible for them. That is, each of us is at once byproducts of, characters in, and authors of, our own experiences. We can comprehend, evaluate, and change our mental models. Not to do so, is to misunderstand how important human choice and responsibility is to our lives (Werhane 1999). Thinking of ourselves as responsible choice-makers should enable us to project that onto those with whom we interact, even strangers and thus acknowledge strangers as equal human beings.

Globalization and Other Models

It would be unconscionable to criticize Wal-Mart without presenting a viable model for corporate governance that does not merely recommend closing this company. Its focus on low prices and the job opportunities it offers cannot be ignored. So let us take the case of Nike. Nike makes nothing it sells, nothing. All of its goods are produced by independent suppliers, most of whom are in developing countries. Recently Nike made headlines by being accused of buying goods from plants producing its products under sweatshop conditions where allegedly at least in Indonesia, women workers were beaten if they did not keep up their productivity. (Hartman *et al.*, 2003)

Nike, as Hartman, Arnold and Wokutch write (2003) has had a similar sweatshop problem. Nike owns almost no factories; rather it buys its goods from numerous manufacturers around the world. So it would appear that what these manufacturers do to get Nike goods to market has nothing to do with Nike. Often Nike had little knowledge of what went on in the plants that produced its shoes and other products. This changed, of course, when the media began to focus on the working conditions, pay, and safety in plants producing Nike products. Still, why is Nike, rather than these plants responsible, and what is the extent of that? As a result of public pressure Nike began to 'look in the mirror' at its mission, corporate image, and challenged itself to think about extending the scope of its responsibilities, engaging in what has become a concerted effort to improve sweatshop conditions not merely in the factories from which it buys but also with the suppliers to those factories. But Nike did not see this problem as merely *its* problem; rather it has taken what I called a systems perspective. That is, it sees its responsibilities as extending beyond its own employees to the system in which its products are produced. It not merely developed a strong Code of Conduct. It has expanded its influence, its employee standards, and monitoring system to its franchises and gradually, to their suppliers as well (Hartman *et al.* 2003). In this sort of case one might think of Nike's scope of responsibility in terms of gradually widening concentric circles. Its first responsibility is to its employees, customers, and shareholders; its next circle is to its contracted suppliers, the third to the suppliers of materials for those suppliers. It is again tempting to conclude that Fig. 4 depicts those relationships. But Nike has developed a model of relationships between stakeholders in a global economy where the company, Nike, is not the only focus, thus not in the center of the graphic. (Fig. 6)

In revamping their vision, Nike put names and faces on its suppliers and their workers. Moreover they formed an alliance with their primary stakeholders using their mission and code, not their organization, per se, as the binding factor. Today they are working to get commitments with their sub-contractors, those companies that supply materials to the factories making Nike goods. Nike cannot monitor everything; it is not and cannot be responsible for everything that goes on in the countries in which it has suppliers; but because of its buying power it can leverage influence and affect supplier conduct. Not to do so would be, from its own perspective, avoiding its obligations (Hartman *et al.* 2003). Interestingly, this year, 2007,

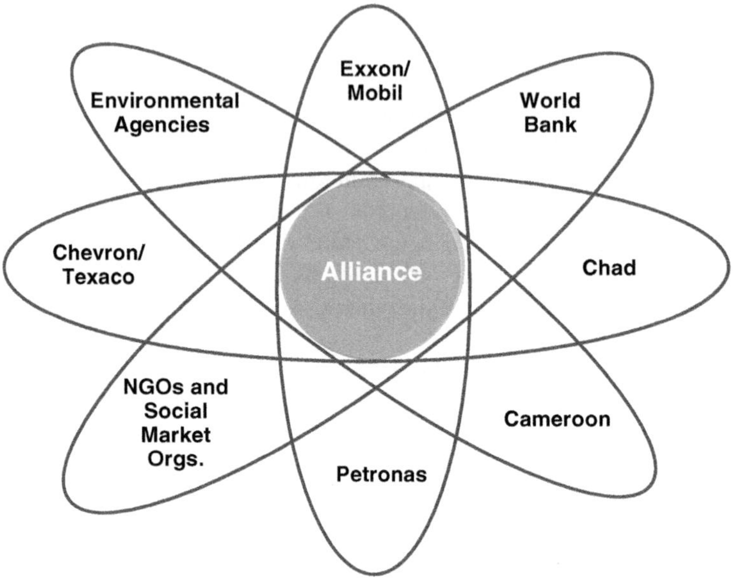

Fig. 6 ExxonMobil's Alliance Model (Model Courtesy of Mary Ann Leeper, COO, Female Health Company)

Wal-Mart has contracted with a non-profit organization in Bangladesh, the Institute for Integrated Rural Development (IIRD), to purchase clothing manufactured on a non-sweatshop factory operated by IIRD scheduled to open next year in Dhaka. (IIRD 2007) We shall see how this project evolves.

To illustrate that Nike's approach is not unique, let us look at another company, The Female Health Company (FHC), an over-the-counter publicly held for-profit

Fig. 7 The Challenge: Poorest nations and largest markets (from Prahalad 2005, p.4)

corporation. FHC began as an ordinary United States based pharmaceutical company focusing on female health. Its first and only product was and still is a female condom, the best of its kind, for which FHC holds the patent. What the Company discovered, however, was that middle-class women in developed countries have no interest in this product, and their efforts to market the female condom in the United States, despite various movie star endorsements, failed. In 1996, as the company threatened to close its doors, the COO of the company, Mary Ann Leeper received a call from the woman health minister in Zimbabwe. It seemed that women in that country had signed a petition asking for help against HIV infections, since men in that country did not practice protected sex. Daisy Nyamukapa, Manager of the HIV/AIDS Coordination Programme for Zimbabwe's Ministry of Health and Child Welfare, explained why she had called. Over 30,000 Zimbabwean women had signed a petition demanding that the government bring Leeper and her company's product, the female condom, into their country. As the President of the Chicago-based Female Health Company, Leeper was stunned and encouraged by Nyamukapa's extraordinary request. Based on her recent experience in developing an entirely new approach to marketing the female condom, Leeper had a newfound appreciation for the cultural and communication intensive nature of her company's product. But the challenge would be worthwhile only if they could reach a population that desperately needed this product.

Zimbabwe is about the same size as California and has a population of almost 12 million. The official language for governmental and business purposes is English. Approximately 19 percent of the population spoke Ndebele and 77 percent speak Shona. The urban population (3.6 million) is vastly smaller than the rural population (8.2 million).[4] The urban population is employed in the developed sectors of the economy with varying levels of education and skills, while a large portion of the rural population is engaged in subsistence agriculture.[5]

Initially Dr. Leeper thought that she could market this product in Zimbabwe in the same way she had tried in the United States. But she shortly realized that this was a grave error in reasoning. First, the country of Zimbabwe is very poor so it could not fund condoms. Thus Leeper had to find funding through international aid and development agencies and social marketing agencies in Africa. Even more difficult, she had to figure out how to reach this diverse population and various cultural and language groups and penetrate the almost universal dependence of women on their spouses. Thus she had to partner with NGOs who were familiar with customs and cultures of each village in the rural areas as well as the urban populations. Zimbabwean women were especially susceptible to risk due to their economic and social dependence on men. Most Zimbabwean women were completely financially dependent upon men, and often sex figured into that dependence.[6] For example, Leeper recalled, "In Zimbabwe, women are totally dependent on men for their well being. Most women do not earn money. The men bring in the money and help keep shelter over women's heads. It is an extremely traditional society." In many African cultures talking about sex was taboo.[7] Culturally, women were not expected to discuss or make decisions about sexuality.[8] So gradually, and with many wrong turns, Leeper developed what she later called an alliance model. She rethought her fund-raising, marketing and distribution strategies and realized that she was no longer selling a product, but was, rather, engaged in a program that marketed the female condom but had as its mission female health.

Today the female condom is sold at low cost or given away in over 100 countries, through NGOs and social marketing mechanisms customized to fit the culture and taboos of each individual, each village, and each community where it is marketed. Pricing varies depending on need, country economic development and international funding. The female condom is also marketed through social agencies in the United States to protect women in various sub-cultures in this country when men have multiple partners and do not protect themselves. Leeper's goal is to make all women independent and in control of their lives, their reproductive functions, and their health, and with Mary Robertson she has started a global female health initiative. Last year, in 2006, the company made a profit for the first time.

The Global Challenge

The Female Health Company, like Nike, had to rethink its approach to its product, to distribution, and to female users through developing an alliance model. Employing such models requires proactive corporate initiatives and the adoption of a systems approach to their operations. Still, we must ask, why would any company engage in this program? These programs take a great deal of time, effort, and ingenuity, and positive outcomes are slow to be realized. Nike has not 'converted' all its suppliers to a gentler work environment. Other companies who are engaging in these processes are also finding that this enterprise is enormously difficult. Why, then persist? Why not revert to an older model of focusing on maximizing shareholder value?

There are a number of good reasons why a systems approach is worthwhile. First, and most obviously, with the globalization of capitalism, for better or worse, corporations are now required to take into account all their primary internal *and* external stakeholders. Many companies have always done so. The difference, using this model, is the adaptation of multiple perspectives, trying to get at the mind set of each set of stakeholders from their points of view. Secondly, an alliance model brings into focus the responsibilities as well as rights of various stakeholders, not merely the corporation, but also to the individuals who affect and are affected by corporate actions. It takes seriously a "names and faces" approach.

Third, if C. K. Prahalad is correct, global marketing to what he calls 'the base of the pyramid,' the less economically developed but most populous countries, is critical for the survival and well-being of global markets. (Fig. 8) (Prahalad 2005; Ahmad, et al. 2004) Only a systemic approach will be successful in those markets. A company like Wal-Mart will defend itself in this regard, since by ordering from factories in less developed countries, they are thereby providing jobs and contributing to the economic growth of that country. But let us think about that claim, a claim commonly made by global corporations. As we learned from Adam Smith over 200 years ago, "by uniting, in some measure, the most distant parts of the world, by enabling them to relieve one another's wants, to increase one another's enjoyments,

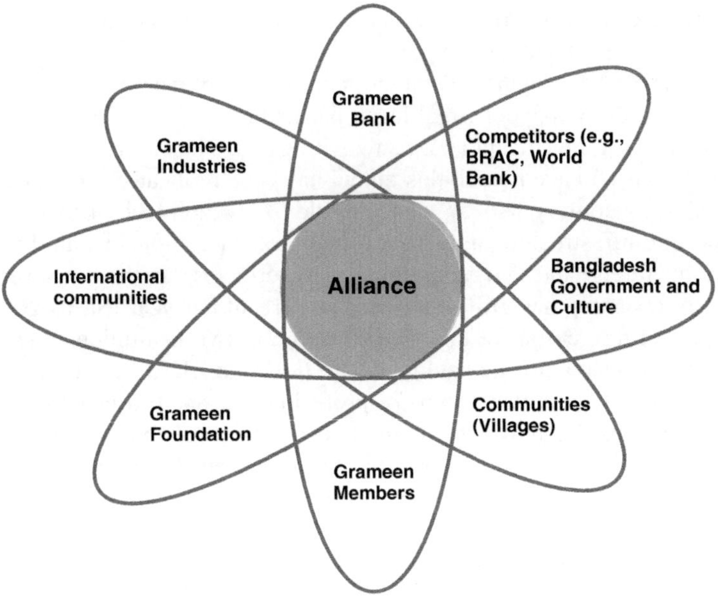

Fig. 8 The Grameen Bank Model for Poverty Elimination in Bangladesh

and to encourage one another's industry, their general tendency would seem to be beneficial" (Smith 1776; rpt. Sachs 2005). If workers are paid less than a living wage or worse, below minimum wage in the country where they live and work, particularly in a less developed country where these wages are very low,[9] they are very unlikely to have any funds left over after basic food and shelter. So they have no economic purchasing power, thus cannot contribute to increasing the demand curve necessary for economic growth. What sweatshop work does is actually take labor resources out of LDCs without increasing purchasing power in those countries, just as in earlier times colonial powers often exported natural resources from those countries they controlled. Thus economic development was not possible, and was even truncated and resources are funneled back into developed countries in the form of cheap goods, services or natural resources. (Fig. 10) Stuart Hart argues, for example, that in the 18th and 19th century what is now India, Pakistan and Bangladesh was an area rich in natural resources and primed for economic development. All of this was halted and set-backs occurred that lasted almost two centuries when the East India Company, a British company, virtually invaded the area. (Hart 2007)

If a global economy depends on new markets and if these are increasingly at the base of the pyramid as Prahalad demonstrates, how should these markets be developed? Jeffrey Sachs and others have argued that the rich nations have not given enough in various forms of focused long-term foreign aid to improve country transportation, agriculture development and land reform, water, sanitation, and other macro development initiatives, health care improvement, nutrition and education, and protection against natural disasters (Sachs 2005). These proposals depend on stable government/public-private partnerships and a developed rule of law. In many countries of the world neither is possible.

In addition, Sachs recognizes the importance of microfinancing and public/private partnerships on the village or tribal level, particularly in countries where the government is likely to be corrupt as we saw with Chad. Thus all is not without hope. Returning to our alliance model, this model has been replicated with great success in Bangladesh, a country with an unstable rule of law and lack of financing to develop a decent infrastructure, a welfare system, transportation, etc. all the elements necessary for foreign aid to have an impact. Nevertheless, in the last several years, Bangladeshi economy has grown at over five percent per year (Sachs 2005, p.13). At least part of the reason for this growth is due to two institutions: the Grameen Bank of Bangladesh, a private banking institution, and BRAC, the Bangladesh Rural Advancement Committee, a not-for profit internationally funded organization. Their contributions that have contributed to economic growth can be found primarily in their massive microfinancing projects throughout the rural communities in this over populated extremely poor flood-infested country that Transparency International yearly ranks at the bottom of the corruption index (Transparency International 2005). Again, these are alliance projects, as illustrated by the Grameen Bank's lending microfinance initiatives, which to date has moved over two million women and their families out of poverty and given them lives of dignity and self-respect. Yet, the Grameen Bank is a for-profit enterprise that has never lost money (Fig. 10).

Conclusion

In a global world where companies are exploring as well as exploiting new markets, such development requires new ways of thinking, what I have described as systems thinking. The use of moral imagination helps managers to question and revisit their traditional and sometimes parochial models for corporate governance and valuation, changing the focus of attention from the company at the center to its alliance partners. While this way of thinking might appear to belie profitability, with an unexplored and underdeveloped market at the 'base of the pyramid,' companies engaged in long-term strategies for survival and growth might want to heed the possibilities in this market sector (Ahmed *et al.* 2004). But without recognizing the value of workers as people and their contributions and the positive market effects of paying workers living wages, this exploration will merely be exploitation to improve the lives of the most fortunate. As developed markets become saturated, this strategy is bound to lead to corporate failure. At least, that is my conclusion.

Notes

1. Churchill is quoted as claiming, "It is said that democracy is the worst form of government except all those other forms that have been tried from time to time" (Churchill 1947).
2. This section on mental models derives from my earlier work on this topic. See Werhane 1999, Werhane 2002.

3. This section on systems thinking is a revised version of a previous publication. See Werhane 2002.
4. *National Health Profile* (1996) <http://209.88.90.4> (accessed on 17 November 2000)
5. *Doing Business in Zimbabwe* (PriceWaterhouse: 1995): 7.
6. *Women and HIV/AIDS* Fact Sheet No. 242 World Health Organization, <Http://www.who.int/inf-fs/en/fact242.html> (accessed on. June 2000).
7. "Leaders: The Battle With AIDS," *The Economist* 15 July 2000:17.
8. *Women And HIV/AIDS* Fact Sheet No. 242 World Health Organization. <Http://www.who.int/inf-fs/en/fact242.html> (accessed on June 2000).
9. The counter example is the existence of foreign workers in industrialized countries. Although often paid poorly by those country standards, if these workers come from poor countries they are able to save, living by their native country standards.

References

'The Costco Way'. 2004, *Business Week.* April 12, 49.

Ahmed, P., Gorman, M. E., and Werhane, P. H.. 2004. 'Hindustan Lever and Marketing to the Fourth Tier', *International Journal of Entrepreneurship and Innovation Management.* 495–511.

Arnold, D. and Hartman, L.. 2005. 'Beyond Sweatshops: Positive Deviancy and Global Labor Practices', *Business Ethics: A European Review,* 14, 425–6461.

Benhabib, S. 1992. *Situating the Self.* Routledge, New York.

Churchill, W. 1947. *Speech to the House of Commons*, November 11.

Emanuel, L. 2000. 'Ethics and the Structures of Health Care', *Cambridge Quarterly,* 9, 151–168.

Freeman, R. E. 2002. 'Stakeholder Theory of the Modern Corporation', in T. Donaldson, P. Werhane and M. Cording, (eds.), *Ethical Issues in Business,* 7th ed. Upper Saddle River, NJ: Prentice Hall. pp. 38–49.

Gentner, D. and Whitley, E. W. 1997. 'Mental Models of Population Growth', in M. Bazerman, D. Messick, A. Tenbrunsel and K. A. Wade-Benzoni (eds.) *Environment, Ethics, and Behavior.* New Lexington Press, San Francisco.

Gorman, M. 1992. *Simulating Science.* Indiana University Press, Bloomington, IN.

Hartman, L., Arnold, D. and Wokutch, R. 2003. *Rising Above Sweatshops.* Praeger Press, Westport, CT.

Hart, Stuart and Sharma, S. 2007. *Capitalism at the Crossroads.* Second edition. Upper Saddle River, NJ: Wharton School Publishing.

Johnson, M. 1993, *Moral Imagination.* University of Chicago Press, Chicago.

Laszlo, A. and Krippner, S. 1998. 'Systems Theories: Their Origins, Foundations and Development', *Systems Theories and a Priori Aspects of Perception,* J. Scott Jordan (ed.) Elsevier: Amsterdam.

McVea, J. and Freeman, R. E. 2005. 'A Names-and-Faces Approach to Stakeholder Management', *Journal of Management Inquiry,* 14, 57–69.

Mitroff, I. and Linstone, H.1993. *The Unbounded Mind.* Oxford University Press, New York.

National Labor Committee. 2000. *The Hidden Face of Globalization: What the Corporations Don't Want us to Know,* Video documentary.

National Labor Committee 2005 www.nlc.org (accessed April 5, 2005)

Plsek P. 2001. 'Redesigning Health Care with Insights from the Science of Complex Adaptive Systems', *Crossing the Quality Chasm: A New Health System for the 21st Century.* National Academy Press: Washington, DC.

Prahalad, C. K. 2005. *The Fortune at the Bottom of the Pyramid.* Pearson Education: Upper Saddle River, NJ.

Sachs, J. 2005. *The End of Poverty.* Penguin Press: New York.

Senge, P. 1990. *The Fifth Discipline.* Doubleday: New York.

Smith, A. 1776 and 1976. *The Wealth of Nations,* R. H. Campbell and A. S. Skinner (ed.) Oxford University Press: Oxford.

Smith, S. D. 2006. 'Wal-Mart gets 25 Thousand applications for its Evergreen Park Store', *Crain's Chicago Magazine* January 25, p. 1.

Transparency International, http://www.trans.de/index.html, accessed 2005.

Waddock, S. 2007. 'Corporate Citizenship: The Dark-Side Paradoxes of Success', In Cheney, G., S. K. May, and J. Roper (eds.): 2007. *The Debate Over Corporate Social Responsibility.* Oxford University Press: New York.

Werhane, P. H. 1999. *Moral Imagination and Management Decision-Making* Oxford University Press: New York.

Werhane, P. H. 2002. 'Moral Imagination and Systems Thinking', *Journal of Business Ethics*, 38, 33–42.

Werhane, P. H. 2004. 'The Principle of Double Effect and Moral Risk: Some Case Studies of US Transnational Corporations', *Responsibility in World Business: Managing Harmful Side-effects of Corporate Activity,* Lene Bomann-Larsen and Oddny Wiggin (ed.). United Nations University Press: New York and Japan.

Werhane, P. H., R. Velamuri and E. D. Boyd 2005. 'Corruption', *The Responsible Corporation. Volume II,* Kirk Hansen (ed.) Sage Publishers: London.

Wolf, S. 1999. 'Toward a Systemic Theory of Informed Consent in Managed Care', *Houston Law Review,* 35: 1631–1681.

World Bank 2002. www.worldbank.org/afr/ccproj/project/pro_overview.htm (Accessed January 15, 2002)

Business Ethics Beyond the Moral Imagination: A Response to Richard Rorty[1]

Paul T. Harper

Introduction

In August of 2005, Richard Rorty gave a keynote speech to the Society of Business Ethics entitled, "Is Philosophy Relevant to Applied Ethics?" My aim in this paper is to build on Rorty's talk, and to imitate some of his argumentative method. Rorty explored two distinct but related dimensions of moral discourse, e.g. the philosophical and the pedagogical. He comes to the important conclusion that if applied ethicists are going to effect a change in the ethical culture of institutions and participate in the progress of moral development of individuals, then the ethics curriculum must come in for some overdue scrutiny.

Theorists who engage in moral philosophy seek to understand what constitutes an ethical outlook and also how that outlook can change over time and across space. Similar to Rorty, ethicists in a philosophically speculative mode do the important work of attempting to articulate what is always already beyond the horizon of human knowledge. Though speculative ethicists are dubious to the attempts to separate claims of "what there is" from claims of "what we can know about 'what there is,' " they do hold out for the hopeful chance that claims of "who we are" can be meaningfully separated from claims of "who we can be." Theirs is a contingent future with an ever-broadening moral horizon. The speculative mode of theorizing has the advantages of being able to provide a richer account of human ethical behavior that is also pragmatically prudent. As I will argue, if there is such thing as moral progress, and I hope there is, it is probably the result of these speculative efforts.

The second dimension I'll call pedagogical because it augments the speculative dimension by considering the means for the moral improvement of people and their attendant institutions. The Greeks placed a high premium on theories and techniques of moral education precisely because they always assumed the priority of a thoughtful citizenry as the most important precondition for a flourishing democracy. From the bardic performances of Hesiod and Homer, to the performance of the dithyrambic tragedies of Aeschylus, Sophocles, and Euripides at the annual festival

P.T. Harper
Doctoral candidate at the University of Virginia
e-mail: harperpos@gmail.com

M. Painter-Morland, P. Werhane (eds.), *Cutting-edge issues in Business Ethics*,

of Dionysus, through the literary dialogues of Socrates and Plato and the peripatetic dispatches of Aristotle, the ultimate contribution of the Greeks was to make clear the intimate connection between ethics and education. Rorty revives some of the Greek spirit by querying whether we are being well served by the dominant mode of philosophical education. I will argue that not only is the content of moral education a central consideration for any ethical theory, it will also prove to be the bedrock to any theory of leadership.

This paper will progress as follows. In the first section, I will reproduce Richard Rorty's argument for moral progress from his Society of Business Ethics address. He grounds his theory in the notion of moral imagination and, therefore, it is that concept that I will scrutinize. My argument will be that his notion of the moral imagination is not robust enough to procure the kind of moral progress he desires. In the second section I will explicate the intellectual paradigm that I think both explains and produces the desired innovations in our moral understanding: critique. Through a consideration of Michel Foucault, I will demonstrate why critique allows for a broader and clearer pedagogical platform for moral development and leadership. In the third section, I will outline the shape of the pedagogy that I think would not only serve to reinvigorate business ethics and make ethical discourse more of a reflection of our contemporary concerns. We must differentiate ourselves from the past so not to repeat it.

The embrace of "difference" that I am calling for has many pedagogical implications and, therefore, must be reinforced by the leadership curriculum. Specifically, we need to find ways to identify and then listen to the people at the margins because there is something about being on the borders of ethical conversation that provides insight about the assumptions operating within the moral core. Not only must we find ways to incorporate the experience of marginal people, we also need to experience what it means to be marginalized. My leadership prescriptions, then, will be a set of exercises where leaders can gain an intimate knowledge of life on the ethical frontier.

Richard Rorty and Patricia Werhane on the Moral Imagination

In this section I will cover Rorty's argument for moral imagination as the engine of moral progress. The peculiar challenge for my paper is that I need to reference a speech that is not in the public domain. For the benefit of my readers, then, I will reproduce the passages that I think best summarize the portions of his argument that I think are relevant to my argument. Rorty's argument for moral progress runs as follows:

> One great divide in contemporary philosophy is between people who still believe something like [absolute justification], and those who, like me, believe nothing of the sort. For us, there is no particular connection between right action and clear thinking. There were clear-eyed Nazis and muddled saints. There is no connection between the skill of justifying one's beliefs – rhetorical effectiveness – and having the right beliefs. Being able to have the right beliefs and to do the right thing is largely a matter of luck – of being born in a certain place

> and a certain time. For purposes of having true beliefs about the movements of heavenly bodies, Aristotle was born at a bad time and place and Newton a better one. For purposes of knowing whether either torture or sodomy is a moral abomination, all of us were born into a better culture than were those who worked for the Inquisition.
>
> For those of us who hold this view, the obvious problem is how to think of moral progress. If there is nothing of the sort that Plato postulated – an underlying sense of right and wrong that is common to all human beings at all times and places – can we still say that we have made moral progress since the days of the Inquisition? If we do not have a faculty called "reason" that can be relied upon to help us make the right moral decisions, how can we make sense of the claim to make better decisions now than when we were callow adolescents? The best answer to these questions, I think, is that individuals become aware of more alternatives, and are therefore wiser, as they grow older. The human race as a whole has become wiser as history has moved along. The source of these new alternatives is the human imagination. It is the ability to come up with new ideas, rather than the ability to get in touch with unchanging essences, that is the engine of moral progress. John Dewey quoted with approval Shelley's dictum that morality only "arranges the elements that poetry has created" (Rorty 1991).

One of the lessons that Rorty has culled from the study of the history of culture is that our species improves with age, both technologically and socially. In other words, humans are not doomed to repeat the same decisions; we learn. Further, the knowledge available to any person or people accrues over time. We benefit from the civilizations that have passed before ours, and those that come next will benefit from the achievements and the failures of our own age.

Obviously, this line of reasoning has the odor of Hegel's historical consciousness. But, I believe that while Rorty's argument displays his historical consciousness in the passages cited above, I do not think that he believes in an ultimate Historical Consciousness or Absolute Knowledge. Contra Hegel's, Rorty's historical progression includes no eschatology or noble end-state. For Rorty, there is no "end of history" and this poses a particular problem for his theory. Hegelians and Marxists have a built-in culminating point in their philosophies of history that, like inertia, pulls human history towards it. In their theories, the endgame explains the *motion* of history and, with an inertia-like attraction, procures the historical progression. Rorty has to rely on a different kind of explanation. It is the moral imagination that is the engine of progress for his theory of progress.

> Moral progress is not, on this pragmatist view, a matter of getting clearer about something that was there all the time. Rather, we make ourselves into new kinds of people by inventing new forms of human life. We make progress by having more alternatives to consider...
> The emphasis I have been placing on the role of imagination follows a line of thought familiar from the work of Patricia Werhane. But I am inclined to adopt a more radical stance than hers. Werhane says that she realized that "ignorance of moral theory and lack of moral reasoning skills" were not enough to explain "why ordinary, decent, intelligent managers engage in questionable activities and why these activities are encouraged or even instigated by the climate or culture of companies they manage." This realization, she says, led her to realize that "something else was involved: a paucity of what I have come to label 'moral imagination'" Her book argues that "moral imagination is a necessary but not sufficient condition for creative managerial decision-making" (Werhane 1999).
>
> I suspect that it may, in fact, be sufficient, as well. I think of moral imagination not as a supplement to moral theory and moral reasoning skills, but as pretty much all you need. Although an acquaintance with moral theory may sometimes come in handy, you

> can usually get along quite well without it. The principles formulated by thinkers like Kant, Mill, and Rawls provide handy little summaries of sub-sets of our moral intuitions. Invoking such principles speeds deliberation, but it does little to help with the tough cases – the ones where institutions conflict (Rorty 2006).

For Rorty, there is a fairly direct connection between the degree of moral progress a culture can claim and the size of its basket of alternative solutions to hard cases. As is clear from these passages, Rorty believes that modern philosophers have spent most of their time asking the wrong side of the moral question. They are convergence theorists. What I mean by this is that modern ethical theorists have worked hard to promote a method for ethical decision-making that seeks to winnow down the number of possible solutions to any problem. Convergence serves their intellectual goal of producing some sort of uniformity across decision makers. In other words, they have served their moral universe well if through their moral methodologies they can get most reasonable people to arrive at the same reasonable solution most of the time.

Rorty is a divergence theorist and, therefore, brings a more post-modern sensibility to the ethics table. For him, it is not about limiting the number of reasonable responses but precisely the opposite. Divergence theorists are not interested in foreclosing on the future but, instead, find their motivation in the *idea* of a future unknowable in advance and, therefore, ripe with opportunities for novelty. "We create new forms of human life . . ." by not being overly committed to current and past modes of culture, and ". . . we have more alternatives to consider" (Rorty 2006) when we become less satisfied with the alternatives currently under consideration. The divergence side of moral reasoning is more interested in multiplying the number of questions we ask of any one situation than it is interested in trying to posit the same solution to most moral questions.

Further, it is only in an environment where the future has not been foreclosed or colonized that the imagination can play an informative role in the decision making process. The problem of convergence as a theoretical outlook is that in its attempt to eliminate uncertainty of effect it smothers diversity of thought. There is a significant difference between the elimination of uncertainty and the management of uncertainty: Managers of uncertainty are leaders rather than Gestapos. And philosophers that seek to eliminate uncertainty plant the seeds of their discipline's demise.

Rorty believes that moral imagination moves morality forward because by it leaders can grasp a novel solution to customary questions that can then change the way we problematize people, places, and things in the present tense. In other words, the moral imagination can change with the way we think about solutions by changing the way we think about problems. Or, stated another way, we are opened to the future by continuing to struggle and rethink those understandings that have become commonplace and quotidian in the present.

This stance differs from that of the convergence theorist because of its risk profile. Through their attempt to eliminate uncertainty, convergence theorists ultimately hope to eliminate risk. But this is folly for two reasons. First, convergence theorist leave themselves open to the risk that they attempt to sweep under the rug precisely because they did not find a way to convert the risky element from a strategic liability to a strategic asset. Convergence theorists are particularly prone to fall prey to the return of the repressed or oppressed. The second reason why the hope for the elimination of risk is folly is that where there is no risk there is little return. Divergence theorists are willing to risk their comfort and stability for the idea of a better world order. For divergence theorists, then, the risk is that they or their children will end up with a world less attractive than the one they helped to undermine. In their attempt to expand the bandwidth of moral possibility, the starry-eyed divergence theorist can easily become complicit with the creation of a different world that is not at the same time particularly progressive. But, and this is important, divergence theorist are *optimistic* about the future of humanity and, though the path to progress is sure to be fraught with foibles and fall-backs, we believe in the long run humanity is more likely to be better off than worse off.

There is a final distinction of Rorty's that still remains to be explained and that is the difference between his version of the uses of moral imagination and that of Patricia Werhane. He claims that he has "adopted a more radical stance than hers" and only now can I begin to describe the contours of Rorty's supplement. According to the philosophical interpretation that I have laid out so far, it would be best to characterize Werhane as a convergence theorist, one who still clings to the idea that the moral imagination needs to be domesticated by reason to be of use in moral deliberation. While she acknowledges the emancipatory power of the imagination in the service of human affairs, she still trembles in front of the idea an uncertain and risky future. Thus, I detect hesitancy in her moral theory, a theory that points the way out of our current morass but is unable to separate herself from some of our traditional philosophical confusions. Rorty, on the other hand, seems to have purged himself of the traditional modern philosophical confusions and is perfectly willing to risk adopting new ones.

My comments should strike readers as somewhat ironic because no theorist within the field of business ethics has worked harder to get both theorists and managers to take the moral imagination seriously. Out of fairness, then, I want to take a few moments and revisit her paper "Moral Imagination and the Search for Ethical Decision Making in Management." It is this paper where she most clearly defines the moral imagination and also recounts its origins in the Scottish Enlightenment. This is also the paper that Rorty cites when he makes his own contrasting comments concerning the moral imagination.

> The role of imagination is crucial for an understanding of Smith's notion of sympathy and indeed his whole moral psychology. Smith argues that each of us has an active imagination which enables us mentally to recreate feelings, passions, and the point of view of another. In this imaginative process one does not literally feel the passion of another, but one is able to "put oneself in another's shoes," so to speak, and to understand what another is experiencing from their perspective (Werhane 1998, p.6).

Werhane follows David Hume and Adam Smith in their desire to provide some sort of explanation of how humans grow to care about persons other than themselves. These philosophers theorize from a position that assumes humans are fundamentally social creatures. But, their position does not take it for granted that the fundamentally social nature of humanity also makes the species fundamentally *communal*; the fact that humans are social creatures is only the beginning of the moral inquiry, not its end. Therefore, their studies of ethics center on moral psychology because that is the mechanism through which they believe the fundamentally social character of humanity gets refined and subsequently expressed in the achievement of community.

Sympathy, according to Werhane, is the lynchpin of Smith's moral theory. She characterizes this attitude as the result of an active imagination reaching out and latching on to the lives and experiences of others; it is a moral intuition of sorts. Though she is careful not to overstate the knowledge that one can gain from the moral imagination, e.g. one cannot know that their intuition of what another person is actually experiencing or that one's interpretation of another's experiences maps on to the interpretation the other person is making about their own experiences. But, that is not the point. The moral imagination is more or less an attitude. It reflects a desire, whether large or small, of a person to consider the experience of others in coming to our own understanding of the world. The moral imagination, in this sense, also plays a strong revising role in that how we intuit the experience of others challenges the understanding of the world we would have otherwise. What else could sympathy be if not the ability we have to value another person's experience as much as our own and sometimes even more.

"Smith breaks with a rationalist tradition by linking moral judgment to moral sentiment. Moreover, it is moral imagination along with sympathy that helps to discern what society ought to approve of, thus shaping moral rules out of community rather than individual values" (Werhane 1999, p.94). For Werhane it is the ability for us to sympathize that is paramount when it comes to codifying some sort of guidelines that will function as the basis, or contract if you will, of a community. A human community that flourishes is one where the constituents feel for their fellows. Again, it is the moral imagination that underlies our ability to sympathize with others and, therefore, it is the moral imagination that for Werhane is the iconic expression of our social natures.

> But Smith's work is limited by his assumption that all of us deal with the world in the same way – through the conceptual scheme of a Scottish gentleman. So, on that assumption one can more easily project and sympathize with another person or make self-evaluations, and actually be correct a good deal of the time. But each of us functions from a set of conceptual schemes, schemes which most of us are only vaguely aware. And these schemes are not identical to those through which others experience. Smith's analysis introduces the notion of moral imagination, but it cannot take into account how one sympathizes with others whose view of the world is not that of a Scottish gentleman, nor can it account for how it is we can reshape our own conceptual schemes" (Werhane 1999, p.96).

In this passage, Werhane introduces the problem of "difference" and frames it as a limit on the abilities of the moral imagination. She considers the possibility that moral conclusions supposedly based on sympathy among people who are identical may not be very sympathetic at all but, rather, uncritical assumptions based on perceptions of sameness. Therefore, sympathetic intuitions resulting from an active moral imagination cannot be the only basis of community and civil agreement. For

Werhane, sympathetic moral intuitions must be *domesticated* by some proxy for rationality before they can be of use in the process of social construction. It is precisely this domestication that I think Rorty is criticizing when he states: "I think of moral imagination not as a supplement to moral theory and moral reasoning skills, but as pretty much all you need" (Rorty 1991).

It is the search for moral minimums that separates Werhane from the pragmatists she cites. The moral minimums show up in many places within Werhane's work. One can find them in the tropes under consideration, e.g. such as the overlapping Venn Diagrams of Michael Walzer and the intersecting sets of interests (imaginary or real) representing John Rawls' reflexive equilibrium on the Cartesian plane. The moral minimums are necessary because Werhane is a "rights" theorist and, as such, is involved in a project that attempts to articulate the least that we should be able to expect from each other regardless of cultural, racial, ethnic, national, sexual, or economic backgrounds. Hers is a moral theory of the lowest common denominator. In contrast, the pragmatist project is an attempt to articulate moral maximums.

Pragmatists want a society not based on the minimum that we can expect from the group but instead based on the maximum that we can expect from each other. Our ideals need to be somewhat idealistic. Also, it is by having expectations that seek to maximize an individual's contribution that we embrace the kind of diversity so often enumerated in social theory but still so neglected in social composition and so misrecognized in social interaction.

The problem that both Rorty and Werhane are left with is that moral imagination, while a useful bulwark against theories promoting pure or extreme rationalism or empiricism, may not provide the most useful foundation for a moral philosophy that seeks not only to provide for human survival but also to promote human flourishing. Rorty, unlike Werhane, has an entire corpus replete with contributions of the kind that I am promoting. Werhane, on the other hand, has done much to help us understand the modern philosophical categories but, unlike Rorty, she has not deconstructed them all the way down. In other words, she gives a very modern critique of modern philosophy. I think that this poses significant limits on her moral philosophy.

If, as Werhane suggests, the moral imagination is insufficient to the task of ethical and political reasoning – e.g. its "sympathetic" intuitions did not stop European imperialism – it is not because it needs to be domesticated by some form of rationality but because we need to start the ethical inquiry with a different conception of human *thought.* I think that the real problem for the procurement of progress is not whether there is an absence or surplus of moral imagination but something much more fundamental than that. *What moral progress needs is thought of a particular kind.* In other words, I want to move beyond or underneath the problematization of rationality in relation to imagination and toward a conception of thought that renders that relationship uninformative. To frame this up a bit, it is not a matter of 'to imagine or not to imagine' but 'to think or not to think.' Further, and in contrast to most narratives of the history of modern philosophy, it is not about thought that can be characterized as either rational or empirical, but about thought that can be characterized as traditional or innovative. I believe that we need to theorize more about the conditions under which this kind of thought becomes possible.

Rorty's professional project has been to provide the intellectual basis for theorists to push beyond the shopworn conventions of modern traditionalism toward a reinvigoration of the grand philosophical tradition. Thus, inspired by his example, I want to change the frame of this conversation about moral progress from one of the legitimacy of modern philosophical categories and concepts in the service of moral progress to a discourse concerning the critical role *thought* plays in the movements of the world and the vacillations of its citizens. To this end, I will divert the stream of philosophy under our consideration. The time has come to make a Continental excursion.

The Three-Dimensions of Moral Progress: From Enlightenment to Critique

> Kant ... describes Enlightenment as the moment when humanity is going to put its own reason to use, without subjecting itself to authority; now, it is precisely at this moment that the critique is necessary, since its role is that of defining the conditions under which the use of reason is legitimate in order to determine what can be known, what must be done, and what may be hoped (Foucault 1997, pp.303–304).[2]

French philosopher Michel Foucault expands on the notions and possibilities of moral progress by reinvigorating the modern critical tradition that has its genealogical roots in Immanuel Kant. This is most clearly exhibited in his article "What is Enlightenment?" (Kant 1784) which is a direct allusion to Kant's earlier work of the same title. I find Foucault's essay on Kant useful for the way it provides an alternate characterization of modernity, one that is particularly useful to me in my desire to change the conversation.

I have privileged Foucault's inquiry into the notion of Enlightenment because he is roughly our contemporary and, therefore, has the advantage of having the benefit of a couple of hundred years of social, cultural, political, and military history. Where Kant is trying to understand how something novel could change the way we experience the world, Foucault is trying to understand how something that was *supposed* to be new never really materialized. If Kant is asking "What difference does today make with respect to yesterday?" Foucault is asking "Why is today no different from yesterday?" Both theorists were seeking to understand progressive change, but from a different place of enunciation and with different hopes. Kant hoped that he could be the impetus of progress by exhorting the masses to move ahead. Foucault hoped that we could better reconcile our espoused ideals with our own histories. Kant's perspective was that of a philosopher or theologian, Foucault's was that of a historian.

The question "What is Enlightenment?" and the question "What is Moral Progress?" are two sides of the same coin. I will be suggesting that moral progress is served by the tension between two perspectives on Enlightenment: the "speculative" of Kant and the "historical" of Foucault.[3] The challenge of identifying and analyzing our own moral problems – of "problematizing" the present, to use Foucault's jargon – is simply our attempt to represent the overlapping portions of these two perspectival dimensions. So, in the mode of classic dialectics, I am claiming that when it comes to moral progress *the struggle is the thing*. Critique, then, is the theoretical offspring of this process (Hoy 2004).

In his interpretation of Kant's essay on Enlightenment, Foucault makes three insights into the relationship between social thought and morality: Enlightenment is an activity, Enlightenment requires courage, and Enlightenment is experimental. It is important to note that these insights could easily be attributed to Kant himself. I will be calling them Foucault's because it is through his work that these organizational tropes in Kant's text became clear to me. In the remainder of this section, then, I will describe each of these tropes in turn and then provide a larger reflection on the effect they have on the theory of moral progress expounded by Rorty.

Enlightenment is an Activity

> Thinking back on Kant's text, I wonder whether we might not think of the age of modernity as an attitude rather than as a period of history. And by "attitude," I mean a mode of relating to contemporary reality; a voluntary choice made by certain people; in the end, a way of thinking and feeling; a way, too, of acting and behaving that at one and the same time marks a relation of belonging and presents itself as a task. No doubt, a bit like what the Greeks called an ethos. And consequently, rather than seeking to distinguish the "modern era" from "pre-modern" or "postmodern," I think it would be more useful to try to find out how the attitude of modernity, ever since its formation, has found itself struggling with attitudes of "countermodernity" (Foucault 1997, pp.309–310).

In this passage Foucault is trying to account not only for the energy that infused Enlightenment thinkers and their systematic forays but also the healthy self-doubt that many of them had toward their own thought (Kant was no exception). Natural philosophers were no longer satisfied with the mechanistic descriptions of the world they inherited, theologians were no longer satisfied with the notion that people had no volition, politicians were no longer satisfied with their subordination to the church, and the expanding middle-class was no longer satisfied with the goods and services readily available in their home towns and countries. In light of all this dissatisfaction it is no wonder that Foucault would seek to characterize it as an age where most people's desires appear to have been unrequited.

But, simply pointing out that the general will in the West was one of dissatisfaction does not capture the impetus of Kant's exhortation or Foucault's critique. If it was David Hume that Kant credits for shaking him out of his dogmatic slumber, it was just as surely Kant whose literary bolt of lightning functioned to wake up a populace, a region, a nation, and an idea called the "West." In other words, Kant was not just dissatisfied with the philosophical tradition but with the general malaise that he perceived to be covering his cultural contemporaries. Unlike other philosophers, though, Kant had grown impatient with the mere fact of dissatisfaction and, therefore, made his theoretical consideration of the notion of the Enlightenment a strong critique of its benefactors.

Consider the following passage from Kant's essay:

> Laziness and cowardice are the reasons why such a large proportion of men, even when nature has long emancipated them from alien guidance (naturaliter maiorennes), nevertheless gladly remain immature for life. For the same reasons, it is all too easy for others to set themselves up as their guardians. It is so convenient to be immature! If I have a book to have understanding in place of me, a spiritual adviser to have a conscience for me, a doctor to judge my diet for me, and so on, I need not make any efforts at all. *I need not think, so long as I can pay*; others will soon enough take the tiresome job over for me... Thus it is difficult for each separate individual to work his way out of the immaturity which has become almost second nature to him. He has even grown fond of it and is really incapable for the time being of using his own understanding, because he was never allowed to make the attempt. Dogmas and formulas, those mechanical instruments for rational use (or rather misuse) of his natural endowments, are the ball and chain of his permanent immaturity. And if anyone did throw them off, he would still be uncertain about jumping over even the narrowest of trenches, for he would be unaccustomed to free movement of this kind. Thus only a few, *by cultivating their own minds*, have succeeded in freeing themselves from immaturity and in continuing boldly on their way (Kant 1784).

Here we find the modern philosopher in his most Socratic voice. Kant is clearly lamenting a lack of cultural leadership and political vision. He is also explaining how the new creature comforts available to the newly expanding middle-class have had the effect of satisfying their simple daily needs by simultaneously snuffing out any desire for additional improvement in their notions of what it means to be human and to express humanity. For Kant, and eventually Foucault, the problem with dissatisfaction is that, under certain material conditions, people can be coaxed to live with it and even to prefer it.

Foucault interprets Kant's expression of dissatisfaction with his contemporaries as the Enlightenment attitude. The Enlightenment attitude is one where a person, in this case Kant, becomes dissatisfied with the mere *expression* of dissatisfaction concerning their political and cultural institutions. The dissatisfaction must manifest itself in some sort of action or attempt at action to be of virtue in this schema (Butler 2004; Jameson 1988). This is a reframing of the narrative of modern philosophy because it does not follow either the heroic trajectory of the victory of Reason in the realm of culture or find comfort in an overly pessimistic description of the failure of modernity.

Kant is charting a middle path, one that sees the undeniable success of modern technology and free market economic institutions as *the* philosophical problem of the Enlightenment (Pippin 1999). Foucault, in contrast, is trying to reconcile the espoused ideals of the Enlightenment with two hundred years of European Imperial history, a history where he finds the Jewish Holocaust, the rise of totalitarianism around the world, Christian justifications for the continued enslavement and then lynching of blacks in America, violent homophobia, Hiroshima and nuclear proliferation, capital punishment and torture by Democratic governments, African Apartheid, etc... In other words, both philosophers see the Enlightenment as a problem but they "problematize" the Enlightenment differently. If one way to characterize the Enlightenment is as an attitude, scholars must not assume that the attitude expressed by different people in different places and at different times is the same. Further, as a motivation for critique, Foucault is not seeking an end to dissatisfaction because he recognizes that it could be the wellspring of moral action if understood. In this way, he is like Kant in that he sees satisfaction as the enemy of moral progress.

Enlightened Morality Needs Courage

> From the very first paragraph, [Kant] notes that man himself is responsible for his immature status. Thus, it has to be supposed that he will be able to escape from it only by a change that he himself will bring about in himself... What, then, is this instruction? Aude sapere: "dare to know," "have the courage, the audacity, to know." Thus, Enlightenment must be considered both as a process in which men participate collectively and as an act of courage to be accomplished personally. Men are at once elements and agents of a single process. They may be actors in the process to the extent that they participate in it; and the process occurs to the extent that men decide to be its voluntary actors (Foucault 1997, p.306).

It is a truism to say any age is defined by its exceptional women and men. For Kant and Foucault, though, part of what makes the person exceptional is some show of courage. Kant is re-introducing the heroic code to the West but in a new place. There is an interesting epistemological update here being executed by Kant and, subsequently, Foucault. In the first sentence of *The Metaphysics*, Aristotle proclaimed, "Man by nature desires to know." Kant and Foucault would edit Aristotle's basic formulation by adding one significant word: '*Some* men by nature desire to know.' In fact, based on the swift anthropology Kant provides of his contemporaries, it is not even the average man that desires to know. It might not be an overstatement of his position to say that in modernity, the absence of thought, the ability to pay for somebody else to think for you, had even become a symbol of an elevated status. On this description, then, it is easy to see why Kant would include the desire for knowledge as a heroic virtue (admittedly, some ancient Greeks may have found this characterization of heroism peculiar). Where knowledge is a virtue there thought is an achievement.

Enlightened morality does not just need courage but specifically the "courage to know." In Kant, there is a direct relationship between knowledge and the kind of morality he would want. Critique is a dialectical expression of the struggle in the mind between the achievements of modernity and the attitude of countermodernity. To be clear, critique is not merely an attitude of simple irony, e.g. of taking the opposite position. Using the language of pragmatists, critique is an ironic attachment to the knowledge one has of her or his experiences and the traditions of knowledge she or he has received. Here the irony is complex. Critique does not claim that reality is the opposite of experience but that there could be other understandings of any experience other than the "accepted" knowledge the official promulgators would have you to believe. Moral progress begins, then, with a healthy but ironic attachment to conventional wisdom, and also the individual courage to explore other ways of making sense of the world for oneself.[4]

Enlightened Morality is Experimental

> Yet if we are not to settle for the affirmation or the empty dream of freedom, it seems to me that this historico-critical attitude must also be an experimental one. I mean that this work done on the limits of ourselves must, on the one hand, open up a realm of historical inquiry and, on the other, put itself to the test of reality, of contemporary reality, both to grasp the points where change is possible and desirable, and to determine the precise form this change should take. This means that the historical ontology of ourselves must turn away from all projects that claim to be global or radical (Foucault 1997, p.316).[5]

As I alluded to in the section on courage, Enlightenment is not simply a method of doubt. For Foucault, the attitude of Enlightenment is as dissatisfied with doubt as it is with overconfidence. Kant's critique is not just about beliefs but also about how those beliefs are transformed into action. But, it is a particular kind of action that Kant and Foucault are seeking. *The action must be one of enlivening alternatives.* What I mean by this is that I take Kant's and Foucault's arguments concerning Enlightenment to be both theoretical and practical. The theoretical insight concerns the methods and means for revising our web of beliefs to incorporate novelty. Indeed, Enlightened people have an insatiable appetite for novelty. But, Enlightened people must be the conduit by which these new ideas become manifest in the world. Not because novelty is inherently good or progressive but because it is only by trying out and trying on new ideas that we can determine which ideas are worth keeping and which to toss away.

I want to augment Foucault's notion of this experimental attitude by saying that not only must new ideas be subjected to the crucible of experience but also to the ideas that are received or traditional and, therefore, *assumed* to be valuable. Every generation, indeed every person, must reassess received values.[6] Once again, Kant is frustrated by the lack of innovation in his society due to the blind adherence of his contemporaries to custom and tradition. One solution that Foucault provides is that we need to be more focused on the limits of our knowledge.

> The point, in brief, is to transform the critique conducted in the form of necessary limitations into a practical critique that takes the form of a possible crossing over. This entails an obvious consequence: that criticism is no longer going to be practiced in the search for formal structures with universal value but, rather, as a historical investigation into the events that have led us to constitute ourselves and to recognize ourselves as subjects of what we are doing, thinking, saying. This philosophical ethos may be characterized as a limit-attitude. We are not talking about a gesture of rejection. We have to move beyond the outside-inside alternative; we have to be at the frontiers. Criticism indeed consists of analyzing and reflecting upon limits. But if the Kantian question was that of knowing what limits knowledge must renounce exceeding, it seems to me that the critical question today must be turned back into a positive one: In what is given to us as universal, necessary, obligatory what place is occupied by whatever is singular, contingent, and the product of arbitrary constraints (Foucault, 1997, p.315)?

Foucault's suggestion is that we apply outward pressure on the limits of our knowledge by re-examining what it is that we think we already know.

I want to return to my argument that moral progress needs a particular kind of thought. Now, with the help of Foucault, I can outline the characteristics of the kind of thought that I believe helps to bring about moral progress. *I will call critical those theories or philosophies or literatures that have the attributes of action, courage, and experimentalism.* It is critique that I think will provide, and has always provided, the material for constructive social thought even though its form is necessarily negative and, sometimes, destructive. But, morality needs social thought because ethics needs heroes.

Finally, Foucault's insights allow me to change the conversation concerning moral progress by changing its operative metaphor. For Rorty, moral progress is two-dimensional. By this I mean that his descriptions of progress fit the shape of an upwardly sloping curve on a two dimensional Cartesian plane. Remember that in Rorty's theory Aristotle is at an intellectual disadvantage to Newton because he was unlucky enough to be born before Newton on the same temporal continuum. But, for Foucault, moral progress is not about the distance we have traveled along the same curve but about the size of our moral universe. Foucault's theory allows us to change the progressive trope from *distance* to *volume*. For Rorty, moral progress can be fully charted with (x,y) coordinates. Foucault introduces the z-coordinate. It is through the theoretical method of critique, with its attributes of action, courage, and experimentalism, that we enter into a global discourse, one that exerts pressure on the limits of what can be thought by de-centering and re-evaluating what we think we already know. It is also through the process of de-centering our knowledge that we learn how to incorporate novelty and, ultimately, difference.

Dispatches from the Frontier: Some Pedagogical Implications of Critical Thought

Why do we need theories of moral progress? Theories of moral progress serve as one basis for political and cultural training that assists, many times accidentally, in the procurement of moral progress. Theorists of moral progress believe that progress cannot happen unless someone is thinking about progressive change. For them, there is an inherent link between 'what we think we can be' and 'who we think we are.' This thread can easily be detected by those who are familiar with the Western tradition that begins with Plato's *Republic* and Aristotle's *The Statesman*, through Herodotus' *Histories* and Augustine's *City of God*, to Machiavelli's *The Prince* and Rousseau's *Emile*, and also DuBois's *Souls of Black Folk* to Bloom's *The Closing of the American Mind.* While my list is not meant to be exhaustive it is illustrative of the simple fact that many of the canonical texts in our philosophical tradition are chiefly concerned with the proper training for leadership. Therefore, it is poignant that Rorty takes up the issue of training in his philosophical reflection on moral progress.

Rorty's Rebellion

Rorty is skeptical of the possibility that the current training in professional philosophy departments provides the kind of tools moral theorists need to create thoughtful and novel solutions for today's ethical problems.

> Anyone who holds this view of moral progress I have been offering will be dubious about the relevance of training in the academic discipline of philosophy is relevant to applied ethics. People with views like mine are inclined to see training in philosophy as no better or worse a preparation for work in business ethics, or in bio-medical ethics, than training in anthropology, or social psychology, or theology, or intellectual history, or comparative literature. For advanced study in *any* of these fields helps the student to envisage new possibilities (Rorty 2006).

Rorty has long worked to deconstruct the privileged position philosophy has had in Western intellectual tradition. One can go back three decades into his oeuvre and find important attacks not just on the peculiar rhetoric of Anglo-American analytic philosophy and also the un-penetrable rhetoric of the so-called Continental theorists, but also deep inquiries concerning the teleology and utility of the philosophic endeavor in general. It would be no overstatement to claim – as I do – that Rorty's work was successful with heralding in a general skepticism about professional philosophy both within the academy and throughout society. This has had the corresponding effect of alienating philosophers and philosophy departments from mainstream social thought. Rorty anticipates this victory in the following statement from "Is Philosophy Relevant to Applied Ethics?"

> What would training in philosophy look like after a quietist victory? It is easy to imagine elementary logic being handed over to the rhetoric and communication department, and advanced logic to the mathematicians. Then all that would remain of the traditional four fields of philosophy would be the history of philosophy and moral philosophy. But these are the areas that are already least professionalized, and most thoroughly intertwined with other disciplines (Rorty 2006).

This is basically what has already happened.[7] That does not mean that philosophy departments no longer exist in colleges and universities. But, anybody who has considered joining a graduate department within the last generation cannot help but be struck by the narrowness of the course offerings and the limitedness of what is considered an "authentic" philosophical inquiry. Though it may be somewhat clear which courses one must take to begin their training in philosophy, it is not clear at all what sort of dissertation would constitute a contribution to the field. It is no wonder that philosophers are rarely called upon for an opinion by their colleagues within the university, and are never called upon for an opinion by mainstream cultural institutions outside of the academy. Indeed, Rorty's Rebellion holds the wreath of victory.

That is why I personally find it exhausting that Rorty still takes the time to kick the dead corpse of professional philosophy. Either he does not realize that he has had the victory – highly unlikely – or he realizes that his pet audience never tires of the effective ways that he belittles professional philosophers – highly likely. Whatever the reason, I think that he does himself a disservice by still thinking that professional philosophy is one of the ethical theorist's moral problems. The effect of Rorty's fixation on professional philosophy is that he makes a kind of category mistake by confusing the symptom with the cause.

Racism is a moral problem. Sexism is a moral problem. Imperialism is a moral problem. Cultural Chauvinism is a moral problem. Homophobia is a moral problem. Religious Radicalism is a moral problem. Totalitarianism is a moral problem. Poverty is a moral problem. *Professional philosophy is not a moral problem.* The problems that Rorty laments concerning professional philosophy are symptoms of the fact that racism, sexism, imperialism, etc . . . are operating and have operated stealthily within the Western intellectual tradition from its very start.

Historian Dipesh Chakrabarty has registered a similar complaint against Rorty:

> I register a fundamental disagreement with a position taken by Richard Rorty in an exchange with Jurgen Habermas. Rorty criticizes Habermas for the latter's conviction "that the story of modern philosophy is an important part of the story of the democratic societies' attempts at self-reassurance." Rorty's statement follows the practice of many Europeanists who speak of the histories of these "democratic societies" as if these were self-contained histories complete in themselves, as if the self-fashioning of the West was something that occurred only within its self-assigned geographical boundaries. At the very least, Rorty ignores the role the "colonial theater" (both internal and external) – where the theme of "freedom" as defined by modern political philosophy was constantly invoked in the aid of the ideas of "civilization," "progress," and latterly "development" – played in the process of engendering this "reassurance" (Chakrabarty 2000, p.45; see also Rorty 1991).

Chakrabarty views Rorty's fundamental sin as one of omission, e.g. that Rorty has managed to miss the ways that modern philosophy provided the philosophical justifications and identity classifications that allowed European imperialism to advance unimpeded (Mehta 1999). Further, for Chakrabarty, Rorty's fundamental sin is one he shares with most of his well-meaning colleagues in the academy. I am mostly in agreement with the point that modern political philosophers, as well as economists, social psychologists, and literary critics, are quite naïve about history in general and colonial history specifically, though I am less sure that Rorty is this group's icon. But, one should expect some sort of overstatement of counter-positions now that the empire has the chance to write back, though.

My critique of Rorty is not that he "intentionally" subverts colonial history but that he has failed to utilize colonial history in his effort to deconstruct modern philosophy. I think that Rorty has missed a grand opportunity to be a leader in post-colonial studies and post-modernism when it is fairly clear that these intellectual paradigms fits neatly within the spirit and letter of his general critique of modern philosophy. By focusing too much on the deconstruction of professional philosophy Rorty neglected to re-construct its pedagogy and curriculum along more ethical lines.

It is my goal, then, to cede the victory of Rorty's Rebellion against professional philosophy and to use this as a moment for turning the power of that critical gaze toward theorists across the humanities and social sciences. I want to do this by suggesting ways to make the larger moral constructs, e.g. racism and sexism, more opaque so that they can be deconstructed. It is time that moral philosophers begin to understand the processes though which their own work, and especially their work in ethics, potentially reinforces the pernicious stranglehold racism et al. have on our moral imagination. *In other words, the reason why the moral imagination is insufficient for moral progress is because it is as contaminated with cultural chauvinism as the other mental contributors to the reasoning process.*

Leadership As A Way Of Life

When it comes to the procurement of moral progress, theory and praxis find their nexus in human action that is the result of critical thought. Critical thought, remember, is thought that is active, courageous, and experimental. Now I want to address and make clear how Foucault supercedes Kant's understanding of critique and, as a result, provides the key to the portal connecting moral theory and practice in the service of progress. Remember that for Foucault the attitude of modernity is characterized as a stance we must have toward the limits of our knowledge: "This philosophical ethos may be characterized as a limit-attitude." But what does this actually mean?

Leaders need to be obsessed with limits so that they can learn how to extend those that need extending and also negotiate those that need respecting. At first glance extending and respecting limits may seem redundant, but there is an important difference between the two. Extending limits is about how we increase the volume of our moral universe whereas respecting limits is about how we avoid making our extension a transgression. But, one way or another, we have to theorize ethical limits in ways that are not simply jurisprudential. Therefore, the limit-attitude is about how contemplation of the limits of knowledge and the contemplation at the limits of normalcy and acceptance assist moral progress. The notion of a virtuous limit is similar to Salman Rushdie's "frontier" in the following passage:

> The frontier is a wake-up call. At the frontier we can't avoid the truth; the comforting layers of the quotidian, which insulates us against the world's harsher realities, are stripped away and, wide-eyed in the hard fluorescent light of the frontier's windowless halls, we see things as they really are. The frontier is the physical proof of the human races divided self... (Rushdie 2002, p.353).

In other words, there is something special about limits, and borders, and frontiers, that need to be mined for ethical reasons. And those that seek to transcend limits must find a way to live at the borders and face the frontier.

The pedagogical challenge for leadership training, then, is to create concrete practices that put humans into situations where they experience and then utilize this limit-attitude. All of us need to be de-centered from time to time. This means that while it is often easy and desirous for us to remain within established identity based-enclaves, we grow ethically when we find ways to get ourselves outside of these comfort zones. I believe that the same mindset that allows one to transcend intellectual situations is also a prime resource for one to find innovative practical solutions. *Leaders must be thinkers.*

Curriculum Considerations

There are three kinds of pedagogical activities that I think will cultivate a limit-attitude in our future and existing leaders: clinical analysis, literary analysis, and acting. All of these activities concern issues of character and, therefore, provide a strong intellectual platform for leadership development. While most programs in management and leadership capture and deploy the technical skills needed to perform a function in an organization, they fall flat where there needs to be value driven decisions about when and where to deploy the functional knowledge, let alone how to improve it. It is my belief that if existing training programs were augmented by these more "existential" exercises, future managers would become better leaders.

By clinical analysis I mean that the beginning of leadership studies should include a psychoanalytic evaluation with regularly scheduled follow-ups and check–ins. This is important because these visits to the clinician serve to make one more thoughtful about themselves and they ways that they affect and are affected by their environment.

By being psychoanalyzed potential leaders will have a clearer sense of their blindspots and places for perspectival improvement. Many programs give the Meyers-Brigg survey, but this is far too general a classification scheme to be of much long-term use; e.g. it is just a start. The depth that can be reached by a clinician is much more personalized and provides more specific information about the motivations, assumptions, and chauvinisms of managers.

It may seem curious to some readers that I would put the analysis of literature in the leadership curriculum, but poets and writers have always plumbed the depths of the human condition and their works have yielded important insights into the human psyche. The themes of hubris, evil, treachery, love, deception, and honor have motivated writers and dramatists throughout history, and there is no reason that we cannot learn from these important texts. Further, literary criticism as its own separate literature is important because it helps us to form good ideas about how to read and learn from the texts. Literature, then, should play as central a role in leadership training as it does in the liberal arts.

Finally, the actual act of acting creates in managers practical wisdom, whereby they will have the ability to lead in situations they have never encountered because acting demands that one put oneself to the side and sincerely attempt to become someone else. Managers will be able to think through "difference", e.g. what it means to be somebody else in circumstances other than one's own. And it is by thinking through difference that managers will come to understand diversity. Leaders value diversity for both ethical and strategic reasons because it is through diversity that leaders become ethically three-dimensional and also more innovative in their management practices.

Finally, there is a logic for teaching these techniques in the order I have given. I began this paper with a consideration of the role of the moral imagination in Richard Rorty and Patricia Werhane. My conclusion at the end of the first section was that critical thought was more fundamental to moral development than the moral imagination. But, my position was slightly overstated in order to emphasize the role of critical thought as outlined by Kant and Foucault. The moral imagination becomes increasingly important only *after* critical thought has been inaugurated in the subject. My pedagogical sequence assumes this in its progression: psychoanalysis makes one's thoughts more critical, literary criticism activates the moral imagination, and drama enacts and embodies the ideas that result from the cultivation of the moral imagination through literature. In the end, it is the moral imagination that spans the distance between management and leadership. But, it is critical thought that activates the moral imagination.

Conclusion

> There are many areas that we could choose to illustrate how business and society intellectuals can begin to redescribe business. We shall focus on two areas, namely, feminist theory and psychoanalytic theory, simply because we have some familiarity with them. We could have focused on religious thought, family therapy, mythology, or even an analysis of pop culture like video games and Madonna, and been perhaps fruitful. Both feminist theory and psychoanalysis pay special attention to the concept of "silence," what has not been said. If we can give voice to some silences, we can come to redescribe business in ways that may well be liberating, that enables us to live differently and better (Freeman and Gilbert 1992).

In 1992 Edward Freeman and Daniel Gilbert provided the above reflections on the field of business ethics in what could be called that field's own version of Kant's exhortation towards Enlightenment. He called for a project essentially about the strategic value of diversity, characterized in this passage as "giving voice to some silences." Freeman also saw the value of psychoanalysis for business ethics. My underlying motivation for writing this paper is to play the role for Freeman that Foucault played for Kant. I am not at all sure that Freeman's call for a diversity of thought in leadership training and applied ethics has been met. My impression from analyzing the class/racial/gender/sex/ethnicity identities of those at ethics conferences and in the ethics journals is that we have a long way to go.

I will conclude this paper with one final thought about the moral imagination: *imagining what it would be like to be somebody else is no substitute for the inclusion of other people*. I began with an analysis of Richard Rorty's "Is Philosophy Relevant To Applied Ethics." His answer is mostly "no," or at least he believes that philosophy is no more relevant than all the other disciplines in the academy. I have asked the question differently and, as a result, chosen a different project. "How Is Philosophy Relevant to Applied Ethics" is my question and this paper is its answer. Philosophy is relevant to applied ethics when it serves to create the conditions under which diverse populations are not just subjects but also citizens in our shared moral universe.

Notes

1. This paper is dedicated to the memory of Margaret Dauler Wilson, late professor of the History of Modern Philosophy at Princeton University.

2. Though I will not be discussing his article within this paper I have also been deeply influenced by African-American philosopher Frank Kirkland's very insightful contribution to this critical genealogy. (1999, p.242–310).
3. Surely, there is a speculative dimension to historical understanding and also a historical basis for any speculation. But, for the purposes of this paper, it will be sufficient to overstate the separation of these two outlooks if only to emphasize their relationship.
4. To be critical in this way does not guarantee that you will not make moral mistakes but that is no reason not to forge ahead. For critiques of this position (see Lilla, 2001), and Wolin, 2004. The classic statement is Sloterdijk, 1987.
5. It is important to point out that "Global" here is a synonym for universal or absolute. This is not a critique of contemporary theories of globalization.
6. Consider T.S. Eliot on "tradition" versus "repetition" in the following:
"Yet if the only form of tradition, of handing down, consisted in following the ways of the immediate generation before us in a blind or timid adherence to its successes, 'tradition' should positively be discouraged. We have seen many such simple currents soon lost in the sand; and novelty is better than repetition. Tradition is a matter of much wider significance. It cannot be inherited, and if you want it you must obtain it by great labour." (Eliot, 1922)
7. It is important to note that Hegel predicted this years ago in the introduction to his *Faith and Knowledge*. In that text he makes the valuable distinction between speculative and reflexive philosophy. In his mind, reflexive – systematic – philosophy would end up being perfected within physics and mathematics departments. Speculative philosophy, then, was the only kind of philosophy that he believed would remain.

References

Butler, Judith. 2004. "What is Critique? An Essay on Foucault's Virtue," in the *Judith Butler Reader*, ed. Sara Salih, Malden: Blackwell.

Chakrabarty, Dipesh. 2000. "Postcoloniality and the Artifice of History" in *Provincializing Europe: Postcolonial Thought and Historical Difference*. Princeton: Princeton University Press.

Eliot. T.S. 1922. "Tradition and Individual Talent", http://xroads.virginia.edu/~DRBR/eliot.txt (Accessed July 1, 2007)

Freeman, R, E, and Daniel Gilbert, Jr. 1992. "Business, Ethics, and Society: A Critical Agenda," *Business and Society*. 31(1): 9–17 (Spring).

Foucault, Michael. 1997. "What is Enlightenment?" *Essential Works of Foucault 1954–1984: Ethics, Subjectivity, and Truth*. New York: New Press. pp. 303–304.

Hegel, Georg Friederich. 1977. *Faith and Knowledge*. Trans. Cerf and Harris. Albany NY. SUNY Press.

Hoy, David Couzens. 2004. *Critical Resistance: From Poststructuralism to Post-Critique*. Cambridge: MIT Press.

Jameson, Frederick. 1988. "Metacommentary" in *The Ideologies of Theory, Essays 1971–1986: Volume 1 Situations of Theory*. Minneapolis: University of Minnesota Press.

Kant, Immanuel. 1784. "What is Enlightenment?" http://philosophy.eserver.org/kant/what-is-enlightenment.txt Accessed July 1, 2007

Kirkland, Frank. 1999. "Enslavement, Moral Suasion, and Struggles for Recognition: Fredrick Douglas's Answer to the Question – What Is Enlightenment?" in *Fredrick Douglas: A Critical Reader*. Malden: Blackwell. pp. 242–310.

Lilla, Mark. 2001. *The Reckless Mind: Intellectuals and Politics*. New York: New York Review Books.

Mehta, Uday Singh. 1999. *Liberalism and Empire: A Study of Nineteenth-Century British Liberal Thought*. Chicago: University of Chicago Press.

Robert Pippin, Robert. 1999. *Modernism as a Philosophical Problem: On the Dissatisfactions of the European High Culture, 2nd ed.* Malden: Blackwell.
Rorty. Richard. 1991. "Habermas and Lyotard on Postmodernity" in *Essays on Heidegger and Others: Philosophical Papers Volume 2* Cambridge: Cambridge University Press.
Rorty. Richard. 1991. "Is Philosophy Relevant to Applied Ethics?" *Business Ethics Quarterly.* 16: 2006, 369–380.
Rushdie, Salman. 2002. "Step Across This Line" in *Step Across This Line: Collected Non-Fiction 1992–2002.* New York: Modern Library.
Sloterdijk, Peter. 1987. *Critique of Cynical Reason.* Minneapolis: University of Minnesota Press.
Werhane, Patricia H. 1998. "Moral Imagination and the Search for Ethical Decision Making in Management," *Business Ethics Quarterly Special Issue No. 1*, 5–98.
Werhane, Patricia H. 1999. *Moral Imagination and Management Decision-Making.* New York: Oxford University Press.
Wolin, Richard. 2004. *The Seduction of Unreason: The Intellectual Romance With Facism From Nietzsche to Postmodernism.* Princeton: Princeton University Press.

An Arendtian Approach to Business Ethics

Peter Gratton

After living some ten years under the assumed name of Ricardo Klement, Adolf Eichmann, a former high official in the German army, was aducted by the Israeli Mossad, which transported him in May 1960 to Israel to face charges of crimes against the Jewish people, crimes against humanity, and war crimes. The next year, after an international controversy set off by the abduction that rekindled the memories of atrocities in Europe some believed best forgotten, Eichmann faced a prosecution depicting him as the anti-Semitic mastermind of the final solution. Four months of testimony, hundreds of witnesses, and thousands of pages of documentary evidence, including transcripts of Eichmann's interrogations by Israeli officials, provided the world with stark details about Eichmann and his role in the Final Solution. Eichmann's defense was meager – Eichmann would claim that he was simply following orders, a defense that had been tried and had failed at Nuremburg – and the result of the trial seemed pre-determined from the moment of his abduction. Eichmann would hang for his responsibility in the Nazi slaughter of six million Jews.

With this, we have, I would admit, a most unlikely case study for use in a business ethics classroom. The story of Eichmann is already some sixty years old, and his activities in his career as a Nazi were far beyond the pale of even the most egregious cases found in the typical business ethics case books.[1] There would be, of course, some truth to the view that introducing Eichmann's story into an applied ethics class would inevidibly depict an unseemly analogy between the practices of latter day corporations and the bureaucracy of the Nazi era. My argument here, though, is that Hannah Arendt's well-known *Eichmann in Jerusalem* offers a philosophically cogent account of judgment and ethical decision-making that business managers and employees would do well to heed. *Eichmann in Jerusalem*, originally a series of press accounts for *New Yorker* magazine, deserves consideration alongside Aristotle's *Nichomachean Ethics*, Kant's *Groundwork for the Metaphysics of Morals*, and other classic ethics texts in a business ethics syllabus. Indeed, Arendt's account offers a narrative structure amenable to the story-based pedagogy favored

P. Gratton
Assistant Professor of Philosophy, University of San Diego
e-mail: pgratton@sandiego.edu

M. Painter-Morland, P. Werhane (eds.), *Cutting-edge issues in Business Ethics*,

by a number of business ethicists, who increasingly argue for the importance of such "experiential" knowledge for the effective teaching of business ethics. Charles Watson, for example, argues that stories provide an essential way for students to see the practical import of the ethical theories under study.[2] To use the language of recent pedagogical studies in ethics, through a close reading of Arendt's work and its theory, the hope is that students would be lead from the level of cognitive competence of ethical theory found in the typical ethics texts to a behavioral competence that is the goal of business ethics courses. G. L. Rossouw (2003) contrasts cognitive and behavioral competence as follows:

> Seen from the behavioral competence position, the purpose of teaching business ethics is to develop the capacity of students to behave morally in a business setting. In contrast to the cognitive competence position, adherents of this approach argue that cognitive competence to deal with ethical issues will not necessarily translate into a willingness to behave morally as well. It is possible to score very high on cognitive competence and yet to be a poor ethical performer in business.[3]

Arendt's work is not uncontroversial: there are serious questions to be raised about both her depiction of Eichmann and her conclusions about "the banality of evil." Nevertheless, her account of ethics, which, with its depiction of ethical duties and its case study of Eichmann's character does not fit squarely within either a virtue or deontological ethics, is a warning to readers who would conflate morality with state laws and their duties with the needs of superiors. In short, I will argue that, despite her critique of modern large scale economies and her general avoidance of discussions of post-industrial corporations, Arendt may be a business ethicist of the first order.

Arendt's work is not, though, a traditional work of ethics. *Eichmann in Jerusalem* (1964) is a long study in character – the character of a man Arendt fears is exceptional in his display of symptoms common to "modern bureaucratic man."[4] Conformist to his core, this "modern bureaucratic man" is unable to see beyond the needs and dictates of his career and is ineluctably unimaginative in his consideration of life's deep ethical and political questions. As Michael Marrus puts it, "Eichmann was the quintessential example of the totalitarian bureaucrat – unable to speak except in officialese [*Amtssprache*], unable to think outside the framework of his bureaucratic function, unable to contemplate wider issues of right and wrong or a transcendant morality."[5] In short, he was ignorant "of everything that was not directly, technically, and bureaucratically connected with his job" (Arendt 1964, p.54).

Arendt argues that in modernity, men[6] are exceptionally a-political, viewing their role in the life of their nation and communities as mere cogs in a power structure for which they bear not even the slightest responsibility. Within this structure, the task of thought – defined by Arendt as the ability to see from the vantage point of the other – is displaced onto a system, or worse, a leader-figure that unburdens each man of his individual responsibility. Arendt is scornful of Eichmann's claim that he was simply following orders for which he had no choice, on threat of violence, to obey. Nevertheless, she recognizes in his defense a larger truth about the nature of responsibility in modernity: judgment and decision-making are always the responsibility of others, and thus, no one.

What is particularly dispiriting in Arendt's account is how short a time she believes it takes for one's conscience to be co-opted by a corrupt social system. "It was of great political relevance," she writes about the outcome of the Eichmann trial, "to know how long it takes an average person to overcome his innate repugnance toward crime" (Ibid., p.93). Eichmann accomplished this by elevating the laws of Hitler to the status of a perverse Kantian categorical imperative. For Kant, the categorical imperative, from which it follows that one's maxims for action are such that they can be made into a self-consistent and universal law of nature, is the self-legislated duty of each free being using its practical reason. One's maxims for action were to be aligned with this internal law, even if, as is often enough the case, it called for an action opposed to one's inclinations. Arendt does not, in strict Kantian fashion, argue that Eichmann, because of his inclinations, elevated his hypothetical imperatives relating to his job security over the duties of the categorical imperative. Rather Eichmann, Arendt writes, viewed his moral responsibility to be that he should act in such a way that the *Führer*, if he knew of his actions, would approve of them (Ibid., p.136).

What is often missed in Arendt's analysis is the way in which Eichmann still retains a measure of Kantian freedom to self-legislate. "In his household use [of Kant's categorial imperative], all that is left of Kant's spirit is the demand that a man do more than obey the law, that he go beyond the mere call of obedience and identify his own will with the principle behind the law ... [here] the will of the *Führer*" (Ibid., p.136–137). That Eichmann did not allow, as he admitted, any exceptions to this law, that he acted freely against his "inclination," is proof, Eichmann argued, that he was merely doing what he took to be his duty.

But, whatever the perversity of his modes of thinking, Eichmann never lost the capacity to judge, to say what was and was not in accord with duty (even if his notion of the latter was tragically skewed). It is this point that needs to be underscored. Critics of Arendt too often highlight her strong account of the rampant conformism of modern society and the crushing oblivion of Nazi totalitarianism to suggest that she believed that Eichmann beared no responsibility for his crimes, that the usurpation of his practical reason by Hitler's edicts was inevitable given the time and place in which he lived.[7]

Arendt is certainly interested in Eichmann's "mechanism" and notes that relatively few "still knew right from wrong" under the Nazi regime, or were prepared at least to act upon the innate pity that humans feel in the face of suffering (Ibid., pp.104, 106). Eichmann, she writes, considered himself to be a mere civil servant, and in many ways he was, as he said, "a law abiding citizen" (Ibid., p.24). He was not stupid, but he was thoughtless. He could speak in nothing but clichés, in the officialese and euphemistic language the Nazi apparatus used in the commission of its horrors. What for the Jews, Arendt (Ibid., p.153) notes, was "quite literally the end of the world," was for Eichmann "a job with daily routine and its ups and downs." There was a "remarkable monotony" to Eichmann's job, given what was at stake, but this monotony – the job security and occasional promotions – provided Eichmann with his self-described *Arbeitsfreude*, a certain contentment and satisfaction with his work. And it is notable, as Arendt points out, that Eichmann's faulty memory, even at the trial in 1961, could recall only those events during the Nazi period that directly affected his career: promotions and changes in responsibilities. The evil of Eichmann, Arendt (Ibid., p.82) argues, was his extreme careerism, which kept him focused on the monstrous and "routine" business of the Holocaust that rendered the lives of millions subservient to the utility of his prospects in the Nazi hierarchy. Eichmann's evil, according to Arendt, lies not in some Augustinian stain upon his soul, but rather in his so-called normality, his exceptional attention to being nothing other than normal within even the most extreme circumstances. The judges in the case, Arendt writes, "were too good, and perhaps also too conscious of the very foundations of their profession, to admit that an average, 'normal' person, neither feeble minded nor indoctrinated, nor cynical, could be perfectly incapable of telling right from wrong Eichmann was indeed normal insofar as he was 'no exception within the Nazi regime' " (Ibid., p.26).

Eichmann in Jerusalem, whatever its faults as history or character study, offers an essential rethinking of morality and evil in the contemporary age. Arendt was struck at the trial, she said, "by a manifest shallowness in the doer [Eichmann] that made it impossible to trace the uncontestable evil of his deeds to any deeper level of roots or motives. The deeds were monstrous, but the doer . . . was quite ordinary, commonplace, and neither demonic nor monstrous."[8] Arendt, who had written her doctoral dissertation on Augustine, knew that this formulation ran against an entire current of Western considerations of evil. Though she doesn't find Eichmann to be monstrous, her depiction of his character is just as chilling:

> [W]hen I speak of the banality of evil, I do so only on the strictly factual level, pointing to the phenomenon which stared one in the face at the trial. Eichmann was not Iago and not Macbeth, and nothing would have been father from his mind than to determine with Richard III "to prove a villain." Except for an extraordinary diligence in looking out for his personal advancement, he had no motives at all. (Ibid., p.287)

In other words, Eichmann's evil manifested itself in a very particular way, one that does not mesh with the thorough-going ruthlessness and pathology of an Iago or Macbeth. Arendt notes, for example, that Eichmann's wish for personal advancement would not be exercised in any "criminal" way: "he certainly would never have murdered his superior in order to inherit his post. He *merely*, to put the matter colloquially, *never realized what he was doing*" (Ibid., p.287). This is the great ethical problem of modernity, Arendt claims: "That such remoteness from reality and such thoughtlessness can wreak more havoc than all the evil instincts taken together which, perhaps, are inherent in men – that was, in fact, the lesson one could learn in Jerusalem" (Ibid., p.288). And it is this very banality that needs to be thought, given the *genocidaires* of Rwanda and elsewhere in the past forty years, who have treated their gruesome task as but another nine-to-five job.[9] The evil witnessed in the past century has not always manifested itself through social pathology, as Arendt recognizes in *Eichmann in Jerusalem*, but through its opposite: men and women conforming rigidly to social and political codes even as those codes are turned into the tools of genocide. Like Eichmann, the *genocidaires* of modernity are all too often law abiding citizens.

Arendt claims Eichmann is a symptom of a wider problem in modernity that needs to be thought, the way in which one's normal aversion to pity can be occluded through the mediation of new technologies and bureaucratic language rules. Arendt worries that past is prologue in the Eichmann case, that "it is quite conceivable that in the automated economy of a not-too-distant future, men may be tempted to exterminate all those whose intelligence quotient is below a certain level" (Ibid., p.289); what worries Arendt, then, is the continued privileging of the technical reasoning of the bureaucrat over the thinking and judging of practical reason.

But despite the very banality of Eichmann, Arendt does not claim that he was without responsibility. "The moment you come to the individual person," Arendt later argued, "the question to be raised is no longer, how did this system function, but why did the defendant become a functionary in this organization?"[10] To explain Eichmann's behavior is not to excuse him ethically or judicially. Let me quote from Arendt at length on this point:

> We heard the protestations of the defense [at the trial] that Eichmann was after all only a "tiny cog" in the machinery of the Third Reich.... If the defendant excuses himself on the ground that he acted not as a man but as a mere functionary whose functions could just as easily have been carried out by anyone else, it is as if a criminal pointed to the statistics on crime—which set forth that so-and-so many crimes per day are committed in such-and-such a place—and declared that he only did what was statistically expected, that it was mere accident that he did it and not somebody else, since after all somebody had to do it... [We have grown used] to explaining away the responsibility of the doer for his deed in terms of this or that kind of determinism... No judicial procedure would be possible on the basis of them. (Ibid., p.289–290)

Thus, if it is true that "those few who were still able to tell right from wrong went really only by their own judgments, and... did so freely," the reverse is also true: Eichmann, even against a backdrop where the law and general consensus of his society was murderous, was left to his "own judgment," the kind of judgment that needs to valorized even in an era Arendt sees has reacted coldly to the traditional idea of judging others (Ibid., p.295–296).

This kind of "free judgment," a refusal to conflate one's ethics with the laws of state, is especially necessary in the contemporary era in which modern capitalist enterprises operate, and certainly a necessary update to Aristotle's notions of virtue ethics based upon a certain form of community-based judgment (*phronesis*). Students should not just study Arendt's depiction of Eichmann simply because, as she argues, it raises the central political and ethical issues of our age – though this should be reason enough. Richard J. Klonoski (2003) offers a well-formulated defense of a non-utilitarian approach to teaching business ethics, arguing that ethics courses should provide a broader depth of philosophical study than is typical of most pedagogical approaches, since such an "unapplied" component provides students with a greater conception of the real ethical issues at hand, rather than what Klonoski suggests is the arbitrarily delimited "decision-making" pedagogy of most business ethics courses. After reviewing a business case in which one firm made money in a "death futures market" – betting on the deaths of insurance policy holders – Klonoski argues that a business ethicist would be remiss in leading a class on the morality of such a market without first discussing the real human issues at hand.

> In reflecting on the myriad ethical questions surrounding such deals, I am prompted to return to classical philosophy and to ask about the nature and meaning of human mortality. I am prompted not to let the most important questions revolve around legal ins and outs, and thin ethical arguments about free enterprise rights of liberty and profitability. But rather I ask how does our view of death affect our conception of what it means to be human and whether such a view alters culture for better or worse. I ask [in my classes] what this latest commercialization of death signals for the way in which we will come to understand human mortality and the value of human persons.[11]

The example cited by Klonoski is, of course, not fortuitous to the case of Eichmann. Nevertheless, I would argue that students should not just study the Eichmann case because it raises the specter of *the* ethical and political catastrophe of the past century. They should also study the case since it raises the central tensions – between technical and practical reason, between utility and moral consequence – that they will face as workers in the contemporary economy, one that moves across a number of legal and national boundaries, such that workers need to make decisions without the guidance of local laws: "Companies are increasingly entrusted with their own responsibility to contribute to a balanced social, ecological, and economic development. . . . It appears that business is an important, if not the dominant actor . . . in the common responsibility of society."[12]

It is probably no accident that business ethics arose as a discipline during an era in which governments across the West have deregulated industries and provided less oversight over corporations and their activities. Communities and nations are now, it seems to me, more and more at the mercy of the good faith of corporations, since governments are less and less likely to step in on the community's behalf. In other words, without legal constraints that would otherwise coerce them into "moral" behavior, communities must hope for corporations to have the ethical wherewithal to act on behalf of the stakeholders, and not just the shareholders, of a corporation. But the community cannot have this hope if business managers and employees reduce human existence to the march of the technical reason of profits and losses – to the detriment of the deeper aspects of being human about which Klonoski reminds us. Too often, though, this is the case. In an appraisal that echoes, however distantly, Arendt's depiction of Eichmann, Patricia Werhane reminds us of the too-limited moral capacities of modern day managers:

> [S]ome managers . . . lack a sense of the variety of possibilities and moral consequences of their decisions, as well as the ability to imagine a wide range of possible issues, consequences and solutions . . .. Still other managers are so focused on their roles and their responsibilities to a particular organization that they fail to consider simple norms of morality.[13]

In short, too many managers and employees have a "muted conscience" (Maclagan 2003, p.28), experiencing *Arbeitsfreude* even as their firms traffic in sweatshop labor, hide damaging reports from investors, and pollute the local environment, to cite the most recognizable examples. Arendt's *Eichmann in Jerusalem* offers a profound thinking of the systemic problems in modern society that underlie what Werhane references in her discussion of the myopic allegiance of some managers to a particular organization. Despite her systemic critique of modernity, Arendt's extended meditation on contemporary human existence shows the continued viability of the notion of responsibility. After all, even if the example is extreme, is it not in response to the central claim of Arendt's work – to obey evil is to support it – that business ethics classes are offered in the first place?

Notes

1. Patrick Maclagan offers a succinct framework of the standard questions by which the relevance of business ethics' cases studies should be judged: "(1) What are the moral issues? Can we identify the moral agents, establishing the locus of responsibility for things that have happened, and for taking corrective action in the future? (2) Is there also a dilemma? If so, whose dilemmas? (3) What sort of dilemmas are they? Where do they lie on a scale from acute to quasi-moral? Does self-interest enter into the picture, and if so, in what manner? (4) What are the possible functions of moral theory? Distinguish between the evaluation of issues and the resolution of dilemmas. (5) What function might other theory perform, for example regarding the explanation of, or justification for, individual or group conduct? (6) What can we do with the concept of moral imagination? (7) What need might individuals have for other, non-cognitive, attributes? Is there evidence of persons' failure to act on their moral beliefs?" Maclagan, Patrick. 2003. "Varieties of Moral Issue and Dilemma: A Framework for the Analysis of Case Material in Business Ethics Education," *Journal of Business Ethics*, 48: 21–32.
2. Charles E. Watson, "Using Stories to Teach Business Ethics," *Teaching Business Ethics*, V. 7, no. 1 (Feb. 2003), pp.93–105. Watson's approach calls, against what can be expected in teaching *Eichmann in Jerusalem*, for studying exemplary ethical models through "uplifting stories." See also Patrick Maclagan, "Varieties of Moral Issue and Dilemma: A Framework for the Analysis of Case Material in Business Ethics Education." Maclagan argues that narratives (he specifically mentions visual depictions) "may be more relevant in that context than it is to students' understanding of the purely cognitive, theoretical, aspect of business ethics" ("VMI," 25).
3. Rossouw, G. J. 2003. "Three Approaches to Teaching Business Ethics," *Teaching Business Ethics*, 7(2) : 409–432. Needless to say, teaching *Eichmann in Jerusalem* may only help cognitive and not behavioral competence. Within the scope of the classroom, Watson (see n. 2) is probably correct in his suggestion that narrative depictions of ethical and moral deeds are as close as an instructor can come to providing "experiential" learning to prepare the student to be competent in performing morally in the work place.
4. Arendt, Hannah. 1964. *Eichmann in Jerusalem: A Report on the Banality of Evil*. New York: Penguin Books, Revised Edition. See pp.175, 276, and 289.
5. Marrus, Michael R. 1997. "Eichmann in Jerusalem: Justice and History," in *Hannah Arendt in Jerusalem*, ed. Steven E. Ascheim. Berkley, CA: University of California Press. p.209.
6. I will stick to Arendt's gender specific usage in part to highlight Arendt's blinkered approach to the question of the feminine in modernity.
7. For a summary of these critiques, see Richard I. Cohen, "A Generation's Response to *Eichmann in Jerusalem*," in *Arendt in Jerusalem*, pp.253–279.
8. Arendt, Hannah. 1976. *Life of the Mind*. New York: Viking Publishing. Vol 1, p.4.
9. Michael Massing makes a similar point in "Trial and Error," *The New York Times Book Review* (Sunday, October 17, 2004).
10. Arendt, "Some Questions of Moral Philosophy" in *Journal of Social Research*, Winter 94, Vol. 64, p.750.
11. Richard J. Klonoski, 2003. "Unapplied Ethics: On the Need for Classical Philosophy in Professional Ethics Education," *Teaching Business Ethics*, pp.21–35, Vol. 7, No. 1, p.30.

12. Ronald Jearisson and Gerard Keijzers. 2004. "Future Generations and Business Ethics," *Business Ethics Quarterly*, 14(1) : 47–69, p.48.
13. Werhane, Pat. 1999. *Moral Imagination and Management Decision Making*. Oxford University Press: New York. p.11.

References

Arendt, Hannah. 1994. "Some Questions of Moral Philosophy" *Journal of Social Research*, (Winter '94) 64: 750.

Arendt, Hannah. 1964. *Eichmann in Jerusalem: A Report on the Banality of Evil*. New York: Penguin Books, Revised Edition.

Arendt, Hannah. 1976. *Life of the Mind*. New York: Viking Publishing.

Jearisson, Ronald and Keijzers, Gerard. 2004. "Future Generations and Business Ethics," *Business Ethics Quarterly*, 14(1) : 47–69.

Klonoski, Richard J. 2003. "Unapplied Ethics: On the Need for Classical Philosophy in Professional Ethics Education," *Teaching Business Ethics*, 7(1) : 21–35.

Maclagan, Patrick. 2003. "Varieties of Moral Issue and Dilemma: A Framework for the Analysis of Case Material in Business Ethics Education," *Journal of Business Ethics*, 48 : 21–32.

Marrus, Michael R. 1997. "Eichmann in Jerusalem: Justice and History," in *Hannah Arendt in Jerusalem*, ed. Steven E. Ascheim. Berkley, California: University of California Press.

Rossouw, 2003. G. J. 2003. "Three Approaches to Teaching Business Ethics," *Teaching Business Ethics*, 7(2) : 409–432.

Watson Charles E. 2003. "Using Stories to Teach Business Ethics," *Teaching Business Ethics*, 7(1) : 93–105.

Werhane, Pat. 1999. *Moral Imagination and Management Decision Making*. New York: Oxford University Press.

A Marxist in the Business Ethics Classroom

Bill Martin

No one who reads this essay (or this book) will be unfamiliar with the standard quip about business ethics being a contradiction in terms. Our colleagues in philosophy and other fields who believe they are saying something brilliant or even intelligent or clever with this are just too cute, not unlike the person who has never been to Kansas who remarks to the Kansan that "Kansas is flat." Having ridden my bicycle in almost every part of Kansas, and having ridden across the entire state (from the Colorado border to the Missouri border) four times (as of this writing), I have wished many times that these clever folks could be put down right in the middle of it and faced with the necessity of riding about seventy or eighty miles. Yes, there is a contradiction in business ethics, but it is a contradiction that runs right down through the middle of society, here in the United States, and in our "globalized" world. There is a lot to be said for getting right down in the middle of it.

Furthermore, this contradiction would exist in any society that is faced with weighing twin imperatives, on the one hand to run a system of production that responds to the needs and wants of people, and, on the other hand, to respect the basic dignity of human beings, individually and collectively.

Now, as a matter of fact, I do not believe that a capitalist form of productive and social organization can really respond to the second imperative, except in a purely calculative way that runs contrary to my own sense of what ethics is all about. Neither is capitalism fundamentally driven by the needs of the basic masses. But more needs to be said about this, because there are forms of Marxist or otherwise socialist thinking that are not only purely calculative, but that even aspire to be such.

Allow me to take a moment to answer three questions that will provide some context for considering what it means to be a Marxist in the business ethics classroom. First, how did I become a Marxist? Second, what is my relationship to Marxist theory and practice today? Third, how did I find myself teaching business ethics?

The answers to the first two questions are of course long and complicated. I do not want to spend so much time here talking about myself, though perhaps that is all I am going to do. In some respects I began gravitating toward Marxism in college

B. Martin
Professor of Philosophy at DePaul University, Chicago, IL, USA
e-mail: woodbug1@aol.com

M. Painter-Morland, P. Werhane (eds.), *Cutting-edge issues in Business Ethics*,

and even high school. This is an oversimplification, but there is something to the idea that what set me on the course to learning about Marx and the radical critique of capitalist society was the conjunction of my Christian upbringing and the events of 1968, from Paris to Mexico City to Chicago to Prague to Shanghai. I was raised to be a good Christian boy, but I probably took some of the aspects of Judaism and Christianity more seriously than I was meant to, especially the idea of placing questions of justice ahead of those of metaphysics. It was not lost on me that the old Israelites had a practice of "Jubilee" in which slaves were freed and debts were forgiven, or that they had a central concern with usury, whereby money mysteriously and suspiciously comes from other money, and therefore money seems to take on a life of its own. It was not lost on me, especially as the United States was raining napalm on the people of Vietnam and pursuing a policy that even its formulators called "scorched earth" and "lunar landscape," that Jesus had said that anyone who harms a child should be thrown into the sea with a millstone tied around his neck. Nor was it lost on me that Jesus had announced his presence in Jerusalem by chasing merchants out of the temple with a whip, an act with several layers of meaning. (It was somewhat later that I learned that the temple at that time had been co-opted by the Romans, so that it was during this period that Rabbinical Judaism emerged, with lay teachers who would give lessons and sermons sometimes in the outdoors, sometimes from a mount.) Finally, it was not lost on me that the Early Christians were said to have "shared all things in common," that there was "neither rich nor poor among them." All of these things were especially not lost on me in the midst of the jarring juxtaposition of people in revolt across the globe, on the one side, and Presbyterian, Republican, Cadillac-driving Sunday School teachers who every week denounced student radicals, black militants, and women who burned their bras, on the other.

So, from early on I had a feeling for what in more recent years I have called "Biblical Marxism." Perhaps it is significant that I developed this feeling in a context where the corporation and "big business" was rising to the level of dominance in every sphere of life. In retrospect, this could also appear to be a period, the 1950s and 1960s, in which calculation came to not only supplant moral language (however hypocritical in some cases), but where calculation insinuated itself so deeply into our culture that generations began to be formed that are barely aware of any other language. In other words, a context in which the machinations of, say, Enron, are simply commonplace and "natural," at least to those making the crucial calculations.

The form of Marxism that I have worked to develop over the last twenty years or so might be called "eclectic," but I choose instead to think that it is guided by two imperatives: 1) always side with the oppressed; 2) learn from many sources. Under this last heading, I think historical materialism has to be open to being "endlessly adjectival," even while, at the same time, not losing its core sense that the crucial task is to change society. Recognizing, however, that Marxism can succumb to a mere utilitarianism, even if one ramified through class categories, I have focused a good deal of attention over the years on the terms in which social change ought to be understood, including the very idea of the "ought" itself. One thing that Karl Marx shares with Adam Smith is that the *good* society is simply the happy aftereffect of processes that are fundamentally utility-oriented and calculative. There is no need to thematize the good as such, the good will take care of itself in the wake of the work of the invisible hand or of the moment when the expropriators are expropriated. While not denying the genius with which Marx, or Smith for that matter, uncovered the mechanisms that organize society around the problem of material production, I take sharp exception to the idea that ethical categories are epiphenomenal at best.

I would like to acknowledge here that there was a time when I would scoff at the discourse of ethics as much as anyone, more or less in the same way that Marx did. Marx had his arguments, even if they only go so far. The discussion in ethical discourse will not lay bare the motive forces involved in production, and therefore this discourse is either completely ineffectual or even worse, a smokescreen for the horrendous wrongs that are done in the pursuit of profit. Marx was not entirely wrong about this. Neither was he wrong in arguing that the state in a capitalist society serves as the agent for the big capitalists, and this includes the use of the military and various secret police agencies in foreign ventures. Certainly Marx was right to have been deeply skeptical of mere bourgeois moralizing in his own day, and he probably could not have imagined the malarkey that is corporate "ethical" hype (especially of the "we care"- and "we're doing this to make a better world"-sorts). And yet, in disparaging the language of ethics, especially a Kantian language of doing what is right because it is right, Marx (and generations of Marxists of the more orthodox sort) abandoned a terrain that ought rightly to belong to the oppressed of the world. Furthermore, he tied the transformation of the world too closely to the categories of class interests and therefore a kind of socialized utilitarianism. On the other hand, it is deep in the American ideology that there are no classes in America, or that the only classes are of the "socio-economic" type (lower, middle, upper, and so forth).

The problem of being a Marxist in the business ethics classroom might come down to understanding how and why these ideas and questions might be communicated to students. One would think that, if there is truth to these ideas—basically of the mode of production, the commodification of labor power, and the workings of forces and relations of production and the wage system in capitalism—then any teacher of business ethics would want to make students aware of them, whether the teacher is a Marxist or what-have-you. One would think that even the capitalist-minded would have no trouble accepting Marx's claim (from *The German Ideology* and understood to be a turning point in his thinking) that, at any point in the existence of a society, there are definite relations of production. After all, capitalism is very insistent on its own relations, and it goes to great lengths (through its conscious embodiment in the capitalist class and the agents of this class, from the military and police to the ideological) to enforce and extend these relations. And yet, frankly, I do not find it that efficacious to attempt to give students a small taste of the critique of the capitalist system. On the contrary, giving students—who are primarily business students who will, for the most part, take up positions of middle management in the corporate system—a little bit of Marxism just seems to empower them to claim that they have "studied" Marx and therefore know that he is wrong.

I had already had some experience with this problem when I was an instructor in the Western Civilization Program as a graduate student, where we spent a week (two class sessions, in other words, or about three hours) on each of sixteen authors in a term, "Plato to NATO," as they say.

Most of the standard business ethics textbooks I have seen have a "theoretical" section at the beginning, and then a series of cases, and the names that tend to be featured are Aristotle, Kant, Mill, Marx, and Milton Friedman and some sort of "stakeholder" critique of Friedman. More on this latter pair in my concluding remarks. It is interesting and arguably significant that most business ethics textbooks stay away from the rather sticky issue of how well capitalism might square with the values of the Abrahamic traditions, Judaism, Christianity, and Islam, for instance with the condemnation of usury. It is not hard to show that the problem behind usury and the generation of interest more generally is that money can take on a life of its own, over and against the lives of people. (Aristotle recognizes this problem as well, in his distinction between maintaining a household—the stuff of *oikonomea*—and the "mere getting of money." Aquinas also takes up this issue, in the early days of the emergence of a more commodity-based economy, and his answer is an early form of the labor theory of value.) But of course we do not want to complicate the lives of business students with the fact that the workings of the system in which they are seeking to find employment are hardly "Christian" or otherwise "holy."

The exploration of Marx in Prof. Richard De George's book, for instance, raises the question whether "wage slavery" can be compared with "real," chattel slavery. In concluding that the wage system is not in fact a form of slavery, De George offers both a critique of Marxism and a defense of capitalism. However, it might be said that the defense functions on the level of microeconomics, while Marxism works on the macro level. What Marx insightfully called the "dirty little secret of capitalist exploitation" is the basic structural set-up in capitalist social relations whereby the individual capitalist does not have to intend to exploit anyone, but instead only has to purchase labor power in the labor market at the market price. (This is the analytic of social relations quite apart from the fact that capitalists have quite intentionally shaped the labor market, quite often through the violent and illegal abrogation of their own system of rights.) For Marx, the crossing point into capitalism is the commodification of labor power, whereby the ability to labor becomes just another *thing* to be bought and sold in the market. Once this threshold is crossed, the way is open to the commodification of every sphere and nook and cranny of life, even to the point where the idea that everything and everyone has its/his/her price seems natural and even indisputable, and it may be that this goes most of all for the sorts of students who are likely to be in a business ethics class. Everything is commodified—so what?, and ho-hum.

Not to continue much further with Marxism 101, but two things are significant here as regards business ethics. First, one of the ways in which labor power as a living process, and not as an ossified thing, is obscured in the process by which labor power is commodified is that, like everything else (that circulates in the field of exchange value), labor power is produced by a labor process itself. (Indeed, it can be argued—and of course has been argued extensively—that, motivated by masculinist assumptions, women's labor in biological reproduction and in household maintenance is not given the attention it ought to receive in Marx's thought.) This obscuring of the labor process is what Marx calls "commodity fetishism," and it is important to not lose sight of what Marx says in Capital, vol. 1, that "there is commodity fetishism because there is commodity production." What is especially important for the Marxist in the business ethics classroom, however, is that the process in capitalist society by which commodities are produced is very complex and contains within it a mechanism of mystification. And, in fact, the complexity and mystification have each taken quantum leaps since the time of Marx, into levels and areas that Marx could not have imagined, even if the analytical tools that Marx gave us are still essential for uncovering the basic mechanisms. But how far could one really go with any of this in the classroom, given the setting and the amount of time that could realistically be allotted? One might as well present a smattering of quantum mechanics or Freud's theory of the unconscious. And, frankly, as someone who has studied Marx's thought and Marxist thought for many years now, I am very hesitant about playing the role of enabling business students to claim they have studied this thought.

Second, it can be said that the commodification of labor power opens the door to the commodification of people, making persons and every aspect of their lives into mere things. Humanity enters a period where "all bets are off" regarding what can and cannot be commodified and reified. As Marx and Engels put it in the *Manifesto*, all human relationships that had previously been treated with respect and/or sentimentality are now brought under the brutal logic of the "cash nexus"; "everything solid melts into air." *However*, on the whole, albeit with significant exceptions, Marx played down the ethical ramifications of this logic of commodification and reification. Indeed, Marx actively disparaged the ethical response to capitalism (and, of course, in the *Manifesto* Marx and Engels hail the bourgeoisie as the most revolutionary class in history), in favor of an analysis of the capitalist system that shows how its internal contradictions will eventually lead to its undoing and surpassing.

However, it is because of this very process of commodification that a restoration of the ethical dimension is a very difficult task. When it comes to ethics, especially in a world defined by utility and calculation, I think it is very important to insist on the centrality of Kant's approach. Fortunately, it is not hard to make the essential elements of this approach accessible to students, and perhaps this has something to do with the fact that most of them will have some experience with one or another of the Abrahamic traditions (and some will be deeply rooted in one of these traditions, of course). I often explain Kant's argument about intention and the homogeneity of motives by saying that it is a question of doing the right thing precisely because it is the right thing, and not for any other reason. A similar simplification that I present is the idea that a conversation about ethics has to center on what is right (and then of course I attempt to explain the idea of universality), and that a conversation about ethics is one thing and a conversation about happiness or what is pleasing is quite another.

Unfortunately, and Kant recognized this (and it might be argued that Rawls recognizes this in his later work as well), it takes a little Aristotle to get Kant off the ground. This is to say, there is a characterological basis for recognizing the value of the universal. Kant was already concerned in his own time with the increasingly far-flung and international character of social relations, and thus he stressed the centrality of principle. But principles mean nothing to people of no character, and character is often very thin on the ground in this world of ever-accelerating commodity logic—character has about as much chance as poetry in this manic world. This isn't to say that there are no longer people of character in the world, but, on the other hand, it has to be recognized that the corporate world for which most of our business students are training is one in which the pressures to check one's character at the door are overwhelming. And, once left at the corporate door, character becomes increasingly difficult to regain. Indeed, there needs to be more study in the social psychology of the dynamics by which so many people in a rich, capitalist society become outright jerks. (Here again there is more Marxist complication, as the United States is not only a capitalist society but is also the lynchpin of a global, imperialist order—imperialism being, as Lenin argued, capitalism as a global mode of production—not only a superpower, but even what has been called the "hyper-power." But this is another course and term in and of itself.) This may seem harsh, but what other term ought to apply to the sort of person who, confronted with a horrendous incident such as the death by fire of two-hundred young girls in a toy plant in Thailand (most of the girls were in the range of twelve to fourteen years, making toys for a U.S. manufacturer), can only summon the morally-bereft response that "that's the way the cookie crumbles"?

In fact, such a response deserves only harsh curses in retort, it only compounds the insult to engage with such a perspective. And yet we are encouraged to engage, and cursing a student is regarded as bad pedagogy. That some students are so lacking in character, and so lacking in an affinity for the ethical-political universalism that is a legacy of not only Kant, but arguably, the Western Abrahamic traditions and Plato and Aristotle, demonstrates more than the extreme moral impotence of the utilitarian response. Indeed, however, that impotence is demonstrated, and we should remark upon it. To attempt to explain to the "cookie-crumbles" student that holding two-hundred teenage girls in conditions approximating slavery so that their labor can be exploited at a rate that is extremely favorable to U.S.-based manufacturers, and then creating the conditions that allowed them to die by fire (the doors to the factory were locked so that the girls could not take unauthorized bathroom breaks or, quite conceivably, run away, escape) is "bad business" is not only a morally bankrupt strategy, it isn't even necessarily right in its own morally-vacuous terms. (That is, an atrocity of this sort may very well be "good business.") But of course these are the very terms in which the "cookie crumbles" response is formed, in the place of moral character, in the first place, and the corporate world does not have any other terms.

Perhaps, then, it would be good pedagogy to curse such a student, to stigmatize the student, to make it clear that there is a discursive gap between actual concern for moral questions, and the brutal utilitarianism that can summon no more of a response than "that's the way the cookie crumbles." In theoretical terms, perhaps what I am asking for is an ethically-grounded Marxism that, certainly, tries to understand society in systemic terms, but also doesn't fail to identify the scumbags out there as such. In the business ethics classroom, perhaps this latter is the more important and even realistic task, and it might be summed up as helping our students to find (or recover) some moral bearings and to hold on to them.

However, after teaching business ethics for about seventeen years at this point, I no longer have the stamina for confrontations of this sort, and I avoid the situations that would give rise to them. (Most likely, I could never bring myself to actually curse a student, in any case, even the ones who are most asking for it and in fairness ought to receive it.) On the other hand, there is no doubt that our students will encounter situations that will test what moral fiber each of them has, and so it seems right to work through some exemplary cases with them and to thematize for them what it means to actually think about moral questions and to deal with these questions in practice. It does seem to me, however, that the case-oriented class is a situation where there is just not enough time to deal with systemic questions at the necessary depth. So, even as a Marxist, I still think it is more important to teach students some Kant rather than Marx.

Incidentally, to complete the picture, my own path toward teaching business ethics had to do with the fact that Richard De George was one of my professors in graduate school (and a valued member of my dissertation committee). He was one of the ones who challenged me on my previous, "Marxist" tendency to scoff at ethical discourse, and for that, and much else, I thank him.

However, I did not study business ethics with Prof. De George, but instead Marx and figures such as Arendt, Habermas, and Foucault. DePaul has a very large commerce school (one of the largest in the United States), and when I first came to DePaul in 1990, we were having trouble covering the business ethics courses. It was decided, rightly I think, that the members of the department who were working in political or social theory, or ethics more generally, should take a section or two of business ethics a year, so that the two philosophers who specialized in the subject would not have to spend all of their time just teaching business ethics at the 200-level.

As for using continental philosophers in business ethics, I would say three things. First, of course it is a strength of Marx that he does not fit neatly into the continental/analytic divide. There is also perhaps more to be done with Marx, in an analytic vein, than has been done thus far under the heading of "analytic Marxism." (One project that I hope to see come to fruition before much longer would be a translation into English of Otto Neurath's book on Marxism and logical positivism, which is the only major work of the Vienna Circle not yet translated.) Certainly there is more to be done to remind people that the "continental" tradition of philosophical Marxism, from Lukacs to Adorno to Sartre to Badiou, and far beyond, is a great tradition that will continue to bear fruit for a long time to come. There is also much work to be done, in my opinion, to set the record straight about the socialist experiments of the twentieth century, in the face of a capitalist triumphalism that seems to still need to pump itself up with the idea that these experiments were nothing but unending disasters, even though the Soviet experiment effectively ended in 1956 and the Chinese experiment in 1976. However, as important as all of this work is, I don't really see much or any of it fitting very well into a business ethics class.

Second, there are certainly those twentieth-century continental philosophers of a Kantian inspiration, such as Sartre, Levinas, and Derrida, whose arguments ought to be brought to bear on questions of responsibility and the other. Certainly there is no shortage of such questions that students will encounter in the world of business, corporations, and finance. As a larger philosophical project, I think there is still more to be done in demonstrating the fecundity of Kant's project and approach, especially as expressed in twentieth-century philosophy, and as also seen in the work of figures such as Wittgenstein, Carnap, Davidson, and Putnam. Just as there has been much work in the general theme of "Marx in light of Kant," I think a "Marx after Davidson" project could be very interesting. All of this might help to strengthen the idea that ethical questions are "real questions" (on which point Marx is skeptical, at best), and therefore such work might be brought to bear on how we thematize the reality of ethics for our business ethics students.

Third, however, and relatedly, while I think Foucault can and ought to be used to help us understand the ways that networks of power articulate themselves in the corporate world (and therefore in the world more generally), I am skeptical of the sort of "continental" and "postmodern approach" that would speak of "figures such as Foucault and Derrida," who supposedly show how the subject (of ethics or whatever) is "deconstructed" or whatnot, and where the pressure is then taken off of the idea of responsibility and what our students (some of them desperately) need to understand of it.

Having set aside the possibility of teaching systematic social critique in a basic business ethics class, however, there are ways that it might come back in, and this relates to the contemporary debate between stockholder and shareholder theories. These theories map somewhat on to the distinction between utilitarian and what I would call, after Derrida, "calculative" perspectives, on the one side, and a broadly Kantian perspective on the other, respectively. Often, when we have discussed Friedman's famous article in my classes, students have asked if his perspective is influential in the business world. I generally tell them that corporate leaders do not even have to read Friedman to represent and follow (or "enact") his arguments. Friedman's perspective *is* the perspective of the business world. It would be silly to pretend to develop a critique of Friedman here, but certainly it can be said that the appeal of his argument is that, where there is business, there is no ethics, at least in the sense that it is not the place of business to concern itself with normative frameworks in the midst of evaluating schemes of profit pursuit.

Friedman's argument is a remarkably clear example of exactly what needs to be negated, and yet it also demonstrates the difficulty of carrying forward this negation once students leave the classroom and take up positions in the workaday world. Of course, Friedman's argument especially "makes sense" in a world where many have lost, or never had, their moral bearings. I place the term "makes sense" in scare-quotes not because Friedman doesn't make sense, but because it is worth studying the ways and contexts in which its sense is made, indeed made too much and overwhelmingly. The stakeholder argument, as formulated by Edward Freeman and others, doesn't make nearly as much sense in our world dominated by capital and corporations, and this also needs to be studied and this failure to make sense in certain contexts ought to be pressed forward, so to speak. The stockholder argument narrows everything down so conveniently and neatly and forcefully, while the stakeholder argument broadens everything out in a way that no one can really get a handle on, in a way that has affinities to Kant, Sartre, and Derrida. Kant: Ethics sets an infinite task. Sartre: In choosing myself I choose the world, and I am responsible for this world, all of it. Derrida: the calls of responsibility and hospitality are without limit. Part of what the stakeholder argument contributes to this discussion is that this at least potentially infinite task (where, in the end, we all are trying to live on this planet together, and we all have a stake in its future) has to find institutional expressions if it is not to be a mere "empty formalism"—as Hegel said in criticism of Kant, echoed by Marx and Engels (and John Stuart Mill, one might suppose, in his critique of intentions and the good will). One of Marx's contributions to the stakeholder argument might be the *normative* force of the recognition that in the epoch of capitalism we live with the contradiction of socialized production and private accumulation.

The next time I teach business ethics, I might base the entire course on the Enron case. It could be said that, on some level, Marxism just starts from the recognition that the big, bad things that happen in the world are systemic in nature. Even though the people who ran Enron really are bad people, outright scumbags to use a term from Sartre (in "Existentialism is a humanism," the famous lecture from 1945, Sartre gives a technical definition for the idea of scum), the "scumbag theory" (to borrow a term from my superb colleague and brilliant business ethicist Patricia Werhane) by itself will not explain what happened with this or any other corporate meltdown. Neither will any Friedmanesque or otherwise utilitarian/calculative theory of "good business." Many of the people who ran Enron were scumbags who pretty much got away with their schemes and enriched themselves in the many millions of dollars. Even Ken Lay, the close buddy of George W. Bush who died of a heart attack in the wake of his court conviction, got off very easy in comparison with what he really deserved. But to get to the root of things there has to be a discussion of what happens to moral bearings in the capitalist epoch, and here the pursuit of the alternative framework, of the stakeholder, will necessarily engage with both Kant and Marx and more contemporary figures who are carrying forward their lines of analysis.

Index

A

AT&T, 13
Abjection, 59–73
Accountability, 5, 33–44, 177
Age of Reason, 15
AICPA, 56
Alcoff, Linda, 89, 95–96, 99
Alienation, 5, 59–60, 62, 63, 65–66, 128
Allen, Robert, 13
Alliance, 178, 180, 182, 184
Ambiguity, 59–73
American Express Red, 98, 100, 102
Analytic philosophy, 1, 131, 133, 138, 142, 200
Arendt, Hannah, 6, 8, 121–123, 124–127, 129, 139, 207–212, 213, 221
Aristotle, 2, 4, 17, 28, 112, 115, 135, 153, 188, 189, 197, 199, 207, 211, 218–220
Assessment, 83
Authenticity, 62

B

Bad faith, 11 16, 95–96, 99–101
Bangladesh Rural Advancement Committee (BRAC), 83, 184
Bank of America, 25, 31
Baudrillard, Jean, 27
Baumard, Phillipe, 37
Being and Nothingness, 12, 13, 14
Bell hooks, 5, 70, 75–76
Benetton, 99–101, 102
Biblical Marxism, 216
Blacks/black community, 5, 81, 92, 100, 101, 196
Bourdieu, P., 35, 37, 131–132, 138, 140–141, 147
Butler, Judith, 37, 38, 39, 40, 96, 98, 196

C

Capitalism, 5, 12, 60, 69, 76–78, 81–83, 134, 144, 145
Card, Claudia, 97, 103–104, 139, 140
Carr, Albert, 109–112
Categorical imperative, 60–63, 117, 209
Chakrabarty, Dipesh, 201
Character, 16–19, 112
Cheney, Dick, 28
Chowdhury, M. Jahangir Alam, 77, 83
Churchill, Winston, 169, 184
Codes/codes of ethics/codes of conduct, 135, 136
Communalism, 81
Communitarianism, 23
Complex adaptive system, 36, 38, 40, 42, 175
Complexity theory, 13, 37
Compliance, 33, 82, 128
Consensus, 83, 211
Consequentialism and non-consequentialism, 39, 92
Continental philosophy, 1, 2, 3, 9, 10, 11, 60, 131–149
Corporate social responsibility, 104, 139, 145
The Corporation, 5, 11, 16, 18, 28, 43, 44, 47, 48, 49, 50–53, 54, 55–57, 58, 59, 137, 149, 171, 182, 216
Courage, 13, 197–198, 199
Curriculum, 203–204

D

Dante, Sylvio, 23
De Beauvoir, Simone, 5, 60, 63, 66
De George, Richard, 218, 221
Deleuze, Gilles, 93, 117, 118–119
Deontology, 8
Derrida, Jacques, 2, 117, 131, 134, 137, 141, 222, 223
Descartes, 23, 132

Develtere, Patrick, 79–81, 83
Dewey, John, 127, 189
Discipline, 3, 101, 200, 212
Discretion, 40, 41, 42
Diversity, 109, 170, 190, 193, 203
Domination, 65, 68, 76, 77, 79, 81, 99–101
Doris, John, 18, 19, 20
Dunlap, Albert John "Chainsaw" Al, 13

E

Eichmann, Adolf, 8, 207–212, 213
Eliot, T.S., 205
Emanuel, Linda, 175, 176
Emergent values, 132, 142–148
Emotion, 37, 93, 125, 170
Empiricism, 7, 154, 155–156, 157, 193
Enlightenment, 132, 133, 141, 142, 194–197
Enron, 28, 216, 223
Entrepreneurship, 121–129, 160
Enzi, Mike, 163
Epistemic closure, 87, 89, 94, 97, 99
Epistemology, 96, 132, 133, 134, 153, 154
Essentialism/essentialized ontology, 5, 63, 95–96
Estranged labor, 60–63, 71
"Estranged Labor", 60–63, 71
Ethical decision-making or moral reasoning, 38, 112, 189, 190, 193, 207
Ethical risk, 6
Ethics management, 169
Ethics officers, 31
Ethics of representation, 88, 101
Ethics training, 204
Evan, William, 127–128
Evil, 103, 127, 139, 210

F

Fairness, 191, 221
Female Health Company, 180, 181, 182
Feminism, 5, 87, 97
Fetishism, 27, 60, 63–66, 71, 72, 219
Foucault, Michel, 2, 5, 7, 35, 40, 44, 68, 73, 75–77, 78, 81, 85, 117, 140, 142, 147, 149, 188, 194–197, 198–199, 202–203, 221–222
Frankfurt School, 9
Freedom, 11, 16, 51, 62, 66–71
Freeman, Ed, 19, 41, 127–128, 135, 172, 174, 204, 222
Free market, 11, 12, 52, 57, 140, 149
French, Peter, 19, 44
Friedman, Milton, 60, 133, 135, 137, 142, 143–144, 147, 149, 218, 222–223
Friendship, 28

G

Gadamer, Hans-Georg, 113–115, 117
Game, 69, 70, 109–110, 114, 116, 118
Gender, 69, 89, 104, 213
Gilbert, Daniel, 204
Gillespie, Norman, 111–112
Gisele, 94, 98
Globalization, 169–185, 205
Global Reporting Initiative, 43, 44
Goodpaster, 19, 44
Google, 127, 129
Gordon, Lewis, 89, 95–97, 99, 100
Governance, 139, 169
Grameen Bank, 6, 75–85, 183, 184
Grameen Bank, 75–85, 183
Greenspan, Alan, 7, 153–154, 163–165
Grounded theory, 131–149

H

Harman, Gilbert, 17, 18, 19, 20
Hart, Stuart, 183
Heaviside, Oliver, 125, 129
Hegel, Georg Wilhelm Friedrich, 5, 9–20, 47–52, 53–56, 57, 58, 73, 93, 97, 132, 189, 205, 223
Heidegger, 2, 12, 13, 14, 132
Hermeneutics, 3, 113, 117
Hotline/helpline, 27
The Human Condition, 6, 123–124
Hume, David, 17, 19, 51, 191, 195
Husserl, Edmund, 7, 14, 153, 154–155, 156–159, 161–162, 164, 165, 166
Huybrecht, An, 79–81, 83–84

I

Identity, 93–94, 98–99
Individualism, 23, 133, 142
Information technology, 91, 163
Innovation, 7, 36, 44, 79, 83, 87, 132, 163, 188, 198
Integrity, 17, 18, 52, 89, 123, 148
Israeli Mossad, 207

J

Johnson, Mark, 35, 44, 170
Jones, Campbell, 1, 8, 34, 85, 87, 131, 135

K

Kant, Immanuel, 2, 8, 15, 30, 47–50, 57, 59–60, 61, 63, 67–70, 73, 93, 96, 97, 98, 112–113, 117, 131, 132, 135–136, 137, 142–143, 153, 190, 194–197, 198, 202, 203, 204, 207, 209, 217–223
Kennedy, Edward, 29, 163
Keynes, 160

Kierkegaard, Soren, 10–11, 12
Kikoski, C.K. and J.F, 36
Kirzner, I., 124, 129
Klonoski, Richard J., 211, 212
Kristeva, Julia, 5, 60, 63–66, 67–68, 71, 72

L
Labor, 123, 163–165
Leadership, 202
Leeper, Mary Ann, 178, 180–182
Levinas, Emmanuel, 2, 26, 131, 137–139, 142, 148, 222
Liberalism/ liberals, 4, 23, 26, 28, 29, 30
Lippke, Richard, 91
Love, Lisa, 60

M
Maclagan, Patrick, 212, 213
Managerialism, 131, 133, 134
Manheim, Karl, 158
Marketing, 6, 87–104, 181–182
Marxism, 215–218, 220, 221, 223
Marx, Karl, 2, 5, 27, 58, 59–63, 65, 67, 68–70, 71, 72
Media, 100, 102, 144, 149, 178, 179
Mental models, 169–185
See also conceptual schemes
Merleau-Ponty, M., 19, 35, 37, 95
Metaphor, 35, 124, 138, 199
Microeconomics, 218
Mill, John Stuart, 2, 17, 19, 135, 190, 218, 223
Mimesis, 115, 144
Moral agency, 4–8, 10, 11, 33, 34–38, 44, 66
Moral development, 7, 42, 187–188, 203
Moral imagination, 7, 169–185, 187–205, 213, 214
Moral minimums, 193
Moral progress, 7, 187, 188–190, 193, 194–195, 197, 199, 200, 202
Moral reasoning, 189–190, 193

N
Narrative, 3–5, 8, 10, 23, 30, 59, 64, 70, 72, 134, 136, 146, 193, 196, 207, 213
Naturalism, 7, 62, 154, 155
Niebuhr, Reinhold, 13
Nietzsche, 10, 38–39, 71, 117–119, 148
Nike, 178, 179, 180, 182
No Exit, 15
Normativity, 40
Norms, 48, 79, 81, 82, 89, 91, 103, 112, 140, 174, 176, 212
Nyamukapa, Daisy, 181

O
Observations on the Feeling of the Beautiful and the Sublime, 97
Odepis Rex/Oedipus at Colonus/Oedipus Cycle, 72
Ontology, 6, 8, 13–14, 18, 87, 95, 97, 98, 138, 146, 147, 198
The Origins of Totalitarianism, 121

P
Painter-Morland, Mollie, 1–8, 33–44
Paradox, 102, 165, 170–173, 177
Pedagogy, 3, 7–8, 188, 201, 207, 211, 220
Performance management, 34
Petersen, Verner, 35, 44
Phenomenology, 3, 9, 14, 87, 90, 154–155, 157
Philosophy of Right, 49, 50, 51, 57, 58
Phronesis, 211
Play, 109, 112–116
Poker, 6, 109–111, 114
Policies, 16, 18–19, 140, 148, 163, 164, 165, 211, 216
Postmodernism, 9
Poststructuralism, 3
Poverty/the poor, 49, 51, 55, 58, 76, 77, 78, 82, 84, 85, 103, 141, 144, 163, 171, 183–184, 201
Power, 76–78
Powers of Horror, 63
Pragmatism, 42, 144
Prahalad, C.K., 182, 183
Principles, 33, 34–35, 41–42, 61, 93, 97, 118, 132, 134, 153, 154, 156, 157, 161–162, 164–165, 190, 220
A priori truth, 156
Professional, 39, 50, 53, 54, 55, 56–57, 98, 114, 176, 178, 194, 200–201
Profit, 6, 11, 41, 54, 55–57, 79, 82–83, 124, 134, 136, 138, 145, 147, 149, 164, 180, 182, 184, 212, 217, 222
Psychoanalytic approach, 9, 64, 72, 116, 203

R
Race, 59, 69–70, 77, 87, 101, 104, 143, 146, 189
Ramamurthy, A., 99, 101
Rational agent, 34, 40
Rationalism, 193
Rawls, John, 2, 135, 190, 193, 219
Reinforcement, 18, 72, 77, 78, 94, 96–97, 98, 100–101, 188, 202
Relativism, 26, 41, 117, 155–156, 158–159, 161, 166
Reporting, 35, 43

Republic, 48, 58, 199
Resistance, 64, 65, 75–76, 78–81, 85, 87
Responsibility, 11
Responsiveness, 5, 33–44
Reward/punishment, 21, 29–30, 33, 34, 38, 81, 82, 90, 196
Rhodes, Cecil, 122
Rights, 23–24, 29, 34, 48, 54, 55, 56, 70, 125, 127, 135, 141, 147, 182, 193, 212, 218
Ritual, 91
Rivoli, Pietra, 69
Robertson, Mary, 182
Rorty, Richard, 7, 42, 187–191, 193–194, 195, 199, 200–201, 203–204
Rossouw, G.L., 208, 213
Rousseau, 51, 67, 132, 143, 199
Rule-driven, 36

S
Sachs, Jeffrey, 144, 148, 183–184
Sarbanes-Oxley, 56
Sartre, Jean-Paul, 4, 9–10, 11–14, 15–19, 30, 96, 140, 221–223
Scheler, Max, 17, 158
Schumacher, E.F., 11
Schumpeter, Joseph, 7, 125, 129, 153–155, 158–159, 160–162, 165, 166
Scott, Lee, 70–71, 171
Self-interest, 27, 51, 110, 135
Senge, Peter, 170
Sensemaking, 77, 198
Sexuality/sexual relations, 89, 181
Sittlichkeit, 48
Smith, Adam, 2, 17, 19, 51, 57, 94, 131, 135, 143–145, 171, 182, 183, 191, 192, 216, 217
Social constructivism, 169–170
Social justice, 60
Socrates, 48, 188
Solomon, Robert, 4, 9, 89, 93
Soprano, Tony, 4, 21, 22, 26, 30
Stakeholder theory, 41, 135, 145, 172
Story-telling, 43
Subjection, 119
Subjectivity, 5, 8, 60, 62–63, 65, 66–71, 95, 138, 147, 148, 157
Sunbeam Products, 13
Supply chain, 43, 103
Sustainability, 58, 134, 135, 142, 145, 147, 148, 171
Sweatshop, 5, 59–60, 66, 68, 69–70, 73, 171–173, 174, 177, 179, 183, 212
Systems thinking, 169–185, 175–178, 185

T
Tacit knowledge, 35, 37
Taylor, Frederick, 36, 133
Toscani, Oliviero, 99
Training, 103, 163, 164, 199, 200, 202, 203, 220
The Travels of a T-Shirt, 69
Triple bottom-line, 35, 143
Trust, 18, 28, 30, 39, 41–43, 160

U
Unemployment, 49, 51–52, 53, 55, 164–165, 174
Utilitarianism, 8, 47–48, 57, 58, 153, 216–217, 220
Utilitarianism, 8, 47–48, 57–58, 153, 216–217, 220

V
Values, 40
Values-driven, 203
Varian, Hal, 79, 85
Virtue-ethics, 8, 17, 20, 47–48, 57, 135, 153, 211
Visual representation, 87–88, 89–90, 91, 92–93, 94, 95, 99, 100, 103–104

W
Walker, Margaret Urban, 88, 89, 96
Wal-Mart, 59, 170–173, 174–175, 176–178, 179–180, 182
Werhane, Patricia, 7, 148, 169, 170, 173, 177, 178, 184–185, 188, 189, 191–193, 203, 212, 223
Whistle-blowing, 23
Whole Foods, 11
Winnicott, D.W., 116, 117
Wisdom, 2, 13, 75, 129, 198, 203
Wolf, Susan, 175

Y
Yunus, Muhammad, 75–76, 78–81, 82–84, 85

GPSR Compliance

The European Union's (EU) General Product Safety Regulation (GPSR) is a set of rules that requires consumer products to be safe and our obligations to ensure this.

If you have any concerns about our products, you can contact us on ProductSafety@springernature.com

In case Publisher is established outside the EU, the EU authorized representative is:

Springer Nature Customer Service Center GmbH
Europaplatz 3
69115 Heidelberg, Germany

Batch number: 10823775

Printed by Printforce, the Netherlands